D0765449

OUTSIZING

OUTSIZING

STRATEGIES TO GROW YOUR BUSINESS, PROFITS, AND POTENTIAL

STEVE COUGHRAN

This publication is designed to provide accurate and authoritative information in regard to the subject matter covered. It is sold with the understanding that the publisher and author are not engaged in rendering legal, accounting, or other professional services. Nothing herein shall create an attorney-client relationship, and nothing herein shall constitute legal advice or a solicitation to offer legal advice. If legal advice or other expert assistance is required, the services of a competent professional should be sought.

Published by Greenleaf Book Group Press
Austin, Texas
www.gbgpress.com

Distributed by Greenleaf Book Group

For ordering information or special discounts for bulk purchases, please contact Greenleaf Book Group at PO Box 91869, Austin, TX 78709, 512.891.6100.

Design and composition by Greenleaf Book Group
Cover design by Greenleaf Book Group
Author photo by Dan Reynolds Photography

Publisher's Cataloging-in-Publication data is available.
Print ISBN: 978-1-62634-631-4
eBook ISBN: 978-1-62634-632-1

Part of the Tree Neutral® program, which offsets the number of trees consumed in the production and printing of this book by taking proactive steps, such as planting trees in direct proportion to the number of trees used: www.treeneutral.com

Printed in the United States of America on acid-free paper

19 20 21 22 23 24 25   10 9 8 7 6 5 4 3 2 1

First Edition

To my wife, Lalana, and children, Ava and Max,
for motivating me to outsize my life every day.

Special thanks to Sarah Dubetz, for her ongoing
support in bringing my stories to life.

CONTENTS

INTRODUCTION

Does your company have a competitive advantage? If you answer yes, you're in the majority. Over the past decade, I have posed this question to thousands of executives and employees in surveys and interviews. Roughly 75 percent of respondents replied in the affirmative. Additionally, 65 percent asserted that their companies have clear, winning strategies. While strategic confidence is widespread, less than 10 percent of participants reported being highly satisfied with their company's strategies, and merely 29 percent stated that they were somewhat satisfied with their strategies.

In reality, no more than 50 percent of companies have a competitive advantage—a company's ability to earn above industry-average economic profits. Additionally, once a company earns a competitive advantage, it must work hard to keep it. Though not all organizations can concurrently be in the top 50 percent, all can design and implement strategies that help them inch closer to the top tier. Every organization has the potential to outsize—to outgrow limitations, challenge conventional wisdom, and achieve extraordinary results.

Over the past decade, I have worked with companies of all sizes from different industries. I have seen winning strategies catapult companies to new heights of success. I have also seen poor decisions put employees out of work and rob business owners of their life savings. Strategy underpins the future of business. The rampant disconnect between plans and results disables companies from capturing the true value that arises from getting strategy right.

As I discuss throughout this book, my thoughts and research are largely inspired by the people whom I have worked with and my observations of how organizations have adapted (or failed to adjust) to the nuances of our dynamic business environment. In my experience as a business owner, management consultant, and CFO, I have witnessed companies with great capabilities and advantages deteriorate under competitive pressure. I have also seen organizations conform to the modern economy with ease and agility, driving record-breaking success with strategic prowess.

The stark disparities in organizational performance emphasize the necessity of strategy. While our new economy presents challenges to those who fail to change, it exposes uncapped opportunity for those whose strategies embrace change. Recent social, political, and digital shifts are reshaping the ways that businesses win.

In our current business environment, nearly 67 percent of strategies fail.[1] The symptoms of business ineffectiveness are revealed in myriad ways. According to Forrester's American Customer Satisfaction Index, customer satisfaction is on the decline.[2] Employee turnover is the highest it has been in recent years, costing companies a collective $160 billion per year.[3] Financial instability is ubiquitous, as total US business bankruptcies in May 2017 were up 40 percent from May 2015 and 10 percent from May 2014, right after the economy poked its head out from the Great Recession.[4]

The impacts of negative strategy are not contained to the organization. I have witnessed the personal lives of business leaders crumble in the face of a declining business. A failing company can eat away at marriages, family relationships, and mental and physical well-being. Despite the disastrous side effects of detrimental strategy, many leaders prefer the shelter of false confidence. Some would rather believe that their companies have a competitive advantage than admit their need for a time-, money-, and energy-consuming turnaround. Many leaders avoid focusing on strategy because it requires the most patience, diligence, and hard work of any business activity.

Businesses today are operating in the dark. Widespread misunderstanding and apathy toward strategy are unduly exposing businesses to risk. Leaders' obscured, idealistic views of their companies are causing them to accept mediocrity, leaving significant opportunity on the table.

To effectively design and implement an outsized strategy, one that will encourage them to eliminate barriers and push beyond their boundaries, employees must educate themselves on what strategy looks like in the new economy. As the world continues to present new levers of influence and uncertainty, strategy is more important now than ever. To succeed in our modern business environment, companies must become transparent *learning* organizations.

A robust strategy design requires the right balance of art and science. Art ensures that the strategy listens, observes, and empathizes to design exceptional experiences that help customers progress toward their goals. It allows companies to think outside the box, empowering innovation and disruption. It welcomes us to an energizing space where we can challenge conventional wisdom, sparking creativity and creation. Science provides companies with a framework to define strategic problems, craft hypotheses, evaluate options, analyze data, and draw conclusions. Too much of one without the other fundamentally flaws plans, leaving them incomplete.

Strategy is more than just design, however. The tactics that allow a company to win are rooted in strong execution. Most executives recognize the need for both art and science but exclude the critical executional ingredient—discipline. Many companies I encounter are skilled in the art of strategy. Leaders craft ambitious plans to capture greater market share, expand capacity, or develop new capabilities. These companies revel in the strategic daydreaming. However, after the honeymoon phase of the strategy subsides and implementation begins, teams lose momentum, and execution falls flat.

Oftentimes, employees unite around the possibilities and promise of a bright future, but they lack a realistic outlook and a process to vet decisions. Other organizations are without the willpower and follow-through to ensure ongoing attention to the plan. Some approach implementation without formalized structures or governance. These companies struggle with undefined decision rights and unassigned responsibility. Finally, many companies ignore or don't know how to adapt to the changing nature of the market.

Strategy is messy and demands tough tradeoffs, bold moves, and calculated risks. When we outsize our strategies, we free up resources from the negligible to protect our time and effort for our big ideas. We extend our abilities and exhilarate our approach to maximize our impact. Outsizing requires fortitude and strategic discipline, two pervasively absent aptitudes in our modern business world.

As we face societal transformation, fueled by social, political, and digital influence, we must ask ourselves: How do we shift our company's value drivers to align with economic changes? How do we adapt to opportunities without adopting the strategic flavor of the month? How do we rally our teams to implement the proposed strategy when they are already overwhelmed by increasing work demands? How do we ensure that our strategy is creating value for our customers? How can we establish a business model and strategy to support continuous growth and improvement? How do we achieve a true competitive advantage and design and implement a strategy that fulfills our objectives? How do we outsize our results?

This strategic guidebook helps answer these questions and shares a proven methodology to power company success. This book provides timely, research-backed secrets to crafting a successful strategy that will help your company

- deliver exceptional experiences to customers,
- build advantages to fend off rivals,
- capitalize on emerging opportunities,
- unleash the potential of your people,
- create and capture outsized value, and
- increase your company's bottom line.

LEARN FROM MISTAKES

We currently stand at a crossroads of progress and peril. Recent innovations and market shifts, such as consumer demands, AI, technology, and globalization, are inherently impacting business. We are inching into unprecedented territory as our economy evolves and new value drivers emerge.

Change is not a novel concept. The world and market have been changing since the beginning of time, evolving products and processes, empowering business to produce more for less, solve increasingly complex issues, and drive societal advancement. All progress builds upon the previous era's developments, and the dawn of every new period is accompanied by unknowns. To grow and innovate, businesses must temporarily endure discomfort.

For example, in the nineteenth century, the steam engine, locomotive, telephone, internal combustion engine, electricity, and cotton gin transformed millions of lives and fundamentally shifted commerce. As a result, we elevated our manual, agrarian processes for machine-intensive industrial advancement. The twentieth century introduced nuclear power, antibiotics, television, and the internet, developments that modernized society and coaxed us from an industrial to a service economy. Companies that clung to outdated processes and structures in the face of groundbreaking innovation struggled to survive.

At every historical juncture, change and innovation have altered the economic value drivers that enable our companies to create and

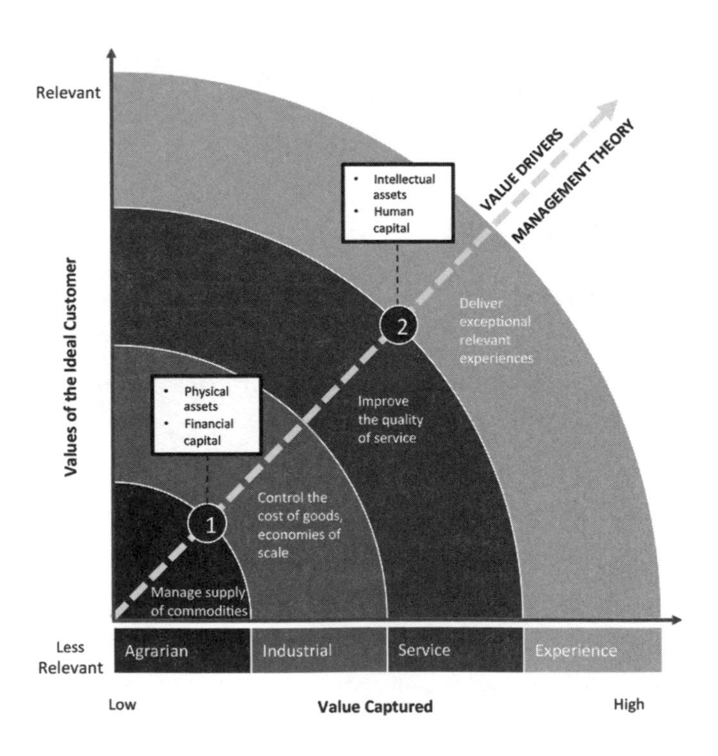

Figure 0.1: Economic progression has shifted the value drivers and strategies of management and buying behavior of consumers.

capture value. The rural agrarian economy revolved around crop production and farmland maintenance. This simple society relied on physical and capital assets to drive success—businesses needed labor and basic mechanization to rear livestock, till the land, and harvest the crop. The industrial economy, sparked by the Industrial Revolution of the early to mid-1800s, introduced more advanced machinery. However, commercial success still hinged on the value drivers of physical assets and financial capital. Those who could manufacture the most for the smallest labor input and capital outlay reigned supreme.

The move from an industrial to a service-based economy, where the "primary economic activity is the provision of services rather than the production of goods,"[5] has been gradual but noticeable, evident as service companies increasingly seize spots once commanded by manufacturers on the Fortune 500 list.[6] Manufacturing jobs have steadily declined, replaced by double-digit growth in service industries such as health care and social assistance. This economic passage has signified the shift of value drivers from physical assets and financial capital to intellectual assets and human capital. This progression is even more dramatic when looking at the transition from the service to the experience economy, where the consumption of goods and services is anchored around creating memorable experiences.

Businesses that have adapted to these recent changes drive greater corporate value, as intangible assets are now a primary factor in company valuations. Over the last few decades, intangibles have "grown from filling 20 percent of corporate balance sheets to 80 percent . . . ergo they're likely to be large drivers of [a] company's stock market value."[7]

As we continue to adapt to the shift in value drivers, we sit at the crux of a blossoming experience economy. As I discuss in chapter 2, evolving consumer demands and priorities affect how businesses create and deliver relevant products and services. Take the act of hosting a party as a metaphor to describe our economy's steady passage from an agrarian to an experience economy. In an agrarian society, the hosts would grow the crops for the food they would serve at a get-together. In the industrial era, a customer would buy ingredients to make homemade food for his or her party. In the service era, a customer might spend some additional money to cater the party. Now, in the experience economy, a customer will pay substantially more to outsource the duties to a party planner who manages the entire experience from location and food to décor and music.

This burgeoning economy has its roots in the entertainment industry, which has always centered on creating memorable experiences for customers. In my first book, *Delivering Value*, I mention Disney as a brand that deeply embodies the experience economy, firm in its commitment to provide a personalized and consistent end-to-end customer experience (CX). The Disneyland theme park delivers on a "wow" factor born from much more than the services it provides. Every touchpoint is imbued with uniqueness and customization. The employees are trained and motivated to serve the customer's every need. Additionally, Disneyland leverages technology

ECONOMIC EXCEPTIONS

Keep in mind that not all businesses evolve in this manner. There will remain industrial and agrarian companies in the service or experience economies. Physical assets and financial capital still drive success for manufacturing plants. Additionally, each country's economy operates on its own timeline. Though the burgeoning experience economy is expanding throughout the US, some developing nations may just now be entering the industrial economy.

like the My Magic+ vacation-planning system, which enables customers to access park information and seamlessly make ride and restaurant reservations.[8] The park gathers and applies customer insights to ensure that each person's visit is distinctive and unforgettable.

The experience economy has expanded beyond entertainment and is infiltrating nearly every industry, impacting what to sell, how to sell, and where to sell in one way or another. I later discuss the criticality of knowing your customer to enable greater customization. Retail has become "shoppertainment" or "etailing," and restaurants have transformed into "eatertainment."[9] Nowadays health care, travel, banking, and even some construction companies are not only evaluated by the services rendered but also by the experiences provided. Commoditized products and services can be revitalized by providing enhanced, differentiated experiences. These memorable experiences are devised, developed, and delivered through intellectual assets and human capital.

What does all of this mean for your business? The new value drivers are transforming strategy. They fundamentally change consumer demands, who and how we hire, the ways we interact with technology and AI, organizational structure, and strategic design and implementation.

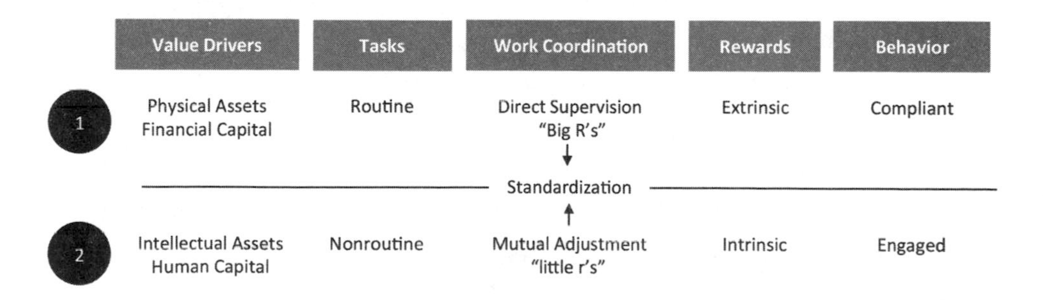

Figure 0.2: The shift in the economy and value drivers has induced fundamental changes in the work employees do and how they're motivated. The transformation demands that companies update management processes, organizational structures, and compensation models.

The experience economy has presented well-adjusted companies with colossal opportunity. Apple, a company built on offering customers a true brand experience, recently broke the stock market record, closing with a market cap of over $1 trillion.[10] However, the chaos of this transition has led some companies to face unforeseen challenges. The most common company mistakes I have witnessed as a result of the economic progress include the following:

- **Lack of understanding of modern value drivers.** Throughout the book, I reference the ideas of many authors and strategists, among them Michael Porter, Theodore Levitt, and Bruce Henderson. My thoughts and research have built upon their decades of insights and well-published knowledge. While their works are astute and imperative to understanding strategy, many leaders solely apply these foundational strategy frameworks dating back to the 1980s, 1990s, and early 2000s. These tools and ideas are not irrelevant, but to be pertinent, they must be updated to account for our new value drivers.
- **Outdated approach to strategic execution.** As shown in Figure 0.2, tasks have shifted from routine to nonroutine and from manual to digital. Yet too many companies continue to focus on supply chain management, cost control, and quality improvement. Although important, these management practices alone are insufficient in the new economy, which demands companies to deliver exceptional experiences to customers. Later in the book, I talk about how companies can prioritize their efforts and resources to focus on what customers truly care about. Outsizing requires companies to exceed the fundamentals of normal business practices and invest in strategic activities that drive differentiation.

- **Inefficient organizational structure.** Company structure has grown increasingly complex, relying on layers of direct supervision for management. While direct supervision works well in a commodities or goods business, it can be expensive and counterproductive in service and experience economies. Additionally, as discussed in later chapters, this structure ignores the needs and wants of the succeeding generations of workers. A stratified structure lends itself to hierarchical command and control management tactics that result in employee compliance rather than engagement. Compliance works in industrial, routine, task-based environments. The new economy, however, calls for engaged employees who can mutually adjust to increase agility in unpredictable environments. It requires a team that can drive speed to value and devise creative solutions to optimize the customer experience.

- **Futile motivational tactics.** Too many companies get strategy wrong because they motivate solely through extrinsic rewards rather than building strategies that prompt intrinsic buy-in. When leveraged in isolation, extrinsic rewards can lead to unintended consequences through what I refer to in chapter 1 as financial arm wrestling, the high jump, and the hockey stick. Extrinsic rewards are quid pro quo and straightforward in the industrial economy. For example, produce twenty widgets at a set profit margin and receive a specified bonus. But what happens when value drivers change, and experience, knowledge assets, and human capital are the cornerstones for achieving outsized economic profits? How can companies reward the intangibles?

- **Company centricity over customer centricity.** In service and experience economies, every decision must revolve around the customer. Too often, leaders choose what to do and how to do it based on their companies' needs. They focus the company inwardly and become distracted by their own mission, vision, and values while ignoring the most important thing—the values of their customers and what motivates them to buy. In the coming chapters, I illustrate the importance of deeply understanding the ideal customer and serving his or her values.

NAVIGATE THE PATH FORWARD

Change is occurring throughout the globe. We are operating in unfamiliar territory. Even Wall Street analysts warn of the current economy, reporting, "this market is weird."[11] While no individual or business has the power to control or prevent these global shifts, leaders do have the ability to shape the futures of their companies.

Our dynamic, unpredictable market and changing value drivers accentuate strategy's significance. Following my employment with professional services giant Ernst & Young, I launched a finance-focused consulting practice. I soon realized that to achieve the desired outcomes on the balance sheet and income statement, I needed to move outside of the bounds of financial statements and into the creative gray area of strategy. While the financials are the measuring stick of strategic success, true organizational value is derived from a broad range of activities that feed into your strategy. Strategy is the multifaceted, living guidebook that leads your business on the road to success. Outsizing requires you to tap into a burning desire for growth and significance. Navigating the path forward can be complicated and challenging, but when mastered and pursued with strategic discipline, it is the key to success.

After a decade of extensive hands-on strategy work and research, I set out to write a book founded on timeless strategic principles.

Too many books promise to share the secret to immediate growth or to sustaining a competitive advantage. They focus on feel-good organizational goal setting. While defining your organizational goals is a critical aspect of strategy, goal setting is not strategy. Accomplishing your goals is the outcome of your organization's efforts. A strategy that is heavy on goals and light on action doesn't drive the fortitude necessary to withstand our competitive, changing market.

As you read this book, remember that outsizing is not a one-size-fits-all solution. It is not doing the same thing you have been doing for years. It does not enable success without a lot of commitment. And it is not internally focused or self-serving. Outsizing is about elevating yourself and your business to achieve more than you ever thought possible. It's about overcoming the inertia and biases that plague transformation to take meaningful strategic action.

As you embark on your strategic journey, understand that strategy is hard. There is no blanket prescription for success. It takes time, dedication, resources, and a willingness to learn and expand your horizons. I hope that this book provides you with the insight and inspiration to move forward on this challenging yet critical path to outsizing your strategy.

As shown in Figure 0.3, this book is organized into six chapters that will help you do the following:

- **Design a robust strategy.** Chapter 1 delves into how to create a strong foundation from which to build your strategy. This entails fostering an intentional culture, eliminating biases, and intrinsically motivating employees to buy into the enterprise's strategy.
- **Understand what customers really want.** Chapter 2 emphasizes strategy design in a CX-driven economy. It teaches you how to define and attract your ideal

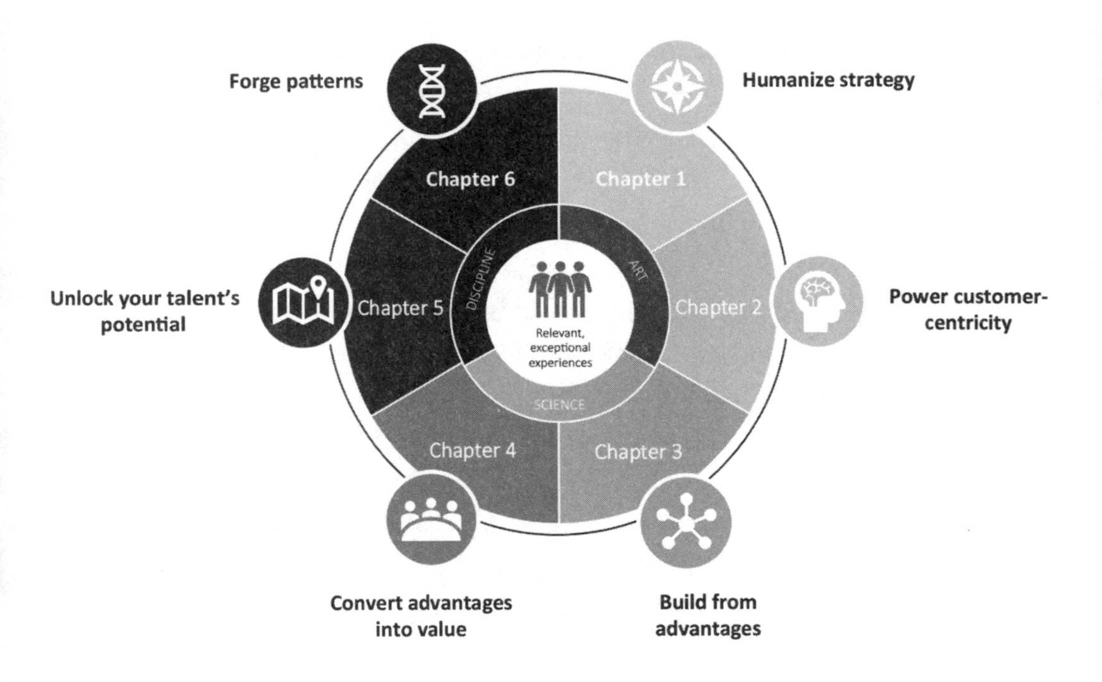

Figure 0.3: The six steps to outsize your strategy

customers by analyzing their buying behaviors and appealing to their values, composed of needs, passions, motivations, and circumstances.

- **Build from positional, asset, and capability advantages.** Chapter 3 introduces how to transform positional, asset, and capability advantages into a competitive advantage by making informed where-to-compete and how-to-compete decisions.
- **Capture financial value.** Chapter 4 instructs on how to align your asset and positional advantages with your corporate capabilities to capture greater value from price premiums, improve cost and capital efficiency, and grow strategically.
- **Empower your team to execute.** Chapter 5 examines how to unlock the potential of your talent. You will learn how to recruit, hire, train, and retain value maximizers, enable teams, and celebrate success.
- **Make strategy a habit.** The final chapter discusses how to create accountability structures and align actions with results to drive ongoing success.

We are operating at an exciting time, standing on the edge of vast opportunity. Adapting to the progress in our global market requires us to shift our thinking and reimagine our businesses. We must make bold moves that support our ultimate quest to outsize our growth, profits, and potential.

1

HUMANIZE STRATEGY

It starts with an intentional culture, deeply rooted in purpose. Outsizing enables you to overcome the inertia and biases that plague transformation. How can you motivate employees to diligently focus on the truly essential activities?

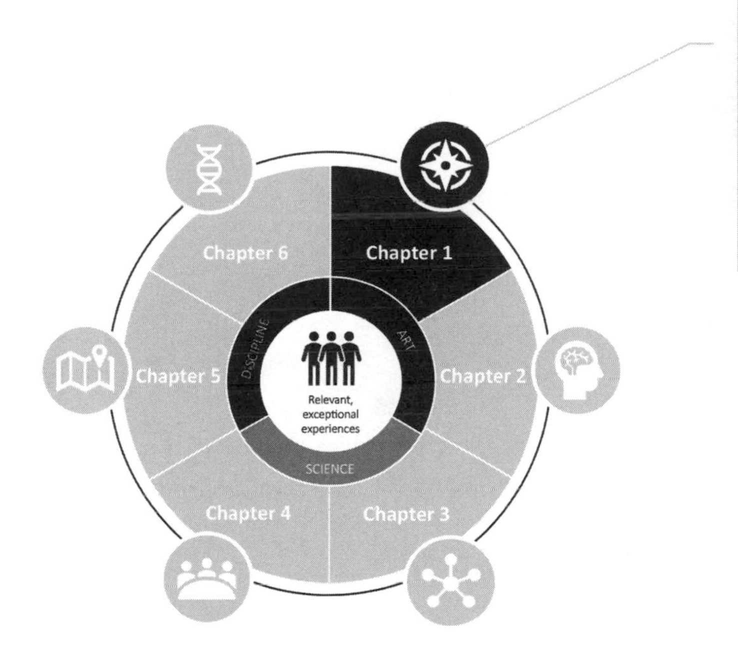

Employees' emotional, passionate, and intellectual insights form the heart of a company, driving innovation, differentiation, and resolution. But human complexity also introduces a unique set of challenges to strategy. To harness the power of our human capital, we must embrace the positive human elements while mitigating ego, misguided emotions, prejudice, and groupthink.

In this chapter, I discuss how to overcome the negative side effects of a humanized strategy to

- transform toxic environments to foster intentional company culture,
- create an objective strategy,
- eliminate rigid bureaucracy,
- resolve power struggles,
- eradicate detrimental budgeting practices, and
- focus on what matters.

BUILD AN INTENTIONAL CULTURE

The internet provides customers with a platform to share their grievances, and it also bolsters the employee voice. Fed-up employees frequently express their frustration with their work environments and unveil workplace ordeals via social media, inviting the public and reporters into their enigmatic company cultures. Neither brand status nor size can shield businesses from negative cultural depictions or litigation.

A story about the $10 billion ridesharing app, Uber, bubbled to the top of 2017 headlines when Susan Fowler, an engineer, published a blog denouncing her former employer. The post candidly detailed Fowler's experiences coping with sexual harassment in an aggressive workplace. She described the sexual advances of a "high performer" who was given a "stern talking to" after she reported his lewd conduct.[1] The company "[didn't] feel comfortable punishing him for what was probably just an innocent mistake on his part."[2] Fowler explained how after interacting with female coworkers, she discovered that hers was not the manager's first reported sexual harassment incident.

Fowler also described the "'game-of-thrones political war" boiling in the company. She depicted the competitive culture where people were shuffled around like pawns, organizational priorities were undefined, and little progress on company-related goals was made. Fowler's blog captured the attention of the *New York Times*, which disseminated Fowler's sentiments and the newspaper's own findings to a broader audience in the exposé "Inside Uber's Aggressive, Unrestrained Workplace Culture."[3] The piece depicted the app's freewheeling, Hobbesian environment, portraying employees' lewd conduct, drug use, and unbridled abuse of power. Uber's culture centers around meritocracy, emphasizing how "the best and brightest will rise to the top based on their efforts, even if it means stepping on toes to get there."

In the article, a few current employees anonymously revealed some shocking cultural concerns. One employee divulged that his manager threatened to beat his head in with a baseball bat.[4] Three female employees reported being groped by a manager at a global staff meeting in 2015. Since Fowler opened the floodgates, Uber has dealt with multiple lawsuits from former employees asserting sexual assault and verbal abuse from higher-ups. Susan's revelations not only exposed Uber to litigation and evoked widespread backlash against the company's culture but also revealed how women are often treated in male-dominant Silicon Valley.

Unfortunately, poor workplace culture extends beyond Northern

California tech firms. For instance, in 2015, Amazon received extensive press for promoting a "bruising workplace" where "workers are encouraged to tear apart one another's ideas in meetings, toil long and late . . . and [are] held to standards that the company boasts are 'unreasonably high.'"[5] As global competition increases, companies shift the burden of enhanced performance and increased production onto employees.

Negative culture doesn't just stem from aggressive behavior and exceedingly high expectations. Every year, the company 24/7 Wall St. aggregates thousands of employee reviews and publishes the report "The Worst Companies to Work For."[6] A variety of companies make the cut for an assortment of reasons. Craft store Jo-Ann Fabrics, Dillard's department store, Dish Network, and Kraft Heinz Company topped 2017's list. In a recent interview, Glassdoor spokesman and list contributor Scott Dobroski explained that the leading indicators of employee satisfaction include "culture and values, career opportunities, and trust in senior leadership."[7] Employees who gave low ratings frequently cited how their employers lacked these core values. One telling comment from an employee at a company that received the second-lowest rating of any US company said, "Corporate leaders don't truly respect or care about their employees. They only care about making money off them."[8]

Cultural warning signs are prevalent, and most of the time, company leadership is aware. Leaders have skimmed employee reviews, witnessed extreme turnover, and even read about their company's cultural slip-ups on social media or in publications. Though many acknowledge that something needs to change, harmful cultures often remain intact. Despite the additional feedback and information that clues leadership in to how *not* to run a company, employee satisfaction remains dismal, and turnover relentlessly climbs.

Amid a changing landscape and labor gap, cultural adaptation is more critical now than ever. People are the source of your

COMPETITIVE ADVANTAGE

I often explain to clients that people cannot be your competitive advantage. This is true because people are not a rare resource—many companies have great people—and people are not durable. They don't stay at your company forever, and they are free to move from company to company.

People are, however, the source of your competitive advantage. They execute your strategy and drive your company toward your desired outcomes.

---

competitive advantage. Employees, not companies, execute tasks, implement strategy, and create value for customers. In my first book, *Delivering Value*, I discussed how employees' diverse skill sets are the primary resources in an organization. Without people, commerce is baseless. Without the right people, company success is bridled. Employees—not companies—have the power. And they're no longer succumbing to virulent work environments. Change is overdue.

Few leaders succeed at transforming their company cultures, because changing behaviors and ideals that have been ingrained over years—sometimes decades—is difficult. This is due primarily to two reasons:

1. **Companies are under pressure to perform.** Most executives don't envision a toxic dog-eat-dog workplace culture when they form a business. Many leaders initially prioritize the health and wellness of their people. They offer generous vacation policies and encourage employees to sleep, exercise, and spend time with friends and family. However, companies are in business first and foremost to deliver results. When inevitable road bumps occur, hindering a

company's ability to fulfill its duty to shareholders, panic sets in, and over time, employee-first culture is gradually replaced with a rank or yank mentality. Employee needs are overlooked or deprioritized in times of crisis. Those who can't compete aren't allowed to play the game. A negative culture evolves as trials cause leaders to tense up and emphasize performance above culture (forgetting that the two are interdependent).

2. **Negative culture is hard to reverse.** Organizations are filled with incumbent players who have constituted and endorsed certain work environments. Oftentimes, a cultural turnaround requires key leadership to transition out of their roles so the company can elevate individuals with fresh perspectives through the chain of command.

While it can be painful to reverse a negative culture, the efficacy of your strategy depends on it. Management guru Peter Drucker famously asserted, "Culture eats strategy for breakfast." While this book is about creating a successful strategy, I cannot emphasize enough the importance of your people and company culture. (See Figure 1.1.) A strategy without people can't exist. If the employees leading your strategy are uninformed, opposed, or apathetic, your company will not succeed. While financial well-being, operational effectiveness, and customer satisfaction are critical pieces of your business, you can't have a business without employees. You must endorse a socially oriented, intentional culture that engages and fulfills the people who are dedicated to making your organizational vision a reality.

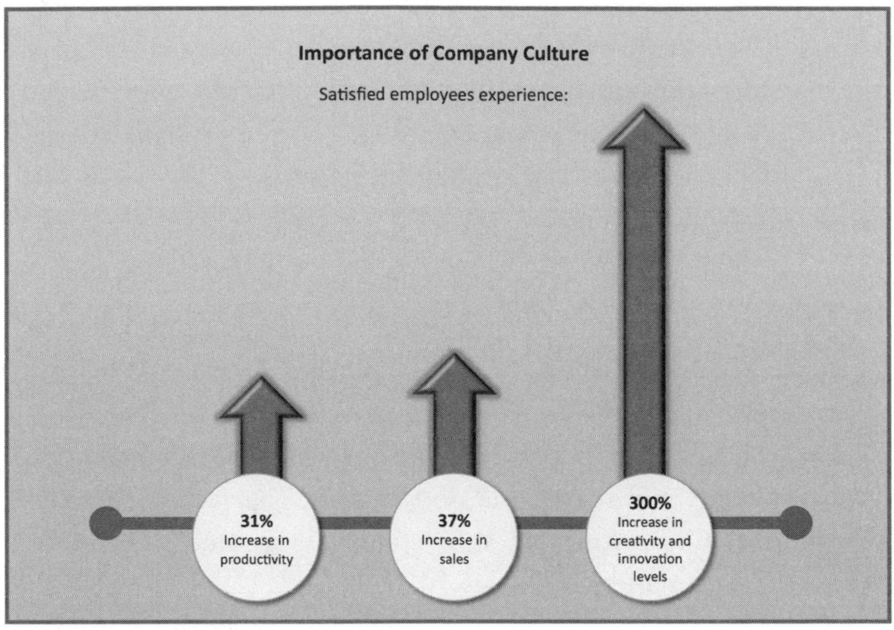

Source: *Corporate Culture Pros*

Figure 1.1: Positive corporate culture results in satisfied employees who are more productive, more creative, and sell more.

To transform your culture, you must first acknowledge your starting point. A simple way to achieve this is by engaging your employees:

1. Ask employees to describe the organizational culture in three words.
2. Request that they anonymously rate your culture on a scale of 1 (ineffective, toxic) to 5 (highly enjoyable, productive).
3. Analyze the results. Are they what you expected? Following these insights, be transparent about the descriptions (not necessarily about low ratings—you don't want to contribute

> to negative feelings about the culture) and ask employees to list up to five things *they* would do if they were in charge of the company. Garnering employee input will provide you with some strong suggestions and open a dialogue around continuous cultural improvement.

Next, you must focus on your company's values and understand how to project them to the rest of the organization through your actions. Culture is defined by how employees interact and behave, and leadership sets the precedent. Employees will mimic their superiors' conduct. If they see a leadership team that puts growth and profits before ethics, they will do the same. Your actions demonstrate the culture you want your employees to build. Therefore, your conduct must be deliberate.

Finally, company culture is built around whom you hire, fire, and promote. Many leaders grapple with this challenge. We are taught that performance always aligns with organizational advancement. However, I have witnessed strong employees—who possess unique skill sets and capabilities—willing to oppose the strategy and poison the culture. I have also observed lower performers who embody the desired culture and project the team-oriented behavioral traits necessary to foster the desired environment. As I highlight in chapter 5, it's fairly easy to train people on skills. Forcing someone to care or attempting to change someone's personality, however, is a futile undertaking.

Ensure that your workforce is established with your ideal culture in mind. By recruiting candidates and valuing employees who exhibit strong behavior and dismissing those who don't, you send a message to the rest of your team and fortify a culture based on shared values and principles.

Former CEO of IBM Louis Gerstner stated, "Culture isn't just one aspect of the game; it is the game. In the end, an organization is nothing more than the collective capacity of its people to create value."[9] Fostering an intentional culture will set the tone for employees' behavior and communication with each other and with customers. Culture is a key tenant of strategy and a driving force within your company. Ensure that your work environment reflects your values and guiding purpose. Promoting a purposeful culture enables you to engage the best employees, attract your ideal customers, and advocate for your desired reputation.

DESIGN AN OBJECTIVE STRATEGY

Have you ever been stuck in a meeting where one person dominates the conversation? Strategy workshops often unveil an organizational chasm born of extreme personality discrepancies. In many cases, a client engages me after their internal strategic process converts to an unproductive argument where a few anchors sway the opinion and muffle the rest of the group. Regardless of the conversation's outcome, hearing one or two opinions is never conducive to a successful strategy. Biases break down the strategic process. To design a focused, effective strategy, you must start with a clean slate and develop an impartial view of the problem or opportunity at hand.

I was working with a mid-size company headed by an intimidating CEO. He stood well over six feet tall and commanded the room with his booming voice and blunt conversational style. His company was experiencing turmoil; the market had shifted, and cross-industry automation was slowly eating away at his revenue. The company needed an immediate turnaround strategy.

He called me in for an emergency strategy overhaul and invited four of his colleagues to join. We were tasked with evaluating an expansion strategy for the business, a necessary but risky endeavor. As we analyzed the options, it became apparent that the CEO's reigning opinion was the only information that mattered. While he was an intelligent, experienced professional, he determined (almost single-handedly) to open a division in an overcrowded, unfamiliar market. He was biased because his brother lived in California and consistently alluded to an economic boom that was generating opportunity for businesses like his own. While this information wasn't untrue, it wasn't the whole story. His explanation excluded key pieces of data, including California's increased cost of conducting business and its overly saturated market.

This strategy session exhibited three common types of damaging biases:

1. **Anchoring:** The tendency to allow the first idea offered to steer the entire decision-making process. The CEO was the first (and one of the only people) to give his opinion at the beginning of the session.
2. **Champion bias:** Evaluating an idea based on the person proposing it rather than by an objective assessment of the idea itself. Because the CEO was a knowledgeable, experienced executive, the team took his word as the truth.
3. **Herding:** People's inclination to side with the majority without taking their own judgments into consideration. It was easy to consent to the CEO's idea. After all, even if his proposition failed, there would be no repercussions for other employees. Sometimes challenging a leader's opinion can seem too big a risk.

The group trusted their CEO. They assented to his ideas without completing any formal analysis or playing devil's advocate. The team had likely been absorbed into a dangerous pattern of groupthink long ago and therefore decided this was a good strategy because everyone else appeared to think so. Due to the volatile combination

TYPES OF BIASES

In addition to anchoring, champion, herding, and optimism biases, other common biases damage strategic decision-making.

Confirmation bias: The tendency to seek and reference information that confirms one's preexisting theories or beliefs.

Correspondence bias: The propensity to inaccurately credit success to observed factors. This bias assumes that by replicating the actions of others, similar results may be achieved. I often see this when companies attempt to "copy" competitor strategies. A company may see its competitor excelling in a certain area and follow the competitor's lead, failing to understand the complex network of activities that enables success for the competitor.

Loss aversion: The impulse to place too much emphasis on avoiding downsides at the peril of not pursuing risks worth taking.

Survivorship bias: The tendency to focus on people or things that made it past some selection process and neglecting those that did not.

---

of biases, the organization's strategy temporarily wandered down the wrong path, costing the company significant time and money.

Bias can take on many forms. One that commonly misleads strategy is optimism bias, such as when a team member proclaims, "We're going to grow by 30 percent next year!" Usually, aggressive growth forecasts such as this don't align with anticipated market growth. This level of growth would require the company to either steal significant business away from competitors by offering a uniquely differentiated product or service or necessitate the company inventing a new piece of the market. Typically, the team will remain steadfast in their bold growth trajectory. They view their strategy and the market through rose-colored glasses because, at the end of the day, it's easier and more enjoyable to maintain a bright outlook.

Optimism bias clouds most people's judgment. Nearly 80 percent of people display an optimism bias, measured as the difference between a person's expectations and the outcome that follows.[10] A recent study asked participants to predict the likelihood of the occurrence of different life events such as receiving a gift, burning dinner, and getting stuck in traffic.[11] Once a month passed, the participants reported back about which events had occurred. The findings demonstrated that people's outlooks tended toward optimism. Regardless of gender, race, or nationality, participants predicted positive events would occur more often than negative or neutral events. Most of us believe that we will live longer, earn more money, and be less likely to suffer from cancer than what reality tells us. In fact, the likelihood of positive, negative, and neutral events occurring is equivalent.[12]

Optimism isn't necessarily bad. Optimistic individuals tend to be happier, and in strategy, a positive outlook may increase a team's confidence, powering performance and results. Optimism is, however, still a bias that can betray strategy. When I encounter overambitious clients, I warn them about establishing unrealistic expectations, so they can avoid disappointment when results don't measure up to projections. While assurance can support strategic execution, nothing is more detrimental to team alignment and energy than a loss of confidence resulting from impractical predictions.

Effective strategic sessions eliminate prejudice. The process should draw out an amalgamation of viewpoints from a variety of key stakeholders at different levels of the company. For example, I was facilitating a strategy session for a highly successful multinational company last fall. While I was there to lead, I was also there to learn. I wanted to understand how the company's approach to strategy had prevailed over its less successful competitors'. When I arrived, I joined eight individuals in a conference room, each a representative from a different level of the company.

Though the meeting started like most—the CEO, COO, and VP guided the conversation—the presence of additional employees shifted the atmosphere and shaped the strategy. About two hours into the conversation, a meek office manager asked, "Have we considered pursuing this market?" Without this frontline manager's input, the team would have continued to circle around the topic and would have arrived at a rather generic strategy. The multilevel representation shaped the team's differentiated approach. The group's willingness to listen to any participant's opinion, regardless of level, distinguished this company's path and separated it from its competitors.

Incorporating a mix of opinions in a strategy mitigates bias, enabling innovative ideas and fresh perspectives to surface. However, engaging everyone in the room requires a thoughtful strategic method. It can be challenging to coax people out of their shells and promote honest conversation, especially when employees are in front of their higher-ups. To attain a balanced variety of viewpoints, teams should fuse a mix of communication styles in their strategic sessions:

1. **Verbal:** Some people process their thoughts by talking others through them. It's important to establish a forum for open verbal communication.
2. **Written:** Some participants shy away from presenting their ideas to the group. At certain points in the day, I pass out sticky notes and encourage everyone to record as many ideas as possible. Participants affix these notes on a whiteboard or poster board where the rest of the group can read them. This method allows participants to share their ideas individually and anonymously.

3. **Dialogue:** At some point in the day, it can be helpful to partner up participants or create small groups. I tend to design groups based on complementary personality traits to encourage blended dialogue. However, be careful not to pair your quietest participant with your loudest.

Though one of these methods might better serve your purposes, it's important to remember your overall goal: to strengthen the voice of each participant in the room. Adjusting the approach to draw out more experiences and ideas will empower a holistic, bias-free strategy design.

ELIMINATE RIGID BUREAUCRACY

While an intentional strategic method supports bias-free strategy, authentic idea sharing is contingent on cultural transparency. If organizational bureaucracy discourages employees from sharing their viewpoints or oppresses opposition, participants are unlikely to openly engage.

Employees want their voices heard and have begun to challenge the hierarchical model. Millennials especially have influenced a widespread conversion from bureaucracy to flatarchy, a model that adopts hierarchy when necessary (for example, during high-intensity projects) but employs a roles-based model for day-to-day operations. However, while millennials are attempting to flatten stratified organizational architecture, the structural transition will be ongoing and laborious. Many corporate cultures remain dictated by inflexible bureaucracy, which can encourage groupthink resulting in deadlock and, in some cases, ethical misconduct.

Following an introductory strategy session with a new client, I schedule one-on-one interviews to confirm some of my initial assumptions. I leverage these interviews as an opportunity to talk with employees from all levels of the organization, customers, and sometimes even suppliers. It also provides an excuse for me to extend my conversation with some of the timid or seemingly disengaged participants who joined the first strategy session.

Typically, when I ask these employees to speak with me further about their opinions on strategy, they circumvent my questions. However, after some coaxing, most usually explain their hesitation by admitting their desire to avoid conflict. "I didn't speak up because I am not about to argue with the CEO," they explain. "I don't want to upset leadership, and if I am wrong, I don't want to ruin my career."

Passive corporate culture corrupts organizational strategy and impedes employee development. In an idle environment, employees rarely dissent from leadership's ideas or actions. Professional advancement requires employees to please their superiors, regardless of whether they agree with the proposed approach. This approval-seeking attitude inhibits growth, as employees spend more time focusing on what the boss thinks and wants than they do forming their own opinions. It also reduces the merit and pertinence of the strategic idea. Playing devil's advocate bolsters strategy, as it identifies potential gaps in propositions and increases idea exploration. When cultures restrict employee questioning, they inadvertently subdue creativity, innovation, and progress.

In some instances, submissive behavior results in moral dilemmas cultivated by employees' unwillingness to speak up, even in the face of fraud. For example, in 2016, Wells Fargo was slapped with a $185 million fine to settle allegations that its employees had established millions of fake bank accounts for customers. A formal investigation revealed that employees had set up 3.5 million fake accounts in total.[13] The fraud was said to have originated when CEO John Stumpf advocated that "eight is great," encouraging employees to sell at least eight products to each of their Wells

Fargo customers.[14] Sales goals were set at three products per customer only ten years prior.[15]

Once the incident went public, many employees came forward, describing how Wells Fargo perpetuated a "toxic sales culture" where if you didn't meet your sales goals, you were "bringing down the team and then you [would] be fired, and it [would] be on your permanent record."[16] Though numerous employees admitted that

BENEFITS OF REDUCING BUREAUCRACY IN YOUR ORGANIZATION

In addition to encouraging multilevel strategic input, limiting corporate bureaucracy will enable your company to do the following:

- **Eliminate bottlenecks to expedite decision-making.** Oftentimes, bureaucratic structures contribute to company bottlenecks. Employees require approval from higher-ups to make even nominal decisions. The back-and-forth between employee and manager results in a lengthy decision-making process. By eliminating extreme bureaucracy, employees are empowered to make relevant decisions, streamlining the process and moving to action faster.
- **Remove unnecessary rules and regulations to increase efficiency.** In every business, there are critical, unbreakable rules. As I discuss in chapter 5 when I introduce little r's, there are also usually some unnecessary or outdated rules. Avoidable rules slow businesses down and burden culture. Once inessential rules are eliminated, employees can focus on more important things like bringing new, innovative offers to market or enhancing the CX.

sales goals were unrealistically high, they didn't speak up for fear of losing their jobs. The pressure to comply with leadership's agenda silenced the employees' resistance. They would rather succumb to immorality than disappoint their superiors.

It's not uncommon for employees to operate out of fear. In one interview, a young worker explained to me how even though she had data to contradict her director's stance during a strategy session, she felt her job was to stroke his ego. She didn't believe that there was anyone else in the higher levels of the firm she could confide in and didn't want to undermine her boss's authority. Therefore, she kept her mouth shut.

Another employee disclosed that he wasn't necessarily scared to disagree with his boss. He simply couldn't risk being wrong. "While I have my own well-thought-out ideas and opinions," he explained, "what happens if the company takes my advice, and I lead it down the wrong path? Do I lose my job?"

If employees believe that they are not working in a secure, constructive environment, they will never feel supported to share their ideas or stand up to wrongdoing. To encourage employee development and contribution, inspire innovation, and strengthen the strategic process, take these actions:

- **Encourage a culture of radical transparency.** This term was inspired by CEO Ray Dalio of Bridgewater Associates, the largest hedge fund in the world, which manages nearly $160 billion. Bridgewater's culture evolved out of feedback that Dalio received early in his career from a confidant who told him he was too brutally honest.[17] His communication with employees was considered blunt. He resolved the issue by meeting with each employee one-on-one and reaching agreement about how they would treat each other. He "wanted to create a culture where employees could have 'thoughtful disagreement' and exchange controversial ideas without creating problems."[18] Nobody is going to—or should—agree on everything. Transparency reduces bias and stimulates conversation, even when it stems from dissent.

A transparent culture will begin to erode the negative side effects of corporate bureaucracy. Once employees and leaders are more honest with one another, they will feel more comfortable sharing their opinions. This openness will begin to break down the ineffective byproducts of corporate hierarchy such as useless, outdated policies instated to further distinguish leadership from subordinates. The superior aura surrounding leadership will dissipate, and employees will be empowered to share ideas and learn from mistakes.

- **Reward those who take action—even when they're wrong.** Whether you reward employees with financial incentive or recognition, praise employees who share their opinions and take action. I know one company that has a "recommendations and tips" box. Employees can write down any of their proposed ideas for the company, whether that involves endorsing the addition of popcorn in the break room or advocating that the company pursue a new lead or mix up the strategy. It can be used for anonymous tips as well. Each month, the CEO shares a few contributions and rewards five employees with gift cards to a retailer of their choice. This approach costs the company little and creates a safe space for employees to share their ideas.

Bureaucracy can have its place in organizations. It allows for scalability and increased control in times of crisis. However, it can build barriers and ravage communication. By remaining aware of bureaucracy's ugly potential, companies can work to develop cultures founded on honest and open communication.

Outsizing is forged through a dedication to clarity and integrity. In settings that encourage transparency, we are free to challenge biases when we feel the company is heading toward danger. A culture of honesty and openness coaxes us to ask difficult questions, reflect on our own interests, and share our intentions with others, therefore establishing trust in both our personal and professional relationships. Where bureaucracy stifles information sharing by creating a divide between employee levels, open and outsized cultures are agile. When we outsize, we clearly communicate our goals and expectations, helping us better understand those around us and encourage each other to reach new heights.

RESOLVE POWER STRUGGLES

Transforming cultural climate also entails eliminating power struggles—the tendency for individuals or groups within a company to battle for control. Power struggles spawn organizational tension, confusing your strategy and employees with contradictory leadership agendas. A company cannot simultaneously serve divergent needs.

Power struggles often arise during a leadership transition. I worked with a thirty-year-old retail company founded by a traditional, principled CEO. The founder had been heavily involved in the company since its inception and was considered the organizational Polaris for the employees.

He was highly respected and set a positive corporate tone and culture. Because of his leadership prowess, when he announced his impending retirement, the company had a crop of deserving and dedicated employees lined up to take his place.

The founder was superseded by a capable leader who had also served the company for many years. His successor had the admiration of his peers and was proving to be a strong replacement.

As the new CEO shifted into the role, the founder retired to the board of directors. This passage proceeded smoothly up until the first board meeting.

The board gathered in the conference room to discuss the direction of the company. The new CEO announced his proposition, to which the founder starkly verbally disagreed. The room looked to the founder for the answer. The team's image of the founder as the strategic decision-maker was etched in their minds, even long after his role was occupied by a new force. This problem escalated as the founder challenged new rules and approaches set in place by his successor, and he appeared sporadically in the

HOW TO TELL WHEN SOMEONE IS INITIATING OR SUSTAINING A POWER STRUGGLE WITH YOU

Some people apply gamesmanship principles to perpetuate an understated power struggle. A few signals that could indicate that colleagues are either starting or perpetuating a power struggle include the following:

- They dance around your request for information. If coworkers are oddly private about their projects or reluctant to share data, they could be storing information that they believe gives them an advantage over you or other employees.
- They publicly disregard your ideas. If they are noticeably brushing aside your opinions or recommendations, it could be their way of undermining your authority in front of your peers.
- Other colleagues shy away from dissenting with these people. It's common for dominant people to assert their dominance. It's likely that you're not the first person your colleagues have tried to undercut.

various store locations, ordering around employees with opposing instructions to what the new CEO had given.

Ultimately, the company came to an agreement. The founder took a step back. While he could remain as an active member of the board, his surprise visits to the stores or the office were not permitted. He had to relinquish control for the new CEO to assert his influence.

While this power struggle was effectively resolved, many are more vehement and result in business termination. One of the iciest and most infamous power conflicts occurred between Adi and Rudi Dassler. The siblings launched the Dassler Brothers Sports Company together in the 1920s but terminated the company in 1948 when jealousy and accusations of Nazi involvement destroyed their relationship. After the breakup of the company, the brothers independently founded two of the largest athletic shoe and apparel rivals, Adidas and Puma. The two vowed never to speak to one another again, and when they died, they were buried at opposite ends of the cemetery, preserving an eternal power struggle.[19] Though these brothers successfully launched independent ventures, power struggles are difficult to overcome and can poison business prospects.

Some detrimental power struggles develop between departments rather than people. For example, sales and marketing are two of the most essential, interrelated functions in any business. While the departments share similar objectives, they often have different perspectives of how to achieve their goals. Marketing is strategically oriented, while sales is typically action oriented. Because of this, the two departments are prone to disagree about how to achieve the end goal of obtaining customers and growing revenue.

A power struggle emerges as each department employs gamesmanship to appeal for a bigger budget and more recognition from the executive suite. Oftentimes, one team is trying to steal away something that the other has. This might escalate as the departments exchange threats and refuse to work together or align on initiatives.

In any power struggle, both parties lose. A lack of alignment cements a company in a strategic stalemate, ultimately leading to its demise. Therefore, it's critical to address power struggles as soon as they begin to appear. To effectively thwart the maturation of power struggles, consider the following:

- If you find yourself engaged in the power struggle, clearly define roles and decision authority. Ensure that you both know where you and your opponent stand in the business, and distribute responsibility. Not all decisions can be made in joint agreement, so separate big choices so that each party has an opportunity to exercise power.
- If you're a witness of another group's power struggle, finding common ground can help ease the tension. Sometimes a third party can bring a fresh perspective to those engaging in business combat. Seek opportunities to bridge the gap with new ideas and quell any bad feelings between people or business units.

ERADICATE DETRIMENTAL BUDGETING PRACTICES

Just as power struggles beget strategic deadlock, misaligned financial goals limit progress and motivation. Too often companies implement unsustainable, unrealistic budgeting practices to define individual and corporate success. Outsizing is not about setting overly ambitious targets or accepting meek projections. When steep goals fail to be obtained, organizational morale is trampled, and companies crawl back to the comfort of mediocrity. Too-low projections applaud average returns from the start. Apathy and stagnation born of poor budgeting methods result in complacency for companies and employees alike, one of the primary killers of strategic advancement. Outsizing is about establishing realistic forecasts to measure your strategy's expected ROI. Budgets alone can't generate outsized results; this is the job of a well-designed and effectively executed strategy.

Early on, I introduced how unpredictable service and experience economies demand that companies move beyond extrinsic rewards and intrinsically motivate employees. That being said, compensation remains an effective motivational mechanism to be used in combination with purpose-driven incentives. However, not all pay plans are equal. A study of nearly fourteen thousand employees found that "performance-related pay [is] positively associated with job satisfaction, organizational commitment, and trust in management" when incorporated in an incentive pay plan driven by strategic motivators. Incentive pay plans increase the stakes for employees, therefore engrossing them in a competition with themselves with a relevant and captivating outcome—a boost in personal income.

Unfortunately, pay-for-performance compensation plans are often poorly designed. Companies must ensure that the compensation methods achieve the desired results and avoid unintended

EXCERPT FROM *DELIVERING VALUE*

To diminish the negative side effects of budgeting, managers should focus on ongoing advancement in the company using continuous planning cycles through a constant twelve-month forecast. As one month drops off, a new month is added to the forecast, so it exhibits at least twelve months at a time. Forecasting is a collaborative, continuous process that motivates employees through future projections. The months furthest from the current date are updated as they approach, based on current market conditions to ensure greater accuracy. Rolling forecasts, not budgets and targets, become the primary managerial tool.

consequences. Incentive-based payment models that involve asking employees to "jump over a stick" can result in many issues. In the jump-over-the-stick budgeting approach, divisional managers hold a hypothetical yardstick in front of employees and challenge them to jump over the target. A back-and-forth discussion between the manager and employee ensues as they determine the appropriate, realistic height or budget they can hit. Typically, the conversation results in some compromise that sets the target at a waist-level height. The employee jumps over with ease and receives a bonus, and both parties are content. The yardstick approach breeds stagnation. The too-low targets fail to push employees out of their comfort zones, undermining their focus on constant learning and continuous growth and improvement.

The concept applies organization-wide as well. An alarming number of strategy conversations conclude with financial arm wrestling. One optimism-biased employee will declare, "We are going to do $150 million in revenue this year!" Another person will chime in, "I bet we will do no more than $125 million," and the conversation continues in this circuitous, fruitless manner until the VP finally decides, "Sure. Let's just plan on $150 million. Please adjust the budget with these updated projections."

The optimism bias is emphasized when employees rely on the unrealistic financial hockey stick approach to budgeting. Hockey stick budgeting refers to the shape of a company's optimistic financial projections if their current earnings and forecasted earnings were charted on a graph. The current year results appear as the toe of a hockey stick, where earnings are relatively flat or dip slightly. The inflection point at the heel of the stick embodies the intersection between historical performance and bullish projections. The forecasted earnings begin to climb exponentially at the inflection point and increase dramatically in the shaft. Thus, the shape of the hockey stick parallels management's argument that although current earnings (the toe) are flat or lower than expected, the company anticipates a miraculous turnaround where revenue and/or profit jumps dramatically, as illustrated by the shape of the shaft.

I worked with a medical device client that, despite the company's unstable condition, was convinced that an extreme financial turnaround was just over the horizon. The employees would reference the prior year's financial statements, strewn with losses, and evaluate the current financials, also stranded in a dismal state. Despite the bleak outlook, the employees assured themselves that the following year would yield significant revenue and margin gains.

During our meeting, the team mulled over a few possibilities. The gregarious VP declared, "We will lose $9 million this year but will produce $15 million in profit next year by making better decisions." The CFO acknowledged the difficulty of achieving the steep margin growth, stating the more likely, less enticing outcome: the company would break even in the following year and achieve incremental margin growth in subsequent years.

The hopeful employees clung to the dramatic hockey stick with the promise of exorbitant margin growth, and not surprisingly, the team failed to meet its targets, losing money in the following year. The team's inability to meet its goals disappointed them and shook their confidence in the company and in themselves. Though the team defaulted on their performance, there were no formal consequences for falling behind; therefore, the company continued to make the same budgeting and operating mistakes year after year.

In the example of the employee and company, the key to engaging in personal and organizational strategy is to set realistic yet ambitious targets. Too often, budgets are built around insignificant projections that are disconnected from strategic initiatives. Take Katie, a company's salesperson, as an example. Katie's personal sales target for the current year might remain the same as last year's, even though she recently completed graduate school and desires to apply her new skills to enhance her performance. Her static sales goals are demotivating. Katie sells just enough to meet her goals and receives a meager bonus. Similarly, a company will throw out seemingly random profit projections that fail to account for its strategic initiatives. For example, let's say a company decides to open a new division. While opening a new division may be a strong, long-term strategic move, it bears a costly short-term impact. The leaders, impatient with results, terminate the division so they can boost the appearance of the income statement.

Too-high and too-low budget projections may at first appear antithetical. Both budgeting approaches, however, serve the same purpose: to mask true financial performance. By establishing unrealistic or easy expectations, companies avoid answering questions about what they should be earning. People opt for mediocrity because it's the safe option. They can preserve their egos. Companies decide not to open a new plant, fire unfit customers, or invest in new offerings, because if they try, there's always a chance they won't succeed. It's easier to stay the course and try to sustain profits.

To be effective, financial objectives must align with the strategy and be realistic. Financial forecasts should drive bold, strategic moves, not encourage averageness. Just as incentive plans for employees must challenge them to learn and improve, an outsizing strategy must propel a company out of its comfort zone and require it to make pivotal tradeoffs. As Mark Zuckerberg stated of strategy, "The biggest risk is not taking any risk. In a world changing really quickly, the only strategy that is guaranteed not to fail is taking risks."[20]

When we couple incremental action with a bold, long-term vision, seemingly impossible targets become attainable. Growth is gradual, and reaping the benefits of a well-thought-out strategy requires patience and discipline. Leading companies and employees take chances. They make strategic bets—and when they win, they win big.

To outmaneuver the competition, you must make some strategic gambles. When I teach companies about taking risks, I share three pieces of advice:

1. **Allow risk-taking to be a learning experience.** Taking risks results in one of two outcomes: either you succeed, or you learn. The best companies are comfortable taking risks that often materialize into lucrative ventures. However, even the highest-performing, most strategic organizations make decisions that don't pan out as expected. Rather than viewing a failed endeavor as wasted time, successful companies regard missteps as educational opportunities. Losses can be fundamental in your company's evolution if you apply the learnings to future undertakings.
2. **Apply a gradual, deliberate implementation plan.** Some teams agree on a bold move and immediately roll out a slew of changes across the entire company. Premature implementation heightens the level of risk and cost, not to mention it irritates employees if the initiative doesn't take. I advise running multiple pilot studies of the program in different parts of the business before full rollout to evaluate feasibility. You will be able to identify issues and make necessary adjustments to reduce the overall risk of investment.
3. **Prioritize when and where to take risks.** This is the most critical piece of advice I can offer. Focus on one new venture at a time. In the coming chapters, I discuss how no company can do everything well. Therefore, you must strategically elect the activities to invest in that will allow your company to excel and differentiate the CX. Conversely, you must also determine where *not* to overinvest. Some areas of your business must remain standard, because additional investment in these areas won't create additional customer

value or allow your company to capture more value. This is especially true when taking risks on new initiatives. Making too many big decisions at once will not only expose your company to heightened liability but will limit the team's ability to focus their full attention on the initiative, reducing the likelihood of success. It's critical to align your strategic decisions with your desired outcomes to determine what needs to happen when.

FOCUS ON THE ESSENTIAL (AND IGNORE THE TRIVIAL)

Once after my wife scolded our four-year-old daughter for misbehaving, I was sent to her room to carry out my fatherly duty of helping her see the purpose and learn the lesson behind the punishment. I asked her, "If something is good, is it right?" Unsure of where I was heading with this question, she paused and responded, "Yes."

She echoed many people's gut reaction to this question. We are often tempted to say, "Yes! It's good, so it must be right for me." We make life-changing decisions based on this misinformed idea that good and right are equivalent. We ignore our natural instincts and convince ourselves that we must do everything good. And each time we do so, we sacrifice our time and energy on pursuits that were never meant to be. We become depleted.

Prioritizing risks, activities, personal matters, and relationships can be one of the hardest things to do. Our culture is founded on a "have it all, do it all" mentality. Consultant and public speaker Greg McKeown explains how we have contorted the word *prioritization* to serve our needs: "The word *priority* came into the English language in the 1400s. It was singular. It meant the very first or prior thing. It stayed singular for the next five hundred years. Only in the 1900s did we pluralize the term . . . [and reason] that somehow we would now be able to have multiple 'first' things."[21]

We can't do or be everything to everyone. We can't be the highly involved parent who works eighty hours a week and volunteers on the side. We can't be in two places at once. This reality hit me last year when traveling to speak at several national conferences. In addition to speaking commitments, I had a plate full of strategy engagements with clients. After one of my speaking engagements concluded in Palm Springs, I flew from Santa Ana to San Francisco and caught the only red-eye that could get me to Nashville by 6 a.m. From Nashville, I embarked on a two-hour Uber ride to Chattanooga, where I was to conduct a strategy workshop for a team of executives. Prior to flying out of San Francisco, I caught a glimpse of myself in the mirror. Dark bags loomed underneath my eyes, and the pallor and exhaustion of my face were exacerbated by the dingy airport lighting. My travel schedule was wearing on me. I missed my family. Travel obligations had forced me to skip out on date nights with my wife and playdates and bedtime stories with my kids. At that moment, I realized I couldn't do it all.

Many confident leaders believe their companies have the power to achieve anything and everything they set their minds to. This assurance can lead to confusing priorities with nice-to-haves. People pile so many things onto their plates that they lose sight of what matters.

McKeown advises people and businesses on essentialism, the art of doing less. Essentialism concerns "how to get the right things done. It doesn't mean doing less for the sake of less either. It is about making the wisest possible investment of your time and energy in order to operate at your highest point of contribution by doing only what is essential."[22] When you outsize, you focus on the essential. You prioritize the very best things (and disregard the insignificant) to achieve impressive results with constrained resources. All companies, regardless of size, must operate within the boundaries of limited means. We only have so many employees, so much money, and so much time. Outsizing your strategy requires you to ask yourself: How can I best leverage my resources to move the dial? What is the anticipated size of the prize for this strategic initiative?

Because we are confined to our available resources, we must prioritize and pursue impactful strategic initiatives. Many companies spread assets too thin across a wide array of activities. When resources are stretched, you might be adequate or even good at a lot of activities. But you are likely not *great* at anything. We may have a plethora of good options. The key to essentialism is determining the best options where we can excel.

Jurist, educator, and religious leader Dallin Oaks describes categorizing our initiatives by "good, better, best."[23] His thought leadership intersects with essentialist principles, focusing on the fact that just because something is or could be good to do isn't significant justification to do it. When we choose good options, we sacrifice our ability to focus on the best. We become too busy to change. We engage in a hectic cycle of focusing only on the good, disabling ourselves from powering our businesses to the next level. Leaders must ask themselves: What is the best choice for our customers, employees, and community? To devise the best option, I always abide by a few key steps:

- **Understand the root of the cause.** It's easy to become preoccupied with surface-level issues. For example, I was providing professional advice to a company that had just released a new product to market. The market response was tepid. The product management team returned to executives with a proposition: "We need to grow our marketing budget by 50 percent to increase customer interest in our new product." The issue, however, was deeper than a lack of market awareness. The sluggish sales stemmed from an irrelevant product. The company needed to spend money on R&D to redesign the offering, not throw more marketing dollars at an uninteresting product. While marketing couldn't hurt, it would detract a portion of the budget from solving the bigger problem. Ensure that you're attacking the root of the cause—not a symptom.

- **Make decisions that increase your odds of success.** Companies often make a list of choices, ranging in degree of risk. I mention that playing it safe can be a risk itself, but on the other end of the spectrum, in some decisions, the odds can be clearly stacked against you. Some of my clients have unsuccessfully entered new market territory because, despite their lack of experience, knowledge of the space, and capability gaps, they thought it was an exciting idea. Don't confuse deliberate risk-taking with leap-before-you-look decisions. You will never have all the answers. Strategy is about increasing the likelihood of success, so make educated bold decisions that increase your chances of achievement.
- **Don't confuse decisions with results.** Sometimes we make good decisions that fail to yield our desired results. Sometimes we make bad decisions that produce favorable outcomes. In some cases, good decisions result in good outcomes but hold you back from making great decisions.

In 2008, my wife and I decided to move from a neighboring city to Littleton, Colorado. We loved the established feel of the community, the proximity to the mountains, and the access to recreational trails. We found a house we liked within our price range and bit the bullet. We prayed about the decision and determined it was the right choice to buy the home. Soon after we purchased the house, Lehman Brothers announced its bankruptcy, the Dow soured, and the economy plunged. The value of our house dropped by 30 percent over two years. In addition to the steep decline in equity, our house gradually revealed many costly defects that had been concealed by the previous fix-and-flip owner.

While our home value has since recovered, I was initially frustrated with my decision. At the time of purchase, we did everything possible to make a good decision. We performed market research, hired a qualified home inspector, prayed for confirmation, and carefully evaluated the pros and cons. We made the best decision for us at the time. Unfortunately, the results did not immediately manifest in the way we had envisioned.

When your best choices lead to disappointing outcomes, you must ensure you don't mistake decisions with results. Sometimes, you get unlucky. Sometimes, your results are not what you expected but lead you to other fortunes. For the longest time, I failed to recognize and be grateful for the intangible benefits we garnered from buying that home. We met neighbors who are very close friends, we are adjacent to the Platte River Trail, which has allowed me to train in tranquility for multiple marathons, and we have been able to serve in a special congregation within our distinctive community. While I was fixated and initially let down by the financial outcomes, I would have missed out on other significant opportunities if not for this home. Sometimes, you must step back and emotionally detach from your expected outcomes to see the true impact of your decisions.

I have also reaped unearned fruit from bad decisions. A few years back, I was presenting at a global contractors' conference. The week of the event, a swarm of client work mounted on my desk, and my focus on the conference and ability to prepare waned. I presented an impromptu session on CX. It was the least prepared I have ever felt as I stepped onto the stage, but following the presentation, I received extensive praise and even won over a new client. My decision to procrastinate conference prep was ill advised, but it worked out in my favor.

It's important to understand how decisions and results differ.

Leaders make a good decision that doesn't immediately generate the desired returns, and they impatiently throw in the towel. Other times, employees positively reflect on a bad decision that produced a favorable outcome and mistakenly repeat the poor choice. The most frequent, oftentimes most dangerous mistake companies make is settling for good decisions that inhibit the organization's ability to pursue greatness.

How do you know you're making the right decision? Making advantageous decisions for your company is easier when you deeply know yourself and your customers. When we outsize, we are left with an eye to what matters most—like people—so we can form strategies that drive unique and relevant experiences tailored to our customers' values. In the following chapters, we will discuss how a customer-centric strategy can guide your decisions and lead you to outcomes that drive value for your business and its stakeholders.

2

POWER CUSTOMER CENTRICITY

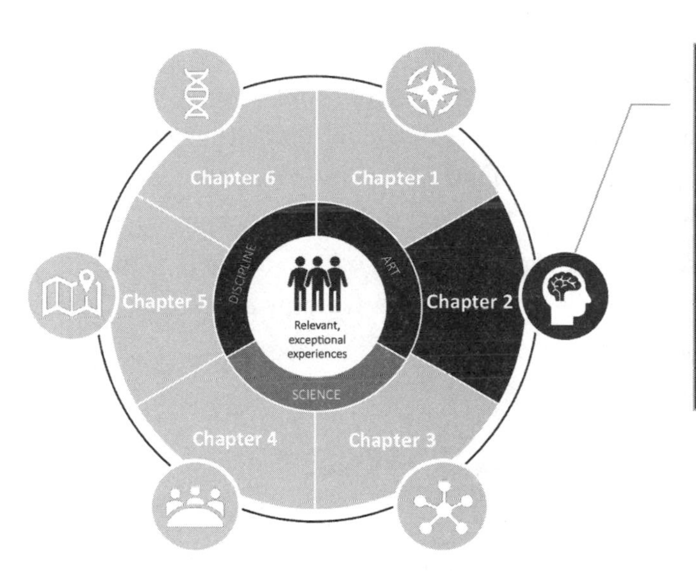

Customer values are the building blocks of customer types. Customer types allow companies to establish a common language that describes groups of customers who have shared values and behaviors. Companies outsize progress and success by optimizing activities to deliver unique experiences and value to distinct customer types.

Perhaps the most expensive strategic design blunder occurs when companies overlook or fail to grasp the customers' complex needs. According to Accenture, in 2017, businesses lost $1.6 trillion due to customers switching to competitors because of poor customer experience—expressed in this book as CX.[1] Many traditional strategy frameworks concentrate on a company's strengths, weaknesses, competitors, market trends, and positioning. These are all important factors that must be acknowledged in the strategic process. However, if the customer isn't the focal point of the company purpose and plan, the strategy likely sways toward irrelevancy.

Unfortunately, companies often mistakenly believe they are customer-centric: they proclaim to love customers and brag about top-tier customer service. As you will learn in this chapter, customer-centric innovation is far more important than customer service offers, customer surveys, or superficial marketing materials. To differentiate and achieve outsized results in our competitive market, companies must deeply understand customers, anticipate their needs, and deliver experiences that align with their values. This requires organizations to stretch far beyond excellent customer service strategies.

DISTINGUISH BETWEEN CUSTOMER SERVICE AND CUSTOMER EXPERIENCE

Customer service receives a lot of buzz, especially since social media has assembled a public megaphone for dissatisfied patrons. Consumers emphasize the importance of customer service in their buying decisions and brand loyalty. Companies often advertise customer service as an essential firm value and allocate significant training funds to the customer support team. While good customer service is integral to customer satisfaction, I often see customers and companies alike mistaking it for CX. Emphasizing customer service is good. However, in today's experience-driven economy, a narrow focus is insufficient. Concentrating entirely on the service element of CX can detract from the big picture. Customer service is one among many in a series of interactions that make up the full CX.

Strong customer service is not always indicative of excellent CX. I witnessed the difference between customer service and CX a few years back when I switched phone carriers. In exchanging phone service providers, I had two requirements: I receive better, more dependable coverage, and I maintain my current phone number. I called the new company to explain my stipulations and was greeted with a pleasant tone and helpful attitude at the other end of the line. "Great customer service. This should be easy," I said to myself.

However, nearly ninety minutes later, even a friendly customer service representative couldn't salvage my poor impression of the company. Due to inefficiency resulting from company-centric, bureaucratic systems, I endured prolonged hold times between a series of transfers. As I slowly wove through a chain of customer service representatives, I recognized the company's structural and operational faults:

- The organizational structure created silos. Employees were working independent of each other, so their priorities were misaligned, and their communication was fragmented. As the customer, I was left waiting while the frantic employees sorted out whom to push me to next.
- The governance structure resulted in a lack of accountability and failed to empower the frontline employees to meet client expectations. Each employee repeated, "I am going to have to pass you off to someone above me." It's more important to give employees the freedom to be helpful than the task of being friendly.

- The process flow was broken. The company's activities, defined as distinct and measurable tasks, mechanisms of work coordination, or steps in the process of making a profit, were not integrated with one another. Each step in the process was inefficient, incomplete, or awkward; therefore, the entire experience felt clumsy. Porting my number was unpleasant at best, and I am sure that the operators on the other end of the line shared my sentiments as they performed daunting, duplicative tasks to confirm information, notify the old service provider, create a pending port while notification was sent, and then activate the port.

The company's customer service was good, and the representatives were kind and genuinely wanted to help. The overall experience, however, fraught with delays and transfers, was frustrating. Following my interaction with the company, I decided to google it. Others' experiences paralleled my own. Customer service ratings were high, even boast-worthy. But the company's scores fizzled in nearly every other category.

This phone carrier likely fell victim to the common misconception that customer service is synonymous with CX. The company's rigid and narrow focus on the service element distracted from the foundational issues plaguing its operational performance. Because the service element is emphasized so heavily—in surveys, in news stories, and by the companies themselves—many organizations misunderstand what it means to have a good CX strategy. They can't see the forest for the trees. There are important distinctions that separate customer service and CX.

Customer Service

Customer service is *reactive*. It's something that companies do to customers. It involves detached touchpoints where companies offer support to buyers; they move customers in and out of a store or on and off the phone and (hopefully) provide helpful feedback in the meantime. For example, when I called the phone company, the employees immediately reverted to problem mode, leading me through a series of questions that impacted how they would approach my situation. Following the call, they invited me to take a survey to score them on their problem-solving abilities. All their actions were reactive, not proactive.

Additionally, customer service focuses on training frontline employees. While it's essential to train attentive representatives, customer service cannot compete with the user experience. In addition to enabling employees, companies must invest in the most impactful activities that drive exceptional experiences for each customer. All the training in the world will make little difference if the organization's structure and activities are not focused on better serving the customer.

Customer Experience—CX

On the other hand, CX is proactive. It is something that clients feel and remember about companies long after an interaction ends. CX entails empathizing with customers to understand their pain points, eliminate obstacles, and deliver relevant solutions. It requires companies to ask customers more in-depth questions to determine the salient activities to invest in to fulfill customers' values.

CX encompasses the whole organization, from the frontline employees to the C-suite, assembling interactions to create a unified customer journey, defined as the compilation of all CX touchpoints. CX is embedded in all the activities of the company. When those activities are optimized and intentionally designed to serve client values, exceptional experiences ensue. It goes beyond isolated events and requires activities, processes, organizational structure, and enabled employees to support a deliberate end-to-end customer journey. When effectively implemented, CX fortifies brand loyalty, differentiates companies from the competition, and stimulates demand for a company's products and services.

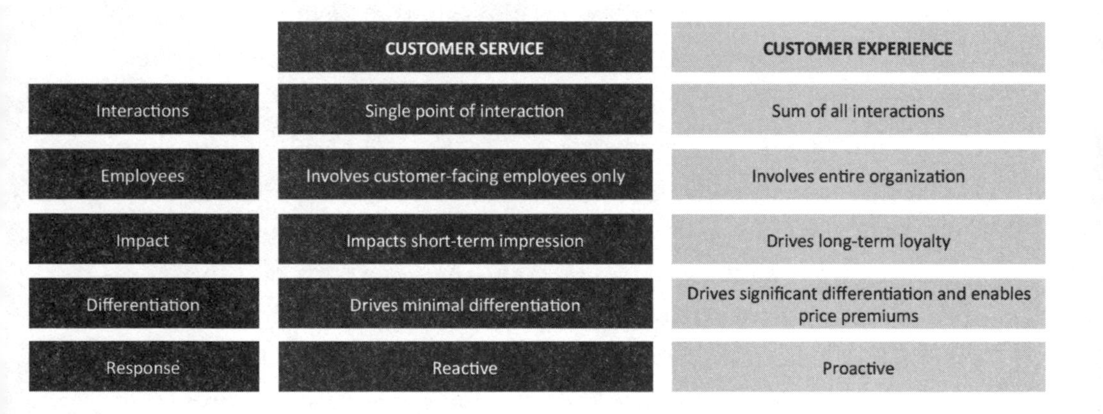

	CUSTOMER SERVICE	CUSTOMER EXPERIENCE
Interactions	Single point of interaction	Sum of all interactions
Employees	Involves customer-facing employees only	Involves entire organization
Impact	Impacts short-term impression	Drives long-term loyalty
Differentiation	Drives minimal differentiation	Drives significant differentiation and enables price premiums
Response	Reactive	Proactive

Figure 2.1: There are distinct differences between customer service and CX, including the nature and number of interactions with customers, the level of involvement throughout the organization, and the outcomes that customer-centric activities can drive.

While I have worked with many organizations weighed down by underdeveloped CX strategies, I can also testify to the fact that some companies are knocking CX out of the park. One company that offers an exceptional CX is Hammer Nutrition. I am an avid runner and have completed four marathons. Because I don't have the typical runner's physique—I am shorter and bowlegged—I prioritize rigorous training and nutrition. I have tried dozens of supplements, gels, and sports drinks to fuel my long runs, many of which taste awful or are pumped with so much sugar and caffeine that they make me sick.

Hammer is the first sports nutrition company I have tried that gets it—and more importantly, gets me. The products are more expensive than alternatives, but I am willing to pay for them because I appreciate Hammer's value proposition: high-quality products, formulated and tested for athletes. Beyond effective products, Hammer has mastered CX for its specific subset of the market. When I ordered a product called Perpetuem, I received a gift bag, free of charge, along with other sample products. When I reordered the product, Hammer sent me a complimentary water bottle and additional products they suggested would benefit my training. The company's nutrition specialist coached me on tips and tricks for staying strong during long runs. Hammer fosters loyalty by providing targeted, personalized CX to each of its customers.

Effective CX like Hammer's is rooted in devout customer centricity—putting the customer at the center of its efforts. The brand supports my specific interests. Hammer's customers compete in a wide variety of sports, but the company knows that I am a runner. Not only does Hammer customize products based on my marathon training, but they also offer me products and advice targeted to my struggles with maintaining my energy levels during long runs. They know what I care about. Providing this level of CX requires companies to deeply understand the customer. This entails

- empathizing with customers to recognize the values that drive their behavior,
- defining and appealing to their multifaceted value systems, and
- serving groups of customers who share similar values with a cohesive strategy and streamlined approach to the customer interface.

As we progress to an experience economy, it is increasingly important to know our customers and understand how to best serve them. This begins with defining who our ideal customers are and aligning our efforts and resources to deliver outsized experiences along the buying journey.

DEFINE YOUR IDEAL CUSTOMER

People love hearing about when CX goes awry. For example, United Airline's recent string of customer horror stories littered the top news headlines in 2017 and 2018. The most notable was the physical assault charge against the airline when it called on aviation security officers to drag Dr. David Dao off a flight between Chicago to Louisville, breaking his nose, giving him a concussion, and knocking out two of his teeth. Protests erupted following the event, as angry activists picketed with signs such as "Beat Your Competition, Not Your Customers" and "United Not Divided," and hordes of disgruntled internet bloggers coined the verbal hashtag #Boycottunited.[2] Though the amount was undisclosed, United had to pay Dao a large settlement out of court for his damages. Greater than the financial burden was the reputational disintegration that United suffered. Before the incident, United was rated the worst full-service airline in the country.[3] The airline's already-low likability plummeted following the circulation of Dao's story.[4]

In most cases, poor CX results in inconvenience rather than trauma. Joanna Vintilla shared her story about a disappointing appliance purchase with the *New York Times* "Haggler" section, an outlet for aggrieved customers. Joanna bought a defective $216 Whirlpool microwave. A Whirlpool technician visited her house on five separate occasions to replace four parts within six months of purchase. The company refused, however, to simply replace the microwave. Once the story went public, Whirlpool offered a refund with terms attached: to receive a new microwave, Joanna was required to pay Whirlpool $75 to remove her defective machine and sign a confidentiality agreement.[5]

In most frustrating instances, companies don't technically do anything wrong. They usually follow the code, elevate you through the customer support hierarchy, and earnestly try to solve your problem. However, while all companies occasionally misstep, CX-focused organizations' proactive, customer-centric approach helps prevent

HOW TO AVOID GENERIC MESSAGING

Mastering messaging strategy requires you to center the value proposition around your ideal customer's needs, passions, circumstances, and motivations—the building blocks of values. Once you have defined your ideal customer, your messaging should do the following:

- **Provide context.** Ensure that your messages are relevant to your target audience by tapping into their momentary thought processes. For example, running a life insurance banner advertisement in an online shoe store distracts your customers from the task at hand and appears out of context. It would make more sense to run such an advertisement on a banking or investment website.
- **Understand the prompt.** In addition to presenting the message in the right context, consider when you should place this message in front of buyers. Customers often trigger potential interest in additional offers. For example, if users upgrade the technology, they may appreciate additional product training. Customer triggers open the door to some of your other products and services.

the escalation of issues. Companies that deliver strong CX possess the structure, processes, and capabilities to mitigate extreme blunders like United's and alleviate customer dissatisfaction in general. When companies fail to deliver CX, it's often due to internally focused strategy.

Organizational narcissism impedes customer centricity. Do you ever get annoyed with a company for putting its own wants and needs before its customers' wants and needs? Take the typical company website as an example. How often do you see web pages that emphasize "about *us*," "*our* values," and "*our* vision"? Companies saturate marketing materials with empty platitudes that proclaim organizational interests, goals, and abilities. I conducted a study of more than 250 organizations and found that some of the most commonly proclaimed values include integrity, value, excellence, honesty, and dedication. These generic, company-centric messages result in a lack of differentiation and often conceal any real value the business can deliver to address a customer's problem. The messaging focuses on corporate values instead of client values. Companies are often preoccupied with internal wants and needs, projecting this self-absorption onto their customer base.

Outsized value is derived by listening to and understanding the customer. I have always believed that the best listeners make the best conversationalists. This adage especially applies in business. If a company doesn't try to understand its customers and instead attempts to force its agenda on the market, it will consistently misfire. As speaker and author Brian Solis stated of companies' frequent misinterpretation of customers, "Ignorance plus arrogance equals irrelevance."[6] This wisdom extends far beyond company messaging. It pertains to the organizational sales motion, positioning, R&D, and customer support.

While a lack of customer understanding can often be attributed to companies' self-created noise, which drowns out their customers' voices, many companies sincerely try to understand buyers; they just don't know how to go about it. When bombarded with data, companies struggle to discern critical customer information from fluff.

Most companies acknowledge that customers should be at the center of every effective strategy, but they stumble when it comes to profoundly knowing them and recognizing their values and behaviors. To focus strategic engagements and help my clients define their buyers, I first introduce the concept of the ideal customer.

An ideal customer is one who understands a company's value proposition and is willing to pay for it. Framing the market in the context of the ideal customer provides a starting point from which companies can gain insight on customer values. As illustrated in Figure 2.2, the ideal customer exists at the center of the bull's-eye. Ideal customers are enjoyable to work and interact with. They rarely challenge you on price, always pay on time, and won't interrupt your Sunday-night family time with semi-urgent requests. The ideal customer provides a reference point that directs organizational focus to the foundation of buyers who will guide strategic decisions and drive success. The goal of the strategy should be concentrated on delivering value to this distinct subset of the market.

Figure 2.2: The ideal customer is at the center of your strategy.

Most companies go astray when they gravitate outside the bull's-eye of the ideal customer. Sometimes companies are forced to shift their strategies. This often occurs during periods of economic contraction. When a recession hits and demand declines, companies are forced to extend sales efforts to those outside their ideal clientele. While periodic shifts may require adjustment to cover costs, long-term adjustments can be dangerous.

As you move away from the bull's-eye, you encounter the outer ring of customers. These customers don't appreciate your value proposition, because your company's activities misalign with their goals and values. As companies lose track of their core customers and flirt with the outer edges of the ideal customer diagram, they establish a following of unfavorable buyers. Since these buyers do not think highly of your value proposition, they can be difficult and unpleasant to work with. Over time, the ideal customer bull's-eye shifts to the exterior ring, and the company's strategy centers around a customer base that is misaligned to its advantages. This trend is hard to reverse, especially for companies with rigid cost structures and high fixed costs, as they must pursue revenue—albeit with the wrong customers—just to keep the lights on.

In good times, it's easy to serve only our ideal customers. It demands strategic discipline, however, to remain true to the ideal customer in times of trial. To outsize our strategies, we must make bold moves and take risks. Outsizing forces us to focus on the essential and disregard the optional. This requires us to commit to trade-offs, and one of the hardest is refusing any customer—even those who we know are detrimental to our business. If we attempt to serve all customers, our strategy will straddle diverse types of customers with different values, and we will pursue multiple strategies simultaneously to no avail.

For example, imagine a restaurant that can only serve one temperature of tea to its customers. It conducts an interview and finds that half of its customers prefer cold tea, and the other half prefer hot tea. To serve both customers, the restaurant must serve warm tea. Instead of delivering on its value proposition to at least one of the customer subsets, it fails to fulfill the interests of both groups.

Knowing your ideal customer, and maintaining strategic discipline, ensures that you build your strategy around the type of customers you want to serve. Additionally, it helps you tailor specific offers to continuously deliver on your value proposition. Defining the ideal customer is the first step in devising your customer types, which we will discuss later in this chapter.

ADAPT TO CUSTOMER TRENDS

Knowing your ideal customers enables you to anticipate what they want and need better than they can do it themselves. However, defining your ideal customer first requires you to understand who your customers are and how they are changing.

Mike recently moved to Boston. After graduating from the University of Iowa with a degree in biomedical engineering, he traded his quaint life in a college town for the excitement of the big city and an appealing corporate job. In his new urban life, he drives to work alongside 4.7 million other commuters in metro Boston.[7] Since relocating from Iowa City, Mike's expenses have drastically increased and been reallocated. He now pays roughly $2,500 per month for a studio apartment in the city (compared to his $750 per month in Iowa), which eats up nearly 40 percent of his pre-tax income. Another 30 percent of his income is spent on food. To avoid the chaos of the grocery store parking lots, he orders groceries online and frequently dines in and carries out. The remainder of Mike's income is apportioned among clothing, transportation, entertainment, travel, and health-care expenses, and he reserves 5 percent of his earnings for his 401(k).

Mike's urban lifestyle is now the norm. The world is expeditiously urbanizing. In 1910, roughly 46 percent lived in an urban area and 54 percent lived in a rural area. By 1950, 64 percent of the US population inhabited urban areas and 36 percent lived in rural locations. By 2010, over 80 percent of all Americans opted for urban dwellings.[8]

Urban migration is impacting our environment, lifestyles, sociocultural climate, and spending habits. Overall, it costs the average American family more to live in the city than the suburbs; for example, it's roughly $71,237 more per year to live in New York City than in surrounding neighborhoods. Chicagoans who live in the city spend roughly $18,500 more per year, and those who opt for Dallas over neighboring suburbs pay about $14,000 more annually.[9] The greatest discrepancy in urban/suburban living is the cost of housing.

Notwithstanding the vast cost-of-living increase, trends demonstrate that millennials, like Mike, will continue to spend their paychecks in the city. Robert Lang, professor of urban growth and population dynamics, describes the "multigenerational pattern of young adults preferring more expensive urban areas over lower-cost rural ones because the lifestyles and opportunities in such places make the extra burden of cost worth it."[10] They prefer cities to suburbs and "subways to driveways."[11]

The white-picket-fence American Dream of the 1950s is transitioning, and the economy is changing right along with it. The urban movement, compounded with technological innovation, is spawning new consumer behavior. Jam-packed cities have introduced additional and changing customer needs, and technology has enabled new solutions.

DRIVE COLLABORATIVE CONSUMPTION

Cities are expensive. Urbanite space and budgeting requirements have erected a sharing economy, also referred to as collaborative consumption or the peer economy. Technology has enabled innovators like Uber, Car2Go, and Airbnb to connect asset owners with others wanting to use those assets. The sharing economy takes these assets and provides them to "renters" at a fraction of the price of purchasing, maintaining, and insuring the assets independently. It maximizes the ROI for the asset owner and provides the user with a less expensive way to access the desired benefits.

The sharing economy is edging into new spaces like co-working, lending, and even apparel. And there are very few things consumers aren't willing to share, indicated by the emergence of "libraries of things." For example, for a $50 annual membership, subscribers to the Sharing Depot in Toronto can rent anything from camping gear to furniture to toys.[12] Monetizing the act of sharing with strangers is revolutionary.

The benefits of collaborative consumption are not limited to cost savings. The sharing economy also enables space saving and maximizes resource utilization. There is a prospering minimalist movement inspired by overpopulation, urbanization, and a refocus on what truly drives value and contentment in life. In our changing economy, people value time and experiences over stuff. The

In later chapters, we will discuss how companies like Uber have succeeded at creating demand in a sharing economy because the founders and employees deeply understand the customer value proposition. Entrepreneurs take a problem that they have experienced and devise a solution. Customer empathy drives relevance, which leads to a better overall customer experience.

minimalist attitude is on the rise, growing increasingly popular among young adults. Millennials don't have the space for stuff, and they don't want to spend their money on accumulating and storing it. Since 1987, the share of consumer spending on experiences and events relative to the total US consumer spending increased by a whopping 70 percent.[13]

This essentialist mindset has presented retailers with a stark challenge. Traditional retailers whose purpose is to create and sell stuff are now struggling to appeal to a younger audience. Department stores, the quintessential stuff peddlers, are fighting to keep up with shifting customer demands. People are no longer buying the furniture, lawnmowers, or tools that built companies like Sears. These retailers are having to compete in the new experience economy. Companies that fail to adjust will lose their edge—and eventually, their customers.

CUSTOMIZE YOUR APPROACH

Future-oriented organizations must cater to the generation of influence. Just as some companies have innovated to foster a flourishing collaborative economy, others are listening, understanding, and driving demand by devising products and services that are relevant to their customers' progress and that address the nuances of changing market trends.

Technology's influence on buyer behavior in the service and experience economies is important to highlight. It is revolutionizing how companies create and deliver offerings and how customers respond. Technology has rewired our brains. One notable factor shaping value propositions is customers' intensified demand for immediacy and customization. Consumers want what they want, and they want it now.

The internet has raised our expectations. When I am shopping online, I quickly grow impatient with stores that are difficult to navigate, contain bugs or glitches, and have complicated checkout processes. I am also unwilling to buy an inferior product or pay more than necessary for something I can order elsewhere. More effective web platforms, greater cost and price transparency, and online comparison mechanisms like peer reviews allow us to quickly assign a value to an offering. If a product or service isn't up to snuff, we can review thousands of other options on alternative sites with the touch of a button.

Our intensified demands are fueled by our vendors, as we are stuck in a cycle of company advancement and heightened consumer expectations. Companies have leveraged technology and big data to progress the CX. Organizations can easily gather and analyze our behavior and feedback to understand what we want on an individual level. Through customizing our options and better understanding our values, companies spoon-feed us exactly what we are looking for before we even ask for it, raising standards across the board. After experiencing an intricate, personalized CX, it's hard to return to generic one-size-fits-all offerings. We demand that businesses continue to offer us first-class service. We become desensitized to the superior service of yesterday and expect that companies provide us with increasingly meaningful value propositions and experiences.

I have noticed my elevated expectations while shopping. One of my favorite clothing retailers has become my personal shopper. It sends me customized coupons and other promotional offers based on my style preferences. This targeted, relevant marketing scheme entices me to buy products that match my style—white and blue dress shirts and dark-colored suits. This contrasts with the advertisements sent to other customers who may receive promotions for yellow dress shirts or pleated dress pants. Rather than simply leading customers to a one-time transaction, as was adequate just a few years ago, personalization takes customers on a buying journey.

Customization is quickly becoming a customer requirement.

Recent studies have shown that customers now expect, if not demand, highly personalized experiences.[14] Big data first powered customization for powerhouses like Amazon, allowing information-rich organizations to present a personalized array of products to their customers. Now brands are taking it a step further and focusing on mass customization. With mass customization, customers can modify products and services to fit their specific requisites. Sperry now allows customers to design unique shoes. Pepperidge Farm customers can even individualize their crackers online.

Personalization strategies generate customer loyalty. A recent survey revealed that customers who tailored a product online engaged more with the company.[15] The results demonstrated that they "visited its website more frequently, stayed on the page longer, and were more loyal to the store or brand."[16] Therefore, a personalization strategy can increase sales and referrals while reducing customer acquisition costs.

Customization is gaining traction and is not limited to web-based transactions. I have worked with several construction clients who differentiate their businesses through robust CX strategies. Customers often view construction offerings as ubiquitous and commoditized, forcing contractors to compete on price. Because customers believe they can achieve the same results from one contractor to the next with low switching costs, they have the power. With razor-thin margins, contractors can't afford profit erosion from a lack of differentiation. To counteract profit decline, winning companies are refining project delivery methods and processes. The approach is two-sided:

1. Companies first leverage lean production models to optimize product fabrication, a method intended to reduce material waste and increase the overall speed of production.

2. Then they invest in activities and develop production models to create products that appeal to different groups of customers. For example, in Japan, contrasting regional influence, climate, and style drastically impact customer values. The prefabrication company Sekisui Heim responds to the cultural and geographic divergences by offering customers a variety of house types to choose from. Some have thicker insulation to withstand colder climates. Others have different roof or window designs to interest customers who have a certain style in mind. Customers can select one of the house types and adjust and customize their houses via an online configuration system.[17]

By implementing technologies, processes, and procedures that align with distinct customer values, construction companies can enhance and differentiate the CX. Customization boosts customers' switching costs, ultimately protecting the contractors' customer base and reinforcing margins.

In addition to customization, customers crave immediacy. Once they design and order something, they don't want to wait for it. Technology fuels our growing culture of impatience. We experience instant gratification from social media, email, and text messages and expect the same speed of delivery from our vendors. Today, 80 percent of consumers report that companies' speed of response impacts their loyalty.[18]

Some companies are responding to the need for speed with accelerated shipping options. Amazon has upped its game from Prime's free two-day shipping; they now offer *two-hour* grocery delivery.[19] Many companies are beginning to recognize speed as the top customer priority. Walmart and eBay are battling Amazon in delivery supremacy, offering same-day shipping for nearly all their products.[20] Even Netflix, which built its movie empire on

DVD delivery by mail, is experiencing customers' desire for immediacy. Less than 25 percent of Netflix subscribers order DVDs by mail, while 75 percent opt for its streaming services.[21]

There are limits to both speed and customization strategies, though. Not all industries or companies are right for mass customization. To be effective, customization cannot be a cost burden to the company. Beyond the initial investment in the engine to drive customization, it should be an effortless plug-in to normal business. This requires that companies possess distinct operational capabilities. Mass customization necessitates seamless processes and integrated technological components to push personalization through instantaneously, without generating excess cost or complexity.

Speed can be a competitive advantage when it's correctly leveraged. It increases a company's throughput, a key capability I will discuss in the next chapter, which measures the rate at which companies can produce products or render services. Additionally, speed is a differentiator for customers. For example, few people would be upset if their products shipped to them faster than they anticipated. But speed to market should not override product or service intention or quality. Nor should any relationship feel rushed. A customer service agent trying to meet speed guidelines and move through calls in a timely fashion to reduce wait time for others risks hurrying the current customer off the phone.

When it comes to customization and speed-based strategies, consider how your company can deliver on customer expectations while maintaining (and growing) your bottom line. In the following chapters, we will discuss how to better understand the customer to design and deliver offerings to meet their specifications. This can be achieved by the following:

- **Deeply understanding customers.** You must listen to your customers to deliver valuable products and services. This entails understanding the forces of buying behavior, which requires you to know their values (composed of needs, passions, circumstances, and motivations).

- **Providing personalized touches.** With all the technology, customers don't want to risk losing the humanity of the buying experience. Though technology is necessary to drive speed and efficiency, ensure that CX has a personal touch that addresses a customer's need to feel understood.

AVOID INFORMATION OVERLOAD

In theory, it should be getting easier to serve our ideal customers with customized strategies. We have an abundance of data to help us understand their preferences. Never in history have businesses possessed so much customer information. The big data revolution has enabled companies to accumulate mass amounts and varieties of customer data. While this information may help a company paint a picture of its typical client—tall, mid-forties, practices law, lives in Minnesota, has kids, enjoys NFL football—without deeper, pinpointed analysis, these customer personas fall flat. Yet this is often where companies stop. Organizations opt for quantity of information over quality.

For example, when Whole Foods announced the opening of its lower-priced sub-brand, Whole Foods Market 365, it announced that it was going to "target communities and demographics that it [didn't] serve with its namesake brand."[22] When looking at the grocer's quintessential customer, you will often find that she is female and between the ages twenty-five and thirty-nine. "Woman One's" general interests include fashion, design, and culture and the arts, and she probably owns a cat as a pet. She cares about the environment, exercises frequently, and drives a Mercedes Benz.[23] On the other end of the spectrum, with the targeted 365 buyer, "Woman

Two," you have the customer who shops at a low-cost supermarket like Aldi. She is over age sixty and drives a Kia. She enjoys gardening, cooking, and has at least two children.[24]

Even if these factors are valid, the two customers' ages or the cars they drive do not likely determine their grocery store preferences. For example, Woman One could end up shopping at Whole Foods because it is within walking distance from her house. She may have an allergy that Whole Foods accommodates. She could like an item from its bakery or rely on the prepared foods to quickly feed her family healthy fare. Similarly, Woman Two may choose to shop at an Aldi because of convenience; maybe it's a smaller store with fewer offerings, allowing her to get in and out quickly.

Organizational strategy is easily distracted when companies focus too heavily on depicting a precise buyer persona, detailing these characters down to the pets they own or their favorite TV shows. More data is only helpful if it's the *right* data. As author and consultant Clayton Christensen says, "After decades of watching great companies fail, we've come to the conclusion that the focus on correlation—and on knowing more and more about customers—is taking firms in the wrong direction."[25]

Understanding what customers want goes much deeper than the typical customer persona allows for. It entails more than demographics, family composition, hobbies, or interests. This information can be necessary but only when viewed as a contributing factor, not the picture itself. Delivering a differentiated CX to your ideal customer depends more on recognizing the desired outcomes for customer types than figuring out the narrow demographic segment where they fit. It requires companies to create ideas, solutions, and opportunities on behalf of their customers. As illustrated in Figure 2.3, the ideal customer is at the center of the strategy.

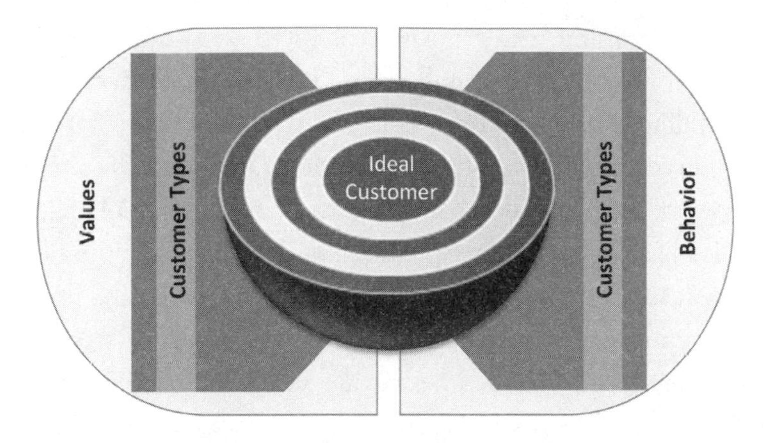

Figure 2.3: The ideal customer is at the core of what companies must understand to effectively message, create, deliver, and serve the market while pursuing the desired organizational strategy. The ideal customer is composed of values and behaviors that feed into customer types.

Customers' desired outcomes are multifaceted and situational. You can only help a customer progress if you understand the nuances of their values, composed of their needs, passions, circumstances, and motivations. The amalgamation of these factors drives customer buying activity and lays the groundwork for your customer-centric strategy. When we outsize, we align our values with our customers' values to develop deeper, more meaningful relationships.

IDENTIFY CUSTOMER VALUES

It was a snowy night in Paris in 2008, and Travis Kalanick and Garrett Camp were struggling to find a ride home. They discussed how nice it would be to hail a cab at the touch of a button. One decade, a billion connections, and $70 billion later, Uber stands as an international powerhouse and emblem of business innovation.[26]

Drew Houston was a student at MIT traveling between Boston

and New York and was growing frustrated with himself for consistently forgetting his thumb drive. He pondered how to solve this problem. He opened the editor and started writing the code that evolved into the file-hosting service Dropbox. Despite Steve Jobs's warnings of the company's demise due to an Apple takeover, Dropbox has been steadily expanding, pulling in $1.1 billion of revenue in 2017.[27]

Solution-inspired innovation paves the way for strong customer-value propositions. The world's most revolutionary companies like Uber, Dropbox, Amazon, Google, and Tesla heeded the ancient proverb "Necessity is the mother of invention." The companies' great success is attributable to their leaders' identification of a customer problem and opportunity. Solution-inspired leaders effectively speak to the customer value propositions they provide because they have experienced the problems firsthand. They know the power of their solutions. They empathized with the market. They recognized that something could work better, and they made their visions of progress a reality.

Customer value proposition is defined as "a positioning statement that explains what benefit you provide for who and how you do it uniquely well."[28] In other words, it's an activity, innovation, or feature that makes a company's products or services attractive to its customers. To develop a potent value proposition, you must understand what your ideal customer cares about. Understanding customer values entails far more than recognizing the superficial interests defined in a customer persona. Shown in Figure 2.4, values are multidimensional and consist of four components: needs, passions, circumstances, and motivations.

Companies typically stumble when attempting to categorize customer values. Organizational analysis of what drives customers to buy is often shallow and underdeveloped. For instance, a company may state that its customers value eco-friendly practices. Green features may or may not be critical factors in your buyers' decision-making processes. I would presume that if given the option, most people would prefer to use an eco-friendly product over a product that damages the environment. However, a small percentage of people are willing to pay the price premium that accompanies the green price tag.

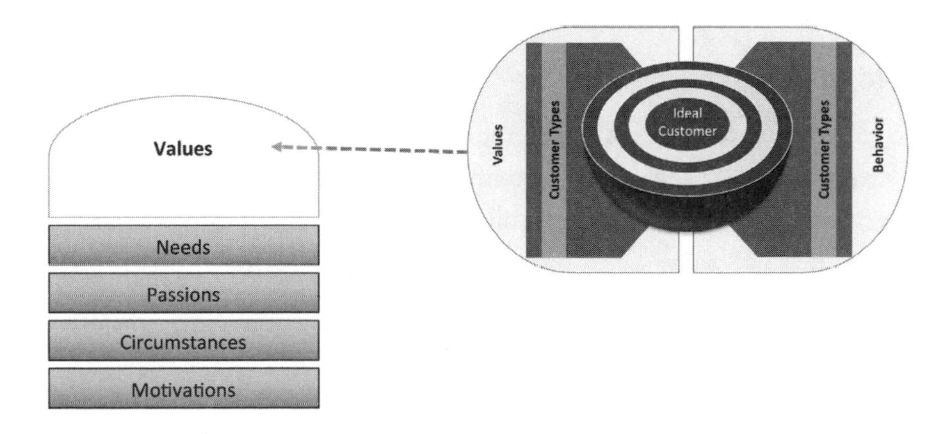

Figure 2.4: The four components that feed into values are needs, passions, circumstances, and motivations.

The environmental value that compels purchases is defined by more than wanting to protect nature. This value must be prioritized over other values shaped by complex factors such as perception and life experiences. Suzie may want to buy green because she genuinely cares about the environment. However, Suzie puts the interests of her seventeen-year-old-daughter, Madison, before all else. Though Suzie is deeply concerned about the environment, family values drive her economic decisions, influencing her to buy standard cleaning products and save a dollar that she can contribute to her daughter's college fund. She is not an environmentally centered company's ideal customer, because she struggles to prioritize a more expensive environmental value proposition over her pile of other bills.

Values-based decision-making is complex and multifaceted. We are products of our environments, as our family, friends, and communities impress their beliefs and values upon our lives. To understand values, you must know your customers' views of what is important in life.

Needs

Needs are the first component of customer values. Understanding customer needs is a critical activity when developing a product or service. However, many companies fail to build client-centric strategies because they stop researching when they acquire a general sense of customer needs. Products and services that solely address surface-level needs quickly commoditize. Comprehending the true customer needs requires companies to dig deep and uncover the covert motives. As American economist and Harvard Business School professor Theodore Levitt famously stated, "People don't want to buy a quarter-inch drill. They want a quarter-inch hole."[29]

You can have the best product or service in the world, but if your customers don't need it, it won't sell. For example, following the introduction of the iPod, Microsoft launched the short-lived Zune. The technology was powerful and rivaled Apple's iconic product, but customers didn't need it. As Robbie Bach, former leader of Microsoft's home entertainment and mobile business explains, "We ended up chasing Apple with a product that actually wasn't a bad product, but it was still a chasing product, and there wasn't a reason for somebody to say, 'Oh, I have to go out and get that thing.'"[30]

The fundamental design principle is as follows: every product or service must serve a purpose and fulfill an essential buyer requirement. People buy products and services to drive change, solve problems, and advance their goals. Basic strategy revolves around meeting such needs. The Zune satisfied an individual's need to listen to music on the go. Yet, it was not differentiated enough to create a compelling value proposition that could lure customers away from Apple. There was insignificant motivation for a customer to switch from an iPod to a Zune.

However, there are many successful "chasing" products. For example, Ford's premier car, the Model T, first produced in 1908, addressed customers' transportation needs. Since then, Ford and other manufacturers have successfully brought to market thousands of other models that serve the same functional need but fulfill other motivations, such as ego. People don't spend $200,000 on a Lamborghini solely to get from point A to point B. They buy it to impress peers, assert their status, and maybe fulfill a lifelong goal or fascination; they buy it for the driving experience and to be seen in a Lamborghini.

When developing a product or service, you must consider the multidimensionality of needs. This can be accomplished in a few ways:

- **Ask for feedback and listen.** Had Microsoft spoken with customers prior to developing the Zune, it likely would have heard what it discovered after investing significant capital and time: customers didn't necessarily want or need an iPod alternative. Garnering customer feedback is imperative for tracking how effective your products and services are at meeting a need.
- **Walk your customers' paths in their shoes.** Knowing your customers entails understanding their problems, as Kalanick, Camp, and Houston did, and evaluating their ecosystem of options. Whom are your customers choosing between, and

how are the value propositions distinct from one another? Take an unbiased approach to reviewing your messaging, calling your customer service, and using the product or service to understand the holistic CX. How does your offering appeal to *your* needs?

Passions

Like needs, customer passion, the second component of values, can be an elusive yet integral element in decision-making. Passion can be described as intense emotion, either positive or negative, that manifests itself in an overwhelming feeling or conviction. When it comes to passions, companies must deeply understand what customers love and hate about the holistic buying experience.

When examining passions, I use the words *love* and *hate* intentionally. Whenever I'm teaching a course or speaking to a large audience, I usually hear a few gasps in the crowd when I say the word *hate*. Some shy away from these descriptors due to their gravity and bluntness. A few participants probably wonder, "Steve, didn't your mom teach you that *hate* is not a nice word?" The challenge with softening the term is that customers like and dislike a lot of things. If a company requests feedback on what customers like or dislike about a certain product, they will provide a variety of responses—make it bigger, thicker, longer, brighter, add this or remove that. Oftentimes, one group of customers' likes and dislikes contradict another group's and send a company focusing on the noncritical, escalating costs to achieve marginal, inconsequential improvement.

Our loves and hates are more deliberate and distinct. I love my church, my family, and my business. I hate poverty, greed, and ego. Customers, too, can identify distinct loves and hates along the purchase journey. These passions dictate their loyalties and fierce company aversions and avoidances. For example, as I define my customer type, you will understand my love for convenient buying experiences. My love of convenience makes me an avid Audible customer. I appreciate Audible's risk-free return policy on its audiobooks.[31] If I buy a book that doesn't pique my interest, or the narrator is hard to follow, I can return the book within seconds, receive a credit, and download another. I love this. This process doesn't require me to speak with a customer service agent or wait for a refund. It's instantaneous and convenient. I am willing to pay a premium to ensure satisfaction with my purchase.

Conversely, I hate inefficiency. For this reason, I am opposed to waiting in long lines for food. Some grab-and-go restaurants have interminable queues, bottlenecked by one or two overburdened cashiers processing orders with clunky, outdated registers. In these instances, when I am bogged down with work and have fifteen minutes before my next meeting, I am forced to leave and choose another restaurant.

One customer journey that often reveals hateful passion is the car-buying experience. In fact, a recent Autotrader survey disclosed that only 17 percent of consumers "like the current car-buying process as it is."[32] The most common reasons that car-buying breeds customer disdain include the following:

- **A lack of trust.** Customers fear that they are overpaying for a car that won't run as promised.
- **Pushy salespeople.** Incentive systems often reward car salespeople based on volume. Because of this, some customers feel pressured to make expensive snap decisions.
- **Fear of additional fees.** Many customers express apprehension that dealerships slip in unexpected costs to already high-priced purchases.[33]

Poor car-buying experiences are cited across the board, regardless of dealership, brand, or location. Yet despite this widely published knowledge, most companies continue to focus on profits over people. Dealerships' marketing materials, promotions, and processes continue to center around the needs of the company instead of the customer.

Why do companies fail to listen or respond to their customers' loves and hates? For one, it can be costly to shift to customer-centric processes. Many "hated" companies make significant money off a lack of transparency. Although 75 percent of consumers stated that they would "consider making their entire car-buying process online," automakers are unenthusiastic about the switch because it would likely result in margin reduction.[34] The truth is, some company models rely on profit at the expense of their customers. For example, the cell phone service industry is notorious for opaque pricing models and taking advantage of customers who fail to accurately predict their monthly mobile and data needs.[35]

Customers *hate* this. But in this traditional model, phone carriers earn up to 50 percent of their income from additional fees like breakage expenses.[36] Customer churn is extensive for phone carriers, so much of these companies' budgets are allocated to customer acquisition costs via expensive advertising campaigns.

The self-centric strategy is unsustainable, as today's customers have access to more information and a broader range of choices. Customers can sense when companies prioritize profits over people, and they will simply take their business elsewhere.

I recently exercised my customer power after experiencing the negative effects of company centricity. My family had vacationed at the same resort in Playa Del Carmen, Mexico, for nearly ten years. Every December we packed up for a week-long stay at this welcoming all-inclusive resort. Upon our arrival, we were greeted by name with hugs and gifts from employees whom we considered family. The resort felt like home, and the CX was exceptional.

A couple of years ago, however, the resort underwent a complete renovation and a strategic redirection, and we noticed a palpable shift in the look and feel of our vacation spot. The quaint buildings lost their historic, authentic charm, as brightly colored exteriors were concealed by monochromatic white hues for a more contemporary feel. A cultural change accompanied the aesthetic alterations. The resort transitioned from customer- to profit-centric. Additional fees were tagged on to our stay. New policies emerged and were strictly enforced. To save a few dollars, the resort ceased placing personalized welcome signs and fresh flowers in the lobby. The company began mistreating and overworking its employees. Many of the employees we had grown to know and love over the years left the company. After this transition, my family and I were resolute against returning to the resort.

As more competitors bring agreeable, honest strategies to market, companies that fail to please the customer will face sizeable obstacles. Companies of the future acknowledge customer loves and hates and innovate activities to maximize the CX. Even industries fueled by customer confusion or misfortune are beginning to change shape. Take Virgin Mobile, a phone carrier that has adopted a customer-centric approach to vastly reduce its churn rate. Most carriers bind customers in lengthy contracts, so even when service is not up to par (which it usually isn't), customers are heavily penalized when they switch. Virgin, on the other hand, offers a mix of prepaid, monthly, and pay-as-you-go plans.[37] The customer love is reflected in sky-high satisfaction ratings that trump Virgin's competitors.

In the hypercompetitive, customer-controlled marketplace, understanding customer passions reduces attrition, drives experience, and secures long-term loyalty. When organizations capitalize on passions, strategy becomes more than what Michael Porter commonly refers to as "the antidote to competition."[38] It becomes the antidote to customer hates and the embodiment of their loves. Once you understand your customers' passions, you can adjust your business model by doing the following:

- **Shaping activities around customer loves and hates.** By understanding what customers love, companies can invest in supporting CX activities that aim experiences at delivering on said passions. By acknowledging what customers hate, companies can innovate with these obstacles in mind to diminish negative experiences.
- **Ensuring your business model empowers your customers.** Ask yourself: Is our company enhancing the lives of our customers, not just through our products and services but also through the overarching experience? Do customers choose us over other appealing, customer-centric options? If the answer to these questions is no, then it's likely time to rethink your business model. If yes, don't allow yourself to get comfortable. Continuously strive to further serve customers' loves and eradicate their hates.

Circumstances

Customer problems, opportunities, and needs are all contingent on circumstances. For example, let's say I am considering where to eat dinner. If I am with my wife, and we are not in a rush, we may choose to go to Rice, one of my favorite local sushi restaurants, for our Saturday date night. However, if it's a snowy Tuesday night and I am taking my young children, Ava and Max, out to get dinner, I will likely choose something fast that doesn't require me to get out of my car.

My circumstances of dining with my wife versus dining with my children impact whether I want a sit-down or carry-out dinner. Circumstances are a powerful lever in nearly every customer decision. Circumstances can be temporary (as in my example) or more defining and abiding. It is essential to understand circumstances, because they can impact short- and long-term buying behavior.

People typically visit McDonald's because it's quick, affordable, and ubiquitous. An estimated 20 percent of meals in the US are consumed in the car, and the low-income and middle-class population consume more fast food than the wealthy.[39] These temporary and more lasting customer circumstances have carved out a distinct audience for the restaurant. McDonald's stumbled when it introduced the Arch Deluxe in 1996. McDonald's aimed the Arch Deluxe at "urban sophisticates," though the company's existing customers valued consistent, inexpensive fast food.[40] McDonald's failed to realize that for its loyal customer base, other value drivers, like low cost and convenience, took precedence over the quality of food it served. The restaurant's $200 million investment turned out to be a total flop.[41]

Though McDonald's misstepped, other brands have capitalized on customer circumstances. Brands like CVS's MinuteClinic are drawing in crowds of customers. MinuteClinic introduced the walk-in clinic concept in 2000 to quickly, conveniently, and affordably treat patients for everything from strep throat to the flu. They grasped the customer circumstances and captured a broad audience of patients who needed to see a doctor when they least expected it. The clinics are conveniently located in retail pharmacy locations so that patients can pick up prescriptions onsite while grocery shopping. These stressed, sick, often underinsured individuals now flock to 1,100 MinuteClinics across the country.[42]

Another timely example of circumstance-powered success has emerged in the grocery industry. Small, innovative startups realized that customers were in a bind for time. They wanted to put fresh food on the table while avoiding chaotic parking lots and interminable lines. Grocers like Webvan or Instacart provided customers the opportunity to grocery shop from the comfort of their own homes.

Larger retailers have taken the cue. Grocery giants Albertsons, Safeway, and Whole Foods have rolled out online ordering and delivery to their customers' doors.

Understanding customer circumstances will not only help you create products and services that address a specific audience's lifestyle, impulses, and situations but will also assist you when messaging your solution's benefits. MinuteClinic's slogan, "Quality Health Care. On Your Schedule," gets right to the point and gives customers control, something their circumstances demand when the flu hits right before the big meeting or a family vacation. Gather information on your customers' lives outside of their internet browser or the four walls of your business. Identify market opportunities that understand your customers as humans who are using your products or services to manage and enhance everyday life situations.

Motivations

Customers are motivated to buy products and services because of the perceived benefits that appeal to their needs, passions, and circumstances. It is imperative to see your customer through the lens of these three factors before defining their motivations. Motivations are the "biological, emotional, social, and cognitive forces that activate behavior."[43]

If my motivation is to save time (due to circumstances, I travel often for work and want to spend my time at home with my family), I will order a book online from Amazon rather than driving to Barnes & Noble. If my motivation is to educate my clients, then I may invest in a survey service to garner customer feedback on topics and courses of interest. If I am motivated to save money, then I will likely prioritize any purchase I make based on price, need, and urgency.

Motivations are influenced by emotional and practical factors. For example, when it comes to my running shoes, my motivations are solely functional—I need running shoes that support good form and prevent injury. I couldn't care less how they look if they suit my functional needs. My wife and kids poked fun at my recent purchase of black running shoes smattered with a colorful fluorescent sprinkle pattern. These shoes are ugly, but they were on sale and completely fulfill my practical motivations. Since I run when it's dark out, either in the evening or early morning before the sunrise, nobody sees me in my running shoes. Practicality drives me to sacrifice style for comfort and savings.

On the other hand, I am choosy about the shoes I wear to work. I am emotionally motivated when purchasing dress shoes—I prefer high-quality, genuine leather shoes and have been known to splurge on a pricey pair before a big speaking event or national conference. My emotional purchase is motivated by my desire to exude a professional, put-together image. Our emotions profoundly impact our motivations. In fact, our response to advertising has more impact on our motivation to buy a product than the content in the ad itself.[44]

Oftentimes, our motivations are the culmination of both internal and external pressures. Let's say I am looking to remodel my back deck. I want to expand it because from a practical standpoint, I need more space for entertaining. However, I opt for the highest-quality deck material for aesthetic purposes. Practical, social, and emotional drivers are at play in this multifaceted decision.

Beyond emotional and practical motivations, we are influenced to buy out of excitement, stress, joy, loneliness, and even fear. For example, after watching a documentary about doomsday, I was motivated to buy a survival kit to store in my basement. All these pressures coalesce to form our motivations, which provide us with our ultimate justification to pull the trigger on a product or service.

Motivation is the composite bow that wraps up values and helps us assemble a holistic view of our ideal customers. Understanding the emotional and practical drivers that compose their motivations allows us to create, message, and position products and services to influence customers' purchase decisions. By acknowledging several factors—buyer needs, what they must have or want; their passions, their emotional, driving convictions; their circumstances, temporary and enduring situational aspects of their lives—we can uncover their motivations, their reasons to act.

These components feed into our customers' value systems that determine their views of the world and what is important to them. Gaining insight into buyers' beliefs helps us better anticipate what people will do and why, enabling us to fuel proactive, customer-centric innovation and outsize our impact.

INTERPRET CONSUMER BEHAVIORS

As I mentioned, strategy is a blend of art and science. Once we grasp the emotional drivers, we can better comprehend the neurological and psychological elements of buying. We must be able to view customers from a variety of angles to derive their customer types and integrate activities to maximize their experiences.

To attract the right clients and drive growth and innovation, leading companies are designing customer-centric strategies focused on delivering relevant value to the end user. Those who employ design-thinking techniques (see text box) to understand buyer behavior will realize the benefits of a loyal customer base, engaged workforce, and financially stable organization. By applying neuroscience and design-thinking methods to uncover human values and behavior, define customer types, power innovation, and align teams around strategic activities, companies will develop competitive advantages that will result in outsized profits. The application of these tools and skills will allow leaders to accelerate their networks and careers. Organizations will increase repeat business, improve employee engagement, and boost the bottom line. Companies have long been

HOW LEADING COMPANIES LEVERAGE SCIENCE TO DELIVER VALUE

- **Neuroscience:** Companies are employing advanced neurotech to understand how buyers' brains function when they shop. This research fuels consumer-related fields like neuromarketing, which employs brainwave technology to guide marketers to the right product designs and marketing messages.
- **Design thinking:** This solution-focused approach utilizes experimentation and empathy to power innovation for future customers.

---

vying for the answer to the question: Why do people do what they do and buy what they buy?

Consumer behavior is defined as the "study of individuals, groups, or organizations and all the activities associated with purchase, use, and disposal of goods and services."[45] This discipline emerged in the 1950s, when two scientists discovered the pleasure center in a rodent's brain, responsible for dopamine release in the nucleus accumbens. Humans and rats share the desire to feel good. But while rats may be stimulated by electrical currents, as they were in this study, we humans often engage in retail therapy.[46]

Uma R. Karmarkar, assistant professor at University of California at San Diego with PhDs in both marketing and neuroscience, explains, "People are fairly good at expressing what they want, what they like, or even how much they will pay for an item. But they aren't very good at accessing where that value comes from, or how and when it is influenced by factors like store display or brands. Neuroscience can help us understand those hidden elements of the decision process."[47]

Karmarkar has conducted studies to observe how consumers'

brains operate while shopping. Neuroscientists scanned customers' brains as they mulled over a wide range of products, and found increased activity in the pleasure center as they debated purchases. As the customers received pricing information for each of the products, their prefrontal cortexes, the part of the brain associated with decision-making, enlivened, as did their insulas, the area of the brain that processes pain. The customers with the most active insulas were far more hesitant to buy. They felt the pain on their pocketbook more than the pleasure of the purchase. Others with lower-functioning insulas behaved more impulsively. Additionally, the individuals who pursued the immediate gratification of shopping released more dopamine than those who decided not to buy.[48]

The magic for companies lies in understanding how and where to strike to light up this pleasure center in the consumer's brain. The reward can originate in an unsuspected product feature or function. Frito-Lay hired neuroscientists to monitor consumer reactions to the world's best-selling brand of cheese puffs, Cheetos. Surprisingly, the subjects' strongest reactions were not in response to the taste or sight but rather the cheese "dust" that lingered on their fingers post-consumption.[49]

Organizations try to uncover the hidden elements of the decision process that make certain products so appealing. The yearning to understand product appeal has resulted in the emergence of design thinking. Design thinking is a "design methodology that provides a solution-based approach to solving problems."[50] It establishes a step-by-step scientific technique that adopts a "hands-on approach in prototyping and testing."[51] Companies apply the following steps to crack the customer code and determine what solutions will resonate and why:

1. **Empathize.** The first step is to understand what you are trying to solve. Put yourself in the customer's shoes and abolish

any of your own assumptions to gain a clear, unbiased image of your audience.

2. **Define.** Once you understand your customer, you can determine the core problem and begin to devise solutions to address the complexities of this challenge. You will decide what elements of your solution will eradicate certain aspects of the issue.
3. **Ideate.** By now, you have a customer-focused problem statement. In this stage, you're applying your knowledge of the customer and the problem to brainstorm new solutions. There are many different ideation techniques, but the overall goal is to bring new concepts to the table, regardless of how extreme or out-of-the-box they may seem. You want to start with as many ideas as possible and methodically narrow them down to your top solutions throughout the process.
4. **Prototype.** Once you have boiled down the options to arrive at your key solution, the design team can assemble some lower-budget, scaled-down versions of the product to investigate how well the prototype addresses the challenges. During this experimental phase, you will evaluate whether to approve or adjust the prototype.
5. **Test.** This final phase is used to "redefine one or more problems . . . conditions of use, how people think, behave, and feel to empathize."[52] You tie up loose ends and ensure you're presenting relevant and effective solutions to your audience.

This approach has captured the attention of many innovation-hungry organizations. The renowned design and consulting firm, IDEO, has leveraged design-thinking techniques to power innovative solutions for megabrands like Apple, Ford, Medtronic, and

Coca-Cola, among others. Other firms that apply this approach include IBM, Marriott, and LEGO.[53]

Once the product is conceived, companies focus on crafting the ideal CX to encompass the new offering. Organizations emphasize the buying experience, leveraging store design, architecture, music, lighting, and sign and product placement to encourage customer spending. They draw on environmental psychology, examining the "direct impact of physical stimuli on human emotions and the effect of the physical stimuli on a variety of behaviors."[54]

Companies leverage a wide range of aesthetic and spatial tricks to encourage buying. Architecture can significantly impact customer behavior, as geometry and space presentation affect the specialized cells in the hippocampal region of the brain that influence mood and well-being.[55] How often do you buy more than you intend to at the grocery store? Supermarkets typically place colorful produce at the front of the store to enhance customer disposition, and situate a plethora of tempting add-on items near the registers to spur last-minute purchases. Grocers hide dairy products and other essentials in the depths of the store, so you must pass through anterior aisles and observe tantalizing nonessentials before you can get what you came for.

Some companies are moving beyond the physical store attributes and tapping into customers' sense of smell. Have you ever noticed how bakeries will cleverly direct fans from the kitchen to the storefront to further circulate the scent of brownies, cookies, and homemade bread? What about the smell of freshly cut wood that consistently permeates a Lowe's or Home Depot store, urging us to buy and DIY. These approaches are effective. Companies like Starbucks, Cinnabon, and Nordstrom have increased sales and enhanced CX with scent-infused strategies. Nike realized an 84 percent increase in a customer's likelihood to purchase when browsing for shoes in a floral-scented room.[56]

Companies have been creating and refining selling techniques like these for decades. While consumer behavior is not a new concept, it is changing. According to Pew Research, 80 percent of Americans shop online, and 43 percent shop weekly or at least a few times a month.[57] The modern economy has introduced new and different behavioral levers. Companies must adapt to evolving buyer attitudes and habits in the age of information.

The internet's primary impact on retail has been revealed in the dissolution of brick-and-mortar stores. In 2017, a record-breaking seven thousand stores closed.[58] For decades, companies have relied on environmental psychology to dictate sales strategy. Customers behave differently in a physical environment than they do in an online setting. Without a tangible backdrop, companies must shift attention to the virtual CX.

Rather than leading customers to purchase by way of sales concierge, store flow, and point-of-purchase displays, retailers are employing social media, targeted ad campaigns, and promotions to drive customers to buy. I am often impressed (and sometimes slightly alarmed) at how well the internet knows me. I will be scanning through Amazon and see a recommendation for the book I mentioned to my wife a few days ago. I will be perusing non-retail websites, reading the *Wall Street Journal*, and a banner ad will appear, reminding me of a pair of shoes I like. My retailers seem to know my color preferences, my size, and my social calendar. From my search history, these companies resolve that I am traveling to a friend's wedding in Guatemala and send me ads featuring ties to match my suits.

While companies have been sending promotional material to our inboxes for some time now, they are beginning to engage our pleasure centers and wallets through other creative techniques. During online checkout, I am frequently reminded of items that I am "forgetting." Or the site may provide me with a helpful notification that if I spend an extra $15 at checkout, I can receive free shipping. These features may seem minor, but they are deliberate and create significant product pull-through for online retailers.

In addition to company influence, our peers impact our thoughts and actions. Online reviews anchor our buying behavior. Where we would historically turn to celebrities, experts, and friends for inspiration, we now reference strangers' opinions. We rely on millions of verified customer opinions floating around the web. Deemed the "new social proof," online customer reviews drive our thinking and influence our restaurant, travel, service, and product purchases. As of 2017, 78 percent of consumers in the US read through customer reviews before buying.[59] As shown in Figure 2.5, younger generations are pioneering this trend; therefore, it's likely that peer reviews will continue to gain traction. We now define the value of a product or service by the number of stars that accompany its description.

In addition to peer-reviewed quality transparency, the internet has enabled more price and cost transparency. An effective pricing strategy aggregates competitor and customer data to establish a sweet spot where the price of the offering aligns with its perceived value. It finds the equilibrium between what the customer is willing to pay for a product or service and what the company is willing to sell it for. If a price is too low, the customer may view the offering as lower quality. If it is too high, the company substantially narrows its market.

While pricing still plays an impactful and intricate role in influencing consumer behavior, the web has introduced additional considerations. The internet allows for easy price comparisons and facilitates a greater understanding of mark-ups and price premiums, reducing a company's ability to procure high margins. Companies are devising more elaborate pricing models to combat the negative implications of price and cost transparency. Dynamic pricing or "smart pricing" applies market-specific insights to tap into consumer behavior.[60] Some companies request that customers enter their zip

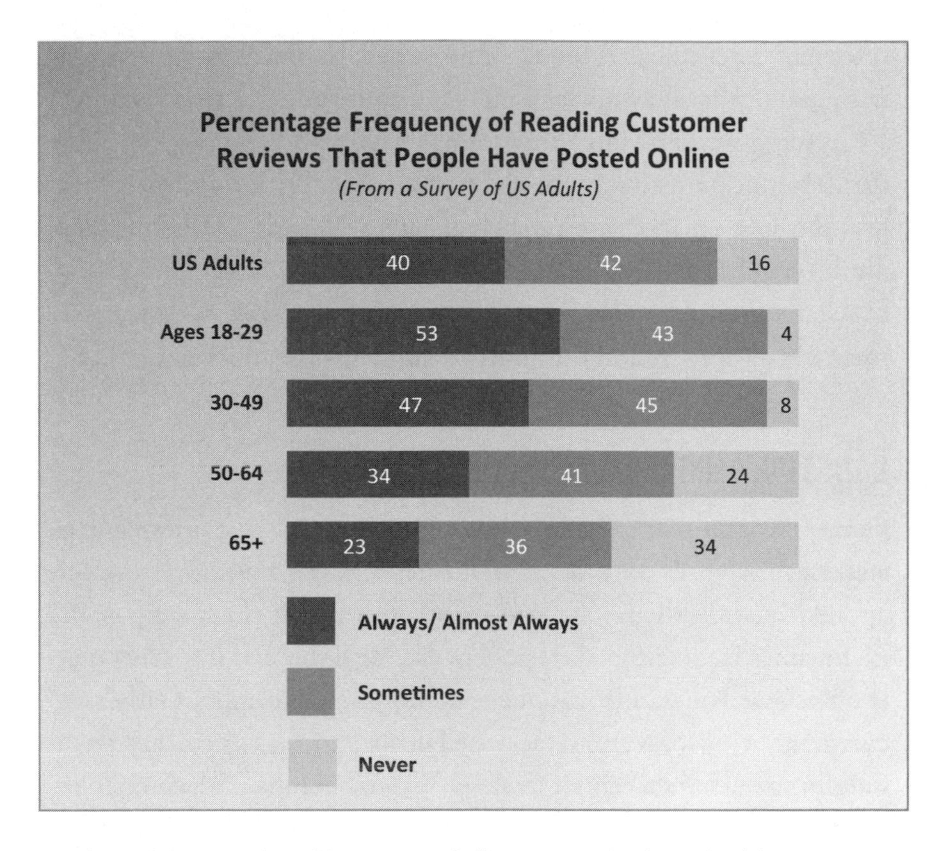

Figure 2.5: More than 80 percent of all customers in the United States at least occasionally reference peer reviews prior to purchase. As the eighteen-to-twenty-nine-year-old bracket—the age demographic reporting the highest frequency of customer review references—continues to exert its influence, this trend is likely to persist.

codes before gaining access to prices. Companies are assembling customers' web histories, social media presence, geographic information, and demographics to mold pricing structures based on their propensity to buy.

While some of these techniques have agitated consumers, the internet is forcing companies to restructure their responses to consumer behavior. To stay up to date with consumer behavior, we must apply neuroscience to understand customer actions and attitudes, integrate scientifically tested approaches to develop new offerings, and never allow ourselves to get comfortable or stop learning. Everything we know about customers seems to be changing every day. It's important to stay attuned to how the internet, global events, and the stock market are impacting buyer behavior. Whether you are leveraging neuroscience research to initiate change or looking at what some of your competitors are doing to reel in customers, maintain awareness and flexibility to adjust to the modern market.

CONSTRUCT CUSTOMER TYPES

Consumer and market research is critical to any customer-centric strategy. However, as I mentioned earlier, when misunderstood or applied incorrectly, it can lead companies down the wrong path. Companies frequently take a pool of data and shape it into customer profiles based on socioeconomic or demographic insights. Gathering customer behavioral and value-based information is a critical step in building a customer-centric strategy. But to be impactful, companies must correctly apply the data. Customers do not buy solely based on demographics or socioeconomics; therefore, the typical, flat customer profiles constructed around age, basic interests, or family composition provide incomplete views of the buyer. Rather, combining needs, passions, circumstances, and motivations with behavioral analysis enables us to conceive customer types.

Customer types are advanced, multifaceted alternatives to customer personas that bundle distinct and critical information regarding values and behavior into a comprehensive customer roadmap. They define the who, what, and why behind the ideal customer, enabling companies to formulate data-based strategic decisions. By boiling down the complexities of buyer behavior and values into a digestible, informative format, companies can leverage customer types to establish a vernacular around a similar group of customers who have shared values and behaviors. This common language allows employees to describe the values and behavioral motivations of clients using one or two words, enabling companies to create scalable, impactful CX strategies to service these distinct buyer segments.

The clearest example of a company that has applied its knowledge of customer types to dominate its competition is Amazon. The organization's recent success has been unparalleled. The e-commerce behemoth captured 4 percent of US retail and 44 percent of e-commerce sales in 2017, bringing in nearly $200 billion in revenue.[61] Amazon's stock increase has paralleled its revenue and net income growth, climbing by more than 25 percent at the beginning of 2018. Investors predict that the company is heading toward a $1 trillion valuation by 2022.[62]

Amazon has been hungry for growth, expanding into territory foreign to any online retailer before it. In addition to retail, Amazon has fueled its growth through its cloud infrastructure (IaaS and PaaS); consumer electronics like the Kindle and the Echo; Amazon content, including Amazon art, games, books, music, and video; grocery services like AmazonFresh and Prime Pantry; and as of 2018, health care. No challenge has been too daunting for Amazon to tackle. The company is demolishing the traditional boundaries of business and redefining the playing field.

I have pondered Amazon's paramount growth and prosperity. How can a $1 trillion company emerge from the humble beginnings of an online bookstore? While today Amazon leverages brand recognition and customer loyalty to successfully enter new arenas, the brand's growth has been highly strategic. CEO Jeff Bezos credits much of the organization's success to its ability to maintain startup culture amid massive growth and accept failure as the price of innovating.[63] While those are both valuable and authentic approaches, Bezos's mention of Amazon's customer centricity as a driver of its achievement most resonates with me. He chalks up Amazon's popularity to its ability to give "customers what they want before they know it." Bezos explains that "even when they don't know it, customers want something better, and your desire to delight your customers will drive you to invent on their behalf. No customer ever asked Amazon to create the Prime membership program, but it sure turns out they wanted it."[64]

Amazon is fulfilling its mission of "[being] the Earth's most customer-centric company."[65] Where other companies have tried and failed to know their customers, Amazon has neatly defined its customer types. The brand has studied, analyzed, and segmented based on consumer behavior. Amazon has gathered more data over a longer period of time and used it more proactively than any other company in the world.[66] The company was one of the first to track not only what customers bought but also what customers browsed. While Amazon gathers an abundance of information, it effectively analyzes and selects what's important to ensure it understands its ideal customers at the core.

Amazon's knowledge of customers has helped it carve out an extremely loyal following. Amazon is my go-to for nearly everything. I choose the site because of its convenience. I can order a variety of items at once from the comfort of my home and have them shipped to me within two days, all while knowing that if any issues arise, I can easily return anything. Its operations are clear-cut, customer service is helpful, and it has a colossal and diverse inventory of products.

My customer type is "Convenient," one of Amazon's most common. My desired CX revolves around ease. I want shopping for products and returning them to be as effortless as possible. I want to easily search and filter to find my product and check out quickly. If any problems arise, I must be able to smoothly resolve them without having to disrupt my day or exert significant effort. Contrasting the traditional approach to defining a customer persona, you will notice my race, income, level of education, and gender do not factor into my customer type.

"Speedy," another typical Amazon customer, has a different value proposition when logging in to the site. This customer type is seeking speed and efficiency. Speedy values Amazon for its Prime two-day delivery option. When shopping, Speedy demands rapid response, checkout, delivery, and communication.

Amazon's customized, customer-centric approach creates a unique, relevant experience for each customer. The company focuses on what's important to each client and delivers value based on a toolbox of activities. The company has excelled in forming activities to serve customer needs. Amazon is the proverbial king of speed and convenience.

In every company, there are hundreds of activities: hiring, processing invoices, training, creating marketing content, product

STANDARD ACTIVITIES

I refer to standard activities as "cooking the chicken." Do you remember when headlines surfaced with news of foodborne illnesses resulting from outbreaks of E. coli, salmonella, campylobacteriosis, and norovirus at Chipotle? Some were reportedly due to undercooked chicken. Chicken is in many of Chipotle's most popular entrees. Cooking the chicken shouldn't even be a consideration for the restaurant. Serving high-quality, *fully cooked* food to customers is table stakes for Chipotle. Cooking the chicken is a standard activity that the restaurant must comply with to remain in business. Chipotle's failure to abide by industry standards derailed its strategy and resulted in litigation and loss of market share.

troubleshooting, schedule management, financial reporting, inventory management, procurement—the list goes on and on. Some companies assume that being the best means being the best at *everything*. Through Amazon's in-depth understanding of customer types, it recognizes what its ideal customers truly care about. This has enabled the company to focus on investing in key activities that support the ideal customer's wants and needs.

For example, Amazon's online platform is incredibly strong because the company understands its customers' desire for immediacy. Amazon calculated that a page load deceleration of only one second could cost the company $1.6 billion in sales every year.[67] Continuously improving the online experience is imperative to Amazon's success and client satisfaction. Some activities, however, are standard. They are table stakes, check-the-box details that must be completed just to play the game. A customer is not going to choose Amazon over the competition because it has a top-of-the-line payroll system. This is not an area where Amazon has or should invest more than necessary, because it does not contribute to its strategic success.

While Amazon hasn't overinvested in standard activities, the company realizes that it can't ignore them either. Companies like Amazon do not win in the market by succeeding at only a few activities. If that were the case, the strategy would be easy for competitors to copy. Rather, Amazon is differentiated through its unique web of interconnected CX and standard activities, referred to as its web of advantages. As we will discuss more in the next chapter, a web of advantages is the combination of activities, and the processes, capabilities, and resources, that allow companies to create extraordinary, inimitable strategies. (See Figure 2.6.)

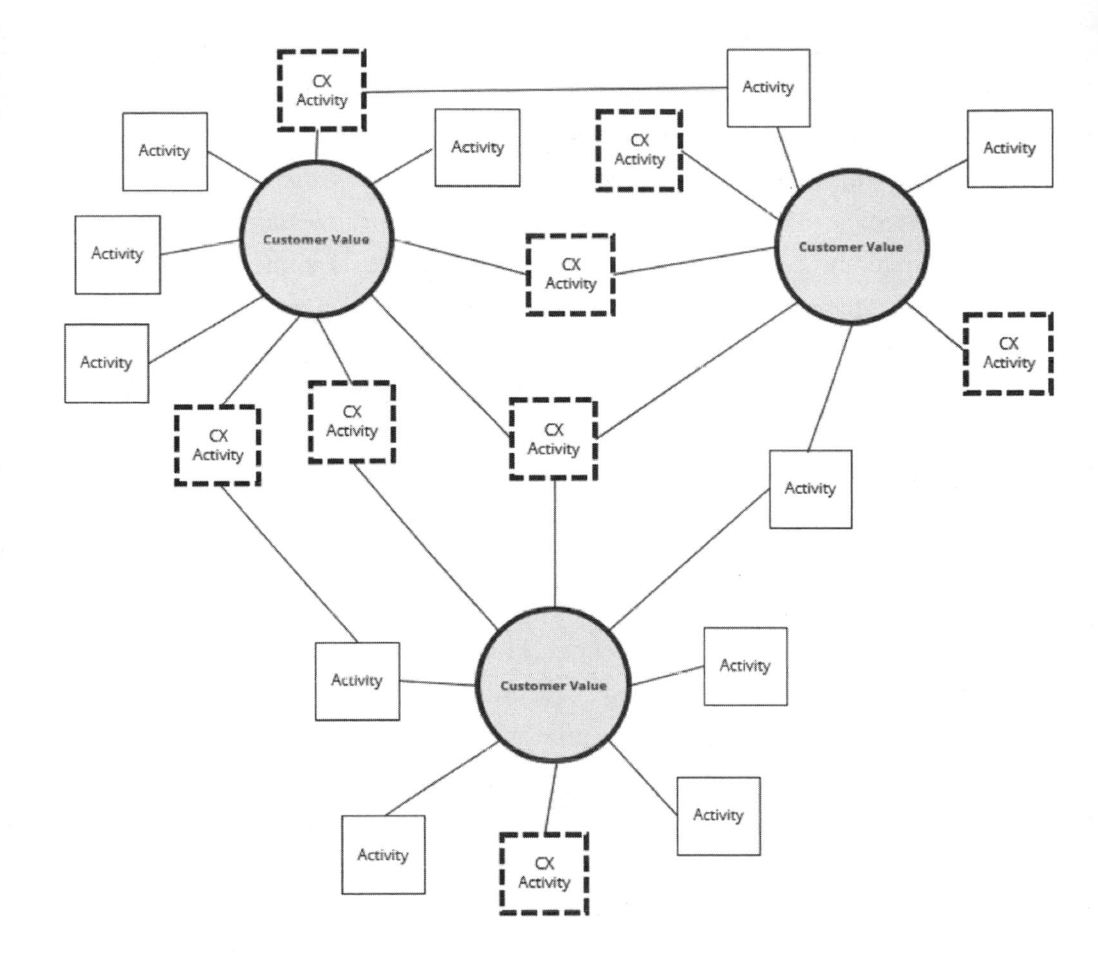

Figure 2.6: The web of advantages is composed of interlocking standard and CX activities.

Amazon executes on its standard "cooking the chicken" activities effortlessly, so it can focus more time and resources on strengthening the CX activities. The company's web of advantages enables it to effectively serve its customer types, carving out a customer-centric competitive advantage.

Though Amazon is distinguished in its ability to serve various customer types, retail is not the only space where customer types apply; industries across the board can capitalize on this customer-centric approach to strategy. Convenience and Speedy are only two examples out of a vast assortment of customer types. While consulting in the construction industry, I have witnessed a wide range of owner personalities. Construction is a low-margin business, so the tendency of contractors is often to assume that low cost is the only factor that matters. However, I frequently encounter other customer types, like "No Disruption," "Deadline," or "Rookie." No Disruption is the owner bidding out a Walmart. No Disruption must keep half the store open while construction is underway, so this type wants to ensure that the selected contractor has a flexible schedule, has a team that is willing to work odd hours, strictly enforces policies around noise, and trains the laborers to be respectful around customers. Deadline, on the other hand, is working off a stringent timeline. This type's priority is finishing the project quickly.

Rookie is new to the game and wants to learn the trade. This type might request that the contractor spend additional time explaining the plans. Rookie may be more heavily involved than other owners and therefore may value more frequent communication.

If No Disruption, Deadline, or Rookie are the contractor's ideal customers, they must ensure that processes are built around their specific types:

- **No Disruption:** To respond to the Walmart bid, the contractor would emphasize its ability to smoothly deliver projects amid the clamor of everyday operations. This contractor might leverage technology to create a detailed logistics and phasing plan to prevent delays and disruption. They could ensure safety with barricades, signage, and daily inspections and engage in daily or even hourly cleanup to prevent any disruptions to the shopping experience.

- **Deadline:** The company could customize its approach to project delivery by investing upfront time leveraging an advanced design-modeling software such as BIM and allowing Deadline to walk through the building to evaluate functionality, lighting, and other finishes so they can make upfront decisions to avoid project delays. The contractor may put a countdown-to-opening timer in the trailer to emphasize the importance of meeting the schedule.
- **Rookie:** To acknowledge Rookie's values, the company could establish weekly status updates to ensure that this type feels like an integral part of the process. They may offer Rookie training or set up regular onsite visits.

Note how important it is to deliver value to the correct customer type. If a contractor misunderstands the customer type, mistakenly believing that it is serving Deadline instead of Rookie, Rookie will receive an adverse CX. Rookie will likely sense rushed communication and will feel excluded from the process.

Customer types are everywhere. They are inherent in every industry. It's the company's job to group consumers based on relevant value systems. "Foodie" has a refined palate and fervent interest in food. Foodies don't simply go to restaurants because they are hungry; Foodies seek exceptional gourmet experiences. Portion size and price are not considerations. Foodie values attentive service, proper atmosphere, and dish presentation to accompany exquisite fare.

"Gadget" has propelled Apple to tech domination. This type is the gadget guru, the first to have every new piece of cutting-edge technology. Gadget views life as being contained in a few sleek devices and therefore researches, invests, and even stands in presale lines to get the latest and greatest technologies.

The modern market has announced the end of superficial

segmentation strategy. Customers are demanding to be treated as individuals, and leveraging customer types is the most cost-effective, scalable, and CX-driven approach. Through values-driven and behavioral segmentation, you can power innovation. Whether you're serving "Price Sensitive" or "Long-Term," you can thoroughly understand your customers and anticipate what they want.

To outsize your strategy, you must put the customer first. Understand the activities that drive value for them. Build your unique web of advantages around them. This will enable you to design and refine on their behalf, striving to better fulfill their needs, inspire their passions, relate to their circumstances, and intensify their motivations. As Bezos explains, "It's our job every day to make every important aspect of the [CX] a little better."[68]

Customer centricity fuels progress.

3

BUILD FROM ADVANTAGES

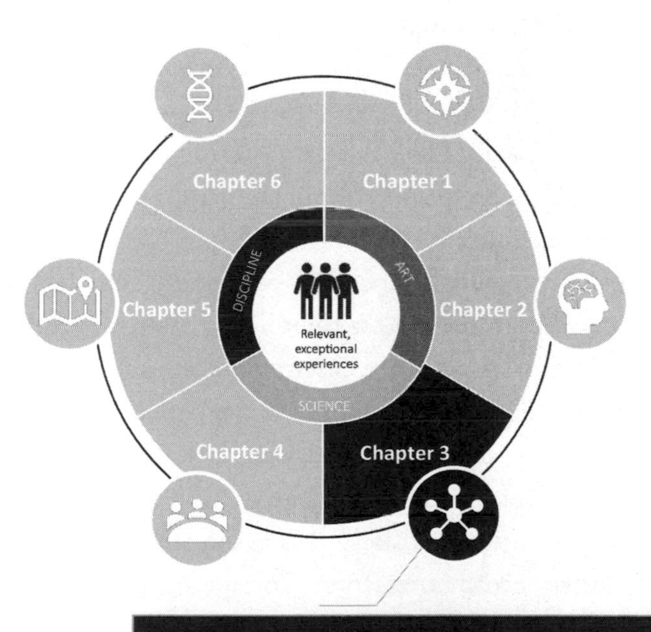

Position-, asset-, and capability-based advantages allow companies to capture a greater share of economic profit. They help companies strategically answer the questions of where best to compete and how to win.

How often do you set out to make an Italian meal and add sushi or enchiladas as a side dish? This disjointed feast would contain few overlapping ingredients, the tastes would not blend, and each dish would likely be of mediocre quality. It would be expensive to make and not very appetizing.

Rather than trying to tackle multiple food cultures in one meal, the best chefs choose a theme and build a menu around a specific cuisine. For example, the UK's Waterside Inn is one of the most renowned French restaurants in the world. It became the first restaurant outside of France to retain all three Michelin stars for a quarter of a century.[1] Described as "unashamedly French, exquisitely executed," the menu applies traditional French cooking techniques to fuse Provençal flavors into unique dishes. The menu includes fare like pan-fried filet of cod and roasted pheasant. While the Waterside Inn presents customers with a lively assortment of options, it never strays from the French theme. The masterful chefs have similar skill sets to ensure consistent quality and complementary ingredients to guarantee a well-balanced meal.

In addition to delectable dishes, fine restaurants emphasize atmosphere. The culinary leaders know their ideal customers expect a complementary ambiance and presentation. For example, the Waterside Inn fuses an "elegant and contemporary" environment to enhance the CX. Emphasizing the old-world appeal, the restaurant sits riverside in the sixteenth-century village of Bray, where chefs take modern twists on timeless dishes.[2] Waterside Inn also offers a private dining experience in the River Cottage to increase the exclusivity of the culinary event, serving the values of Mr. and Mrs. Privilege, the restaurant's elite customer type, who appreciate an undisturbed, customized experience.

Fine restaurants are deliberate in what, where, and how they serve customers. You wouldn't expect a greasy hamburger when dining in the River Cottage. And you likely wouldn't appreciate the cozy, chalet-esque character of the Waterside Inn at a modern rooftop restaurant in downtown New York City. Also, New York City is home to a plethora of French restaurants and many Michelin-acclaimed establishments. It would be harder for the Waterside Inn to differentiate itself in one of the world's most praised food capitals. Where-to-compete and how-to-compete decisions must be carefully evaluated, as these determinations can impact the fate of a business.

Like the Waterside Inn, it's imperative that companies develop a cohesive, complementary "menu" of offerings by carefully analyzing the market; they must remain focused while making tradeoffs to align finite resources. Just as a restaurant's location, atmosphere, and menu determine who it serves and who it competes against, every company must strategically position itself in the market to earn outsized economic returns. Additionally, restaurants must design menus that center around a theme to increase ingredient overlap and maximize the chefs' skills. Strategy must be laser-focused to optimize resource use and enhance the web of advantages.

I mentioned in previous chapters how companies want to do everything. People often think that by doing more, they increase their chances of winning. Too often I see teams cobble together long, strategic task lists, brimming with disconnected and sometimes conflicting agendas. The result is misaligned, fragmented strategy. Cohesive strategy transports companies beyond a random assortment of activities to deliver a congruent and meaningful CX. Because we can't do everything, we should focus on doing things that highlight our strengths.

Your company may be good at any number of things, but what is it great at? For a company to outsize, it must build from advantages—its distinct differentiators that generate value for the customer. Like the Waterside Inn, you must strategically leverage your market position and talent to produce the greatest outcome. This calls for the essentialist mindset, encouraging you to sacrifice the good to pursue the great. When building from advantages, consider the following questions:

- How will you win in your ideal customer's eyes?
- How will you beat your competitive set, the four or five direct rivals who share similarities to you like size, offerings, and audience?
- What unique corporate advantages can you capitalize on to build a distinct web of advantages?
- What activities, capabilities, and teams can you build to strengthen your competitive advantage?

CREATE AND CAPTURE VALUE

In the last chapter, I introduced how companies build a web of advantages by blending standard and CX activities. The unique sequence and connections in this web create a non-duplicatable strategy. Now, we will focus on how to build the web of advantages by uncovering your company's strengths and opportunities and weaving them into a cohesive strategy. However, before determining what to focus on, let's build a foundational understanding of advantages.

I work with many companies that initially insist that strategy comes second to fixing operational "cooking the chicken" issues. Other companies assume that strategy is a plan to strengthen weaknesses and repair shortcomings in the business. While patching weak points in your company is necessary, this should only be one small outcome of your strategy. Fixing what's broken will not give you a leg up on the competition. It'll simply equip your company with a strong base from which to build your advantages.

Strategy must go beyond performing well and must seek ways to differentiate a company. It should consider the issues that need to be fixed while identifying opportunities to exceed customer expectations. Advantages give your firm a leading edge to seize narrow windows of opportunity within a market.

Before diving in to understand your company's advantages, it's important to step back and understand the problem you are hoping to solve with your strategy. As we will discuss in the final chapter, a strategic problem should be viewed as a major, underlying issue that will impact your organization's long-term success and well-being. By framing your strategy as the antidote to this problem, you can devise a more targeted approach to attack the challenges.

Capitalizing on advantages provides the solution to your strategic problem. Advantages accomplish a dual purpose. They allow you to solve the overarching strategic problem and delight customers through enhanced experiences. By investing in the advantages that customers care about, you can deliver exceptional, relevant experiences that compel customers to buy, which ultimately leads to value capture.

Outsizing your strategy requires your company to make strategic decisions that enable you to both create *and* capture value. Nearly every strategy generates at least minimal value for some subset of the market. However, profit is derived from capturing value and should enable an organization to stimulate demand for its products and services. The two related business functions produce divergent outcomes:

- **Creating Value:** To capture value, you must first create value. Every offering and interaction should generate value for your customer. Value creation is defined as the benefit achieved when a product or service enhances the quality of life or satisfies the goals for the end user.

- **Capturing Value:** Capturing value entails monetization of the value created. Your offerings must enable your company to grow and generate cash flow at rates of return that exceed its cost of capital.

Companies often create value but struggle to capture it. This issue has plagued tech firms that provide free access to applications. For example, the popular dating app Tinder has gained widespread usership and a strong brand presence since its launch in 2012. However, in a move to cash in on the value it provides, the firm recently shifted its model by launching Tinder Plus, a premium service that provides new, updated features to users who pay to play. Similarly, Pinterest, a visual social platform, has struggled to monetize its offerings. Although the firm was valued at $11 billion in 2015, it generated merely $169 million in revenue.[3]

Delivering value to customers while capturing value within your company is the essence of strategy. If you don't capture value, your ability to create value is abolished. There are three ways that your company can capture value:

1. **Charging more.** Commanding a price premium by charging more than competitors.
2. **Doing it for less.** Lowering your cost structure by maintaining revenue while reducing expenses through cost and capital efficiencies.
3. **Growing strategically.** Increasing top-line earnings by differentiating and forming brand equity so customers consider only your company in their purchase decisions. Customer acquisition and retention result in volume growth. Acquisition is enabled by getting customers to bypass your competition through a strong network and/or differentiated

> offer. Retention increases with high switching costs—making it expensive or inconvenient for customers to move their business to your competitors—or enhanced CX, which generates customer loyalty, therefore reducing the likelihood that customers seek other alternatives.

This chapter focuses on building strategic advantages rooted in your where-to-compete and how-to-compete decisions. Companies gain a competitive edge through market ownership, acquisition and allocation of assets and resources, and consolidation of individual and team skill sets.

We will also explore how to convert three sources of advantages—positional, privileged tradable assets, and distinctive capabilities (see Figure 3.1)—into a web of advantages that will drive improved customer experiences and holistic value capture for your company and your customers.

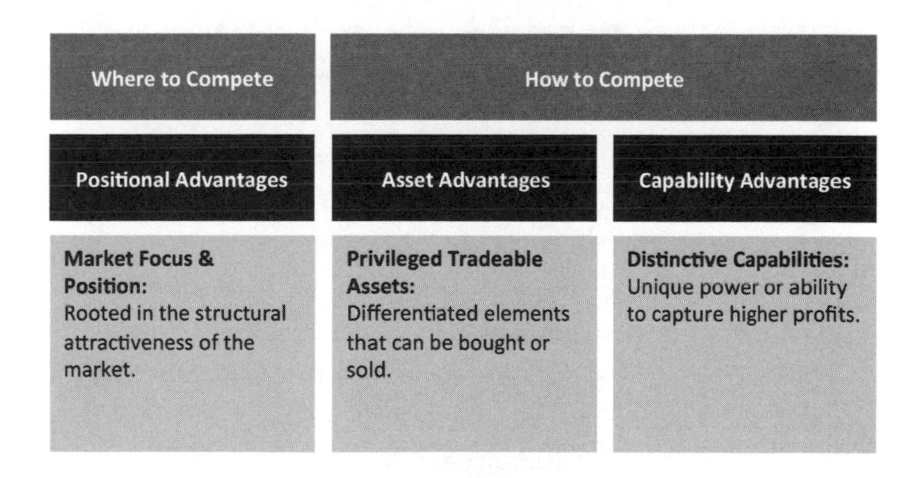

Figure 3.1: Sources of competitive advantage

SECURE POSITIONAL ADVANTAGES

A positional advantage is a company's market focus and customers' perception of a brand and its offerings. Capitalizing on positional advantages leads to price premiums and cost and capital efficiencies. When correctly leveraged, positional advantages yield bottom line growth, enabling companies to capture greater value. However, positional advantages are complex, and companies often apply ineffective frameworks and inadequate or incorrect information when making positional decisions.

The SWOT analysis (strengths, weaknesses, opportunities, and threats) and Porter's generic strategies dominate nearly every strategy-class curriculum. After graduating, bright businesspeople transfer these frameworks to their organizations and apply the concepts to corporate strategic discussions. The problem is not that these frameworks are wrong; it's that they're incomplete. Sixty-year-old frameworks are not always relevant to today's problems. Both SWOT and Porter's models focus on long-term planning. Since the inception of these methodologies, the speed of business has vastly accelerated. Companies can't predict where they need to be and what they need to do in five years if they can't accurately visualize the landscape a year from now. Outdated, static models fail to account for the modern pandemonium that shapes our fast-moving competitive environment.

Even the strategic masterminds of the 1970s and 1980s had to adjust frameworks to make them more malleable and dynamic. For example, the concept for Porter's where-to-compete framework, coined his Five Forces, was pioneered in the 1930s by Edward Chamberlin and Joan Robinson. The economists conceived the Structure Conduct Performance (SCP) model.[4] The SCP evaluates how the competitive, cost, and demand structure of the industry impacts conduct, and how competitors behave toward pricing, investments, and innovation—which ultimately affects the financial performance of the industry. Porter built on the idea of industrial organization economics, defining how five forces—threat of entrants, threat of substitutes, bargaining power of customers, bargaining power of suppliers, and industry rivalry—determine industry attractiveness.

The SCP and Five Forces frameworks should still be considered when determining where to play. It's critical that companies understand

- industry structure,
- market saturation,
- available substitutes,
- who has the power, and
- what the competition looks like and how it's changing.

Applying a dynamic lens to the analysis enables you to understand your market and anticipate imminent industry shifts. Industry trends are critical to understand because, as Porter alludes to, competitive structure will dictate the ease by which new competitors can enter the industry, the power of customers and suppliers, the availability of substitutable products and services, and the intensity of rivalry among other firms. To modify billionaire investor Warren Buffett's quote, I always tell my clients, "When a business with a reputation for brilliance tackles an industry with a reputation for bad economics, it is the reputation of the industry that remains intact."

However, while industry structure plays a large role, I would shift Porter's model slightly and build on it with modern considerations. First, Porter's Five Forces model centers around understanding and managing competition. Knowing the competition in any given market is imperative to determining how you will gain a competitive edge to procure higher-than-industry-average profits. While you can't ignore the competition, as I emphasized in the previous chapter, winning strategy revolves around your *customers*. If you leverage Porter's model, you risk ending up with a rivalry-oriented strategy rather than a customer-centric strategy.

Customers dictate your what-to-do and how-to-do decisions; naturally, they should guide your where-to-compete decisions. Porter's model accounts for buyer power, evaluating the amount of pressure that customers can exert on businesses to enhance offer quality or reduce offer prices.

Customers also impact industries by establishing trends. As I pointed out in the last chapter, robust strategies apply behavior and design thinking and values-based decisions to understand the market. Why do customers buy? How do they buy? What emerging customer trends and behaviors will shape the industry? How can you differentiate and create value to convince customers to bypass your competition? What offers and experiences do customers deem

KEY MARKET CONSIDERATIONS

Selecting key markets to play in is critical. While doing so, ask yourself the following questions to develop foresight around how you will build a strategy to compete and win in your selected segment:

1. What does winning look like in this key market?
2. What resources and capabilities are required for a company to win in this market?
3. Why will my company have a positional advantage in this key market?

relevant and differentiated, therefore enabling you to command a price premium? Buyer power only scratches the surface of customer analysis. If you apply Porter's model in isolation without fully evaluating styles, trends, behaviors, and values, you could be missing an important piece of the puzzle.

For example, according to the US Bureau of Labor Statistics, manufacturing is one of the fastest-declining industries in terms of production. US tobacco production decreased from 180,000 tobacco-growing farms in the 1980s to 10,000 farms in 2012.[5] About fifty years ago, roughly 42 percent of the US population smoked. As of 2016, the US rate of smoking lingered around 15 percent. The largest factor causing the steep industry decline is customers' changing interests and values. Consumers are investing in their health.

The industry is complex, however, and could be considered very attractive through the Five Forces lens. Despite decreased demand, tobacco companies have maintained margins. The small percentage of remaining smokers have succumbed to steep price hikes, demonstrating their lack of power. Barriers to entry are high due to government regulation, thus reducing competition. There are few comparable alternatives to the cigarette, and most competing products, such as e-cigarettes, still contain nicotine, which is derived from tobacco.

On paper, the tobacco industry looks promising. However, the colossal shift in customer values makes it an unappealing place to compete. If we solely analyze the industry from Porter's view without further considering customer values and behavior, we could risk overlooking the severe impact of customer trends. As smoking continues to fade in society, tobacco companies will confront the challenges of competing in a dying industry.

In addition to the lack of customer centricity, Porter's model suggests that industries are relatively stable and, therefore, infers that by capitalizing on a structural advantage, companies can sustain a competitive edge. In my experience, competitive advantage cannot be sustained indefinitely, regardless of industry structure. It must be continuously reinvented and refined, built on strong activities, capabilities, talent, and positioning. Strategies and where-to-play decisions must be consistently revisited to account for shifts that will impact your profits. The model's applicability varies from industry to industry.

Some industries are more stable and predictable. For example, fast-moving consumer goods (FMCG) are considered one of the safest, least volatile industries.[6] FMCG is composed of an array of daily-use products, including toothpaste, soap, and toilet paper. The top FMCG companies as of 2017 include brands like Proctor & Gamble, Johnson & Johnson, Kimberly-Clark, and PepsiCo, all of which made 1970's Fortune 500 list.[7]

The same FMCG conglomerates have reigned for decades and are likely to continue to rule this industry. These companies have successfully preserved a competitive advantage due to size, reach, steady and predictable industry activity, and an unchanged industry structure.

However, the consumer goods industry is somewhat of an anomaly. Very few companies maintain corporate dominance for decades. As shown in Figure 3.2, the Fortune 500 list has experienced significant churn since the 1950s. The persistent turnover of the world's industries ensures innovation and revolution. Choosing a strong industry to compete in is important. However, it will not provide you an indestructible competitive advantage. You must integrate strong market decisions with other positional advantages to increase your odds of winning.

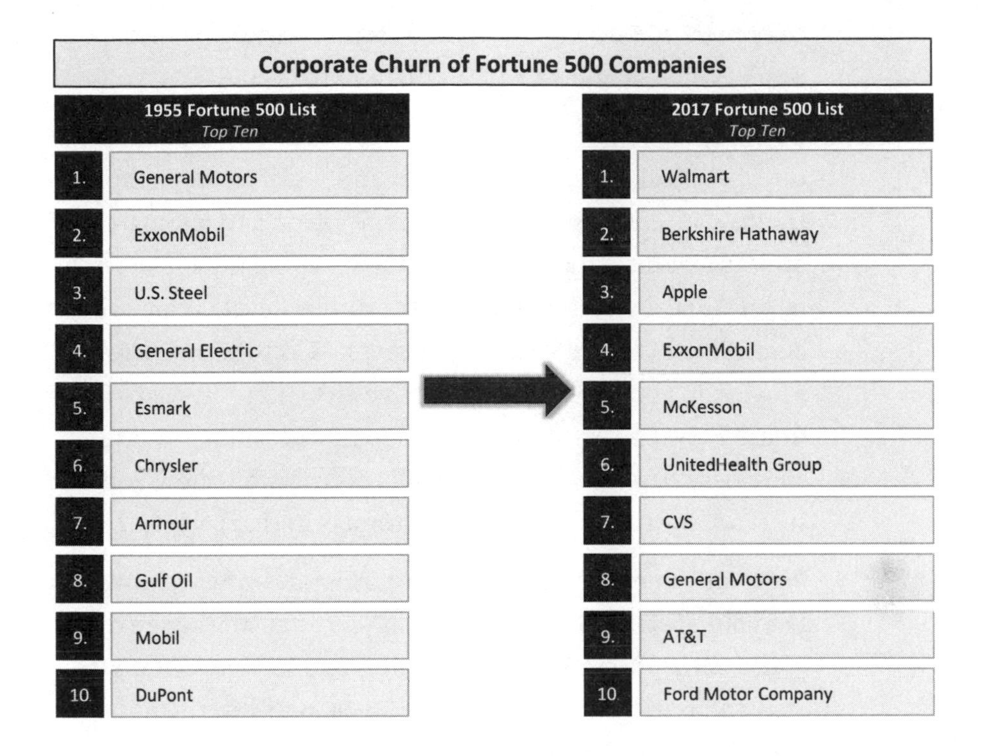

Figure 3.2: Only 20 percent of the top ten Fortune 500 corporations in 1955 remained on the list in 2017.

Additional Positional Advantages

When building your where-to-compete strategy, consider the following factors:

- **Customers.** Those who purchase your offerings. Who are your ideal customers, and where are they located? What trends are shaping their buying behavior? Do your offerings and positioning align to maximize the CX?
- **Channels.** How you bring your product to your customers. Do you deliver your goods and services directly to your end

customer? Or do you leverage intermediaries for distribution? Which channel will lead to an enhanced CX?

- **Geographies.** The geographical area in which you manufacture, sell, and distribute products and services. Geographic trends can encompass a wide range of critical inputs that impact market attractiveness and your company's relevance in an area, including GDP, educational level, population density, or local and state governments. Consider: What territories do you cover? Will you have virtual or physical locations? How can customers be grouped with similar interests and needs based on location? Will this location allow you to successfully attract profitable customers and grow sales?
- **Products and services.** Your offerings to your customer. Do your specific offerings position you at an advantage over your competition? Are your products and services differentiated and relevant? Can you produce or perform them more cheaply or charge more for them than those in your competitive set can?
- **Stages of production.** The different phases of the manufacturing process, originating with the idea and ending with a final product. Do you own the entire manufacturing and distribution process? Or do you participate at a certain juncture near the beginning, middle, and/or end? What are the benefits of being involved or removed from certain points in the process? How do your organizational capabilities align with your responsibilities in the production process? Does it make sense to insource or outsource certain stages of production?

The goal is to determine where you can position your company to capture value and win. For example, Little Man is an ice cream shop shaped like a huge tin milk jug in the Highlands neighborhood on the west side of Denver. While the ice cream is tasty and homemade, the iconic structure, situated at the top of the hill in this unique, hip part of town, sets it apart from competitors. The company has seized a one-of-a-kind positional advantage, attracting a consistent line of locals and tourists alike and serving as one of the most photographed structures in the city. Through its position, this company captures value by charging a price premium.

On a larger geographic scale, Amazon announced its expansion plans roughly ten months in advance of determining where to locate its next headquarters, ultimately deciding on New York City and Northern Virginia. The company was extremely deliberate in selecting its geographic locations, accounting for everything from tax incentives and talent to inventory storage, delivery, and transport. This decision can impact value capture in three ways, determining

- how Amazon maintains status as a preferred brand that influences customers to bypass the competition with a wide range of options and shipping supremacy,
- how it can keep shipping and storage costs low by selecting a central hub with affordable land, and
- the company's ability to hire capable talent to build an operational and efficiency advantage.

Amazon has also attained an advantage from its channel strategy. One of its larger revenue-producing branches is Fulfillment by Amazon (FBA). Amazon stores third-party merchants' goods in the warehouses and helps merchants "pick, pack, ship, and provide customer service for these products."[8] The company's advanced storage and delivery infrastructure has dismantled other distributors. It rakes in third-party fees for selling merchants' goods, which now account for 45 percent of the total number of goods sold on the site.[9] Amazon's decision to serve as a distribution channel for other merchants has solidified it as a logistics titan and positioned it to trounce competitors.

Other companies may benefit from participating in a specific phase of production. For example, Apple has a complex global supply chain. The tech company leverages more than two hundred suppliers to provide components, materials, and support in manufacturing and assembling its products.[10] Firms like Intel and LG strategically enter at the intermediary phases of production and make high margins off low-cost parts like modems and screen glass.

Lumentum is a supplier of 3-D sensors for iPhone. Its tactical position as the provider of 3-D sensor technology (including facial-recognition technology) for the iPhone has increased the company's earnings and stock prices and propelled Lumentum into higher, more profitable deciles.[11]

Of course, when making positioning decisions, there are also critical where-*not*-to-compete considerations. In the previous chapter, I explained how straying from your ideal customer, even temporarily, can drive your strategy into undesired territory. The further you stray and the longer you stay, the more challenging it is to return to your ideal customer base. The same goes for your decision on where not to compete.

For example, Starbucks serves a high-end market segment. The coffee chain prioritizes individuals who are willing to pay $4 for a cup of coffee to ensure consistent quality and invest in a recognizable brand. The brand's high-priced menu dictates its positioning strategy. Starbucks has invaded city centers. When I walk around any major US city, I can normally spot two or three within a few blocks of each other. Its stature as an urban workday oasis aligns with its strategy—entice the price-insensitive young working generation to conveniently fulfill their caffeine fix. As you move into lower-income, more rural areas of the country, you're harder pressed to spot the green-and-white mermaid.

Starbucks locations revolve around their ideal customers. Currently 83 percent of the brand's US coffee stores serve populous, predominantly wealthy and middle-class areas.[12] While Starbucks has received flack for its deliberate tendency toward economic privilege, the company's decision to avoid certain market segments is strategic, conserving resources for locations occupied by its primary customer types. The company's calculated positional strategy enables a price premium, therefore providing Starbucks with a lucrative competitive advantage. In fact, the company's 2017 operating income was roughly 19 percent, while the average coffee shop earns a meager 3 percent.[13]

Conversely, Walmart has positioned itself as the low-cost leader. Walmart has predominantly focused on establishing a presence in rural and suburban areas. The retailer operates with "2.5 times as much selling space per inhabitant in the poorest one-third of states as in the richest one-third."[14] By minimizing property prices through the establishment of low-frills stores in inexpensive areas, Walmart squeezes out an additional cost advantage over competitors.

Additionally, Walmart eliminates the nonessential intermediary wherever possible. In 2013, it announced an initiative to cut out the go-between and purchase 80 percent of its produce from local growers.[15] By focusing on its channel positioning and turning down the intermediary, Walmart further reduces its costs and passes along the savings to its customers, capturing value through consumer loyalty and a less expensive production model than competitors.

Bold and deliberate positioning strategies like those of Starbucks or Walmart are rare, however. I frequently observe companies defaulting to what is most familiar or convenient rather than positioning to attract profitable customers and capture higher value. Construction companies often pursue markets like hospitality, health care, or higher education, not because these firms have an advantage over the rivals but because the request for proposal bid process is standard and widespread. I have witnessed companies investing money in expensive reports that reveal the markets and segments projected to experience strong growth. Keeping up with market forecasts is important. However, when a company pursues growth markets for the sake of riding a market wave without regard to its positional advantages, assets, or capabilities, it runs the risk of competing to compete rather than competing to win.

Across markets, most companies tend toward comfortable choices. Many pharmaceutical companies jump into the saturated generics market because it's familiar. Hotels are frequently positioned near airports alongside tens of other competitors. While the logic checks out, opting for convenience often restrains companies from making the big decisions that outsize their strategies.

Rather than evaluating customer trends or market attractiveness relative to the company's assets, capabilities, and talent, most organizations attempt to penetrate saturated segments where competition is intense and profit margins are lean. To be effective, companies must apply advantages and align market pursuits with unique opportunities that drive the development of distinct capabilities, ultimately leading to above-industry-average profits. For some, this may mean competing in a secondary market where rival firms will be outmatched or pursuing a narrow, neglected segment that is unattractive to larger firms with high cost structures but fitting for the agile startup.

By making specific, strategic where-to-compete decisions, you position your firm to provide value to your desired customers and capture value in your organization. The next step is to align where-to-compete decisions with your how-to-compete decisions: your asset advantages and capabilities.

DEVELOP ASSET ADVANTAGES

In 2016, the US farming industry was facing its third year of financial distress due to a decline in commodity prices and an excess of grain inventory. An agricultural client was struggling with liquidity issues from eroding profitability and production inefficiencies. The land primarily yielded crops like potatoes, sweet corn, and lettuce. While the farmers knew everything about the land (it was a family plot, passed down for generations), they were ardent practitioners of their parents' and grandparents' techniques. They were attempting to compete with archaic production models.

The farmers were relying almost entirely on manual processes. The labor and overhead expenses were ballooning, and the season's crop was not as productive as anticipated. They waited out the season with the same processes, but once the crops were harvested, they developed and immediately enacted a productivity plan focused on technological investment.

Investment in ag tech was booming at the time; it soared to $4.6 billion between 2012 and 2015, so the industry was ripe for transformation.[16] The farmers began by implementing basic precision-farming technology. Using satellite imagery, they could

CONSUMER-CENTRIC ADVANTAGES

Keep in mind that any type of advantage—positional, asset, or capability—is only valuable if the customers care about it. The advantage must provide customers with higher quality, enable lower prices, or offer a desired attribute or experience deemed worthy of passing up competitors and alternatives.

better anticipate where to plant certain crops based on soil levels and weather patterns. They gradually layered on the Internet of Things (IoT) to further oversee production, driving significant productivity enhancement, not to mention reducing their workloads. The technology enabled them to monitor conditions from the comfort of their homes and effortlessly manage water usage and optimize treatments.

Production skyrocketed, and the farmers transformed into true tech enthusiasts. Their tech-fueled strategy enabled them to procure a competitive advantage, surpassing many of their rivals in low-cost production. As the labor shortage intensified and the cost of labor increased, the company relied on its technological edge to diminish the challenges of finding qualified workers. The farmers' rivals were not as fortunate.

It was not the purchase of just one piece of technology that carved out an asset advantage for these farmers; it was the effective execution of a calculated asset investment strategy. The farmers' ongoing investment in new technologies secured an advantage, one that would take years and significant capital for competitors to catch up to.

Companies that make strategic bets with capital expenditures can capture additional value. It's no coincidence that many of the companies topping Strategy&'s 10 Most Innovative Companies list also appear on the Top 20 R&D Spenders ranking.[17] To achieve this type of advantage, companies must apply calculated investment strategies. Realizing an asset advantage may require some companies to double the investment of the competitive set in capital expenditures, especially in equipment-intensive industries like manufacturing or construction. Funds should be funneled to research, technology, and equipment that, when properly implemented, can generate an innovative advantage for a company.

This might entail ongoing investment and refinement of infrastructure. For example, Google, Facebook, LinkedIn, and Amazon have all built asset advantages around distinct, highly utilized technological platforms. These platforms' functionality, usership, and brand equity carve out a unique competitive advantage for the well-known tech empires. Even if a company could copy the site code and algorithms, it would take years to build up the consumer trust and use that these established platforms boast. Consumers bypass the competition to employ these platforms because they're effective, recognizable, and used by most consumers' networks. The increased usership enables the companies to heftily charge advertisers to post endorsements and clickbait.

Asset advantages can come in many shapes and sizes. In addition to having a tech platform as an asset advantage, Google is extremely well capitalized. The company has nearly $90 billion in cash sitting on its balance sheet.[18] The cash surplus gives Google an advantage, as money serves as a privileged asset that enables the firm to invest more in other lucrative ventures than its competitors can. For example, Google can afford to hire more people to enhance the platform, improve the CX, or research new initiatives.

While people are not an asset advantage, they are instrumental in building winning cultures, sharing fresh perspectives, and discovering new ideas. Google has poured extensive resources into pioneering the autonomous vehicle industry. The company's cash has allowed it to invest in and explore new territories, giving it an advantage over less-capitalized firms. In 2012, the tech giant was awarded a US patent for self-driving car technology, which could emerge as a major asset advantage for the company in the coming years.

The patent is one of the most common and powerful asset advantages. The strength of the patent was highlighted in 2016 when the pharmaceutical company Mylan came under fire for spiking the price of its widely used EpiPen. Though the drug Epinephrine was first developed in 1895, Mylan obtained the coveted patent on the EpiPen design, protected through 2025.[19] Mylan raised concerns

ASSET ADVANTAGE LIFESPAN

Asset advantages are lasting—hard for your competitors to recreate or catch up to; however, they cannot sustain a competitive advantage indefinitely. For example, the term of a US utility patent is twenty years. While this patent may secure your competitive advantage for its duration, it's important to invest time and resources into developing new and relevant asset advantages.

when the price of the EpiPen steadily climbed, from $57 to roughly $500 in 2016, making it unaffordable to millions of its users.[20] Because the EpiPen has no direct competitor or substitute, Mylan manipulated its asset advantage (many claim unethically) to power steep margin increases. This enabled the firm to capture value through an acute price premium.

Asset advantages can capture significant value for companies. However, these advantages are not abiding. Equipment and technology eventually become obsolete, capital is invested, and patents expire. Ongoing value capture requires companies to establish additional channels of differentiation. This can be achieved by refining individual, team, and corporate skill sets to produce capability advantages.

CAPITALIZE ON CAPABILITY ADVANTAGES

In eighth grade, I wanted to grow up to be a Major League Baseball star. I had been playing baseball since I was a kid and extoled the sport's greats like Ken Griffey Jr. and Tony Gwynn Sr., who monopolized the sports channels and cereal boxes of my youth. While I continued to play baseball for a few years, the players consistently grew taller and bigger, team tryouts intensified, and my dream career drifted out of reach. By high school, I began devoting my time to other interests, like landscaping, which ultimately led me to my first business venture and unleashed my entrepreneurial spirit. It would have been a disappointing path had I remained committed to my childhood fantasy of MLB greatness.

The problem wasn't that I didn't want it badly enough. It's that I didn't have the tools or talent necessary to catapult me to professional sports stardom. Baseball didn't come naturally to me, as my other interests like finance and strategy have. Unfortunately, regardless of my level of effort, it's highly unlikely that I would succeed at a sport where I lacked a natural ability, facing competitors whose expertise flourished on the field. Pursuing baseball would have been futile and inhibited me from honing my genuine skills.

Each one of us is gifted distinct competencies. We all have strengths and weaknesses. I am not saying that an underdog can't come out on top. There is always room for an unlikely hero in the boardroom or on the baseball field. I am suggesting that leveraging our natural abilities enables us to move faster and further in accomplishing our goals.

This is not just true for individuals. The world's greatest companies are defined by corporate capabilities. While customers aren't always aware of the intangible internal skills, these capabilities build distinct differentiators that generate value for the end user. For example, few people understand the Git, Java, or Python expertise that has been poured into creating Google algorithms. What they do know is that typing a search term into Google quickly and effortlessly produces a set of relevant results. They likely also don't acknowledge the managerial effectiveness of Google's leaders that makes it one of the best companies to work for year after year. However, customers recognize the innovation born of a functional, well-run organization.

Customers appreciate online shoe company Zappos and its speedy shipping policy that promises standard, free delivery to customers within two to three days of placing their orders.[21] Zappos's advanced inventory management and supply-chain capabilities enable expedited shipment. The company has built a strong shipping relationship through its collaboration capability. The team-oriented culture extends beyond internal operations to suppliers. As CEO Tony Hsieh states, "The benefits we've reaped from building relationships with our vendors are endless."[22] The company's fast, free delivery is upheld by its strong relationship with UPS. Because Zappos works exclusively with the carrier, UPS negotiates low rates for Zappos.

While Zappos offers the same brands as many other shoe retailers, it has successfully differentiated itself from competitors by delivering what Hsieh refers to as a "wow" experience to customers.[23] The company's shipment policy, customer service, and pleasant and simple buying experience contribute to its CX capability. By delivering superior value to the customer, Zappos increases the likelihood that customers bypass the competition. Its elevated CX and collaborative capabilities pave the way for value capture, securing the brand a competitive advantage.

Google's talent or Zappos's collaboration and client experience are just a few examples among many other corporate capabilities that enable companies to create and capture unmatched value. Your firm can leverage many unique corporate capabilities to form a differentiated advantage. Developing an advantage simply requires you to understand what you're good at and how to emphasize and continuously invest in your corporate competencies.

Capabilities bundle individual skill sets, managerial techniques, company culture, team ability, and expertise to execute. The strength of your corporate capabilities is a result of the training, leadership, and resources you put into developing them. They define your organizational identity and sculpt a natural path for your organization, answering the questions: What will we do and how will we do it?

Determining what capabilities to emphasize and strengthen (and what capabilities to spend less time and attention on) plays a large role in what you can accomplish. My adolescent dream of playing baseball, despite my inadequate skill set, parallels many organizational endeavors. Time after time, I see businesses with strong, creative talent underachieving because they don't understand how to capitalize on strengths. Rather than highlighting a niche set of capabilities, companies attempt to emulate others' skill sets. They may look at competitors' earnings with envy and strive to recreate their strategies. However, every company has distinct capabilities. When these undertakings fail, it's often because the company lacks the competencies necessary to outperform their competitors. They don't have what it takes to duplicate the competitor's web of advantages.

For example, in 1994, Richard Branson, founder of the Virgin Group, was running a successful business empire when he decided to challenge Coke and Pepsi. Virgin had no experience in the beverage industry; at the time, the Virgin Group was primarily focused on music production. While the team had strong networks in the music industry, employees knew little about competing in the cutthroat beverage market. Branson reflected on his team's train of thought, explaining, "Coke is the best-known brand in the world, and if we could topple Coke, we thought it would be a lot of fun."[24] Unfortunately, Virgin lacked the distribution and marketing capabilities to execute. The business extension turned out to be a flop.

LEGO experienced a similar failure. In 2003, the toymaker was operating on the brink of bankruptcy after unfortunate over-diversification steered the company off track. LEGO lost $240 million. Rumors swirled of a Mattel takeover, and private equity firms encroached, looking to get their hands on the global brand.[25]

Can you guess what caused the demise of the toy-making empire? A lack of capability alignment with its new ventures nearly forced LEGO into insolvency. LEGO was attempting to become a lifestyle brand selling "its own line of clothes, watches, and video games."[26] Its capabilities were planted firmly in the toy industry. LEGO's innovative high-quality toys defined its success. By shifting away from its core competencies, LEGO abandoned the strategy that earned it a competitive advantage. The company has since regained its standing after executing a bold turnaround plan focused on simplification and innovation, and as a result, "more than 60 percent of LEGO Group's sales are new launches every year."[27] By refocusing on its primary capabilities, innovation, and creativity, the company has restored its brand and spiked its sales.

Knowing your capabilities and understanding how to use them can mean the difference between success and failure. To drive results through advantages, you must unleash the power of your capabilities. To understand your capabilities and how to develop and apply them, you can conduct a capabilities audit. Consider the questions listed under each core capability (Figure 3.3), reference the detailed descriptions of the first five, and request that your colleagues do the same. You will see patterns emerge around commonly cited capabilities. These strengths should be at the forefront of your strategy.

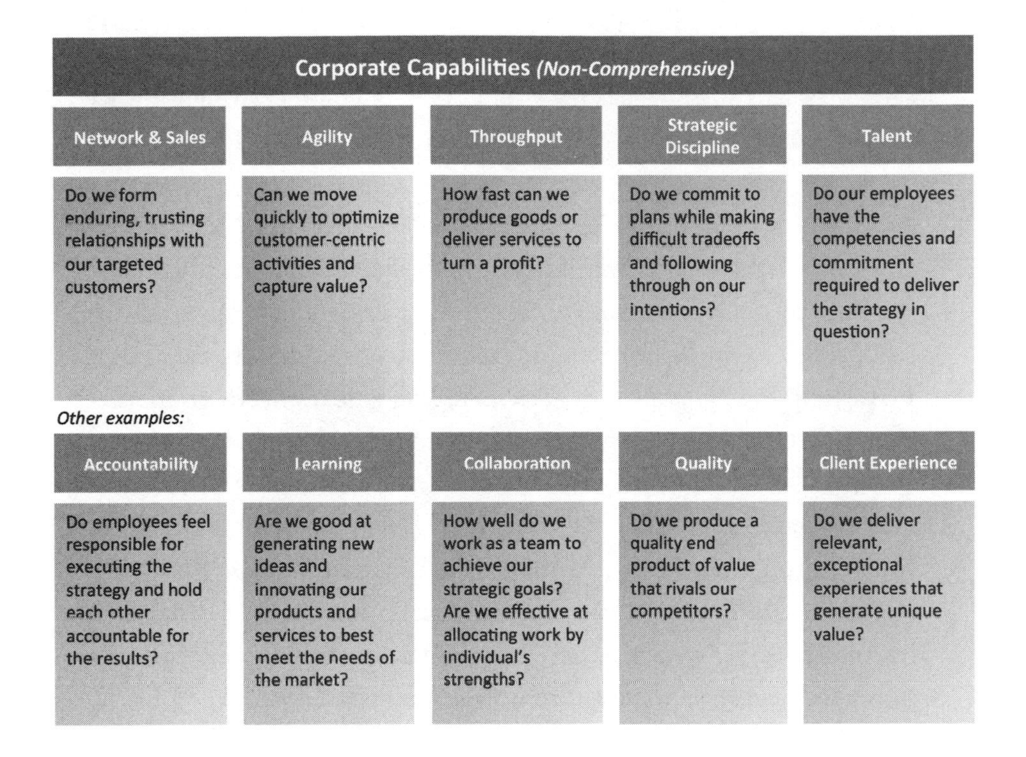

Figure 3.3: Companies can leverage a variety of corporate capabilities to power value creation and capture.

Network and Sales: *Do our processes, employees, and network enable effective sales to relevant customers? Are we gifted at pipeline management?* Some companies possess strong, differentiated offers and the talent to deliver. However, even companies with operational skills and talent may fight slipping margins due to ineffective pipeline management. These companies might lack the sales skills to engagingly position offers to convince customers to buy. On the other hand, there are some companies that have standard products and services that excel with the support of qualified sales teams; scalable, potent processes; marketing aptitude; and connections with the right buyers. Strong sales and network capabilities help companies command a higher price point from customers, therefore increasing profitability. An effective sales process also enhances the overall CX, building customer loyalty and safeguarding business from competitors.

Agility: *Are we able to quickly adapt to market changes to mitigate risk and capitalize on opportunity?* Bulky bureaucracy limits flexibility. Though large organizations often have capital as an asset advantage, smaller companies can compete through an agility capability. Possessing the dynamism to anticipate and adjust quickly to market changes empowers continuous CX improvement.

Throughput: *How fast can you make things happen?* Related to speed, throughput measures the rate at which output is produced. Resources are finite, and the time value of money erodes profitability, so companies that can increase production speed to earn profits faster than competitors capture greater value.

Strategic discipline: *Do we share an intellectual, behavioral, and procedural agenda for our strategy? Do we commit to plans and follow through on our intent*ions? A company can design the best strategy in the world; however, if employees are not in alignment and don't know how to execute, the results won't materialize. Strategic discipline is a distinct capability that differentiates companies. In fact, research shows that executional excellence is the number-one issue facing global corporate leaders.[28] Developing discipline enables companies to ignore distractions and exert full effort toward achieving set objectives. This discipline allows companies to capture value in all three ways (increasing price, reducing cost, or growing strategically) based on the desired outcomes of the strategy.

Talent: *Do our employees have the competencies and commitment required to deliver the business strategy in question?* Earlier, I discuss how companies continue to prioritize traditional value drivers, physical assets, and financial capital over new value drivers, intellectual assets, and human capital. While it's crucial to develop a strong asset-investment strategy, fully developed employee skill sets are often an untapped lever of competitive advantage. Training typically focuses on improving low-performer production or maximizing the skills and abilities of the top 10 percent. Roughly 74 percent of the workforce falls in the middle of the talent spectrum, however. While these mid-level performers compose the largest portion of the labor pool, on average, managers devote only 20 percent of their focus to this group.[29] Empowered with the right tools, training, and technology, these mid-level performers can rise to the top and drive organizational productivity. By strengthening all employees' individual competencies, organizations can establish and fortify corporate capabilities.

Once you have determined your capabilities, you will be in a better position to pursue investments, allocate resources, and make strategic decisions. Aligning your asset and positional advantages with your corporate capabilities will power strategic growth. It will enable you to offer customers a cohesive "menu" of options that will outsize the CX, value creation, and value capture.

4

CONVERT ADVANTAGES INTO VALUE

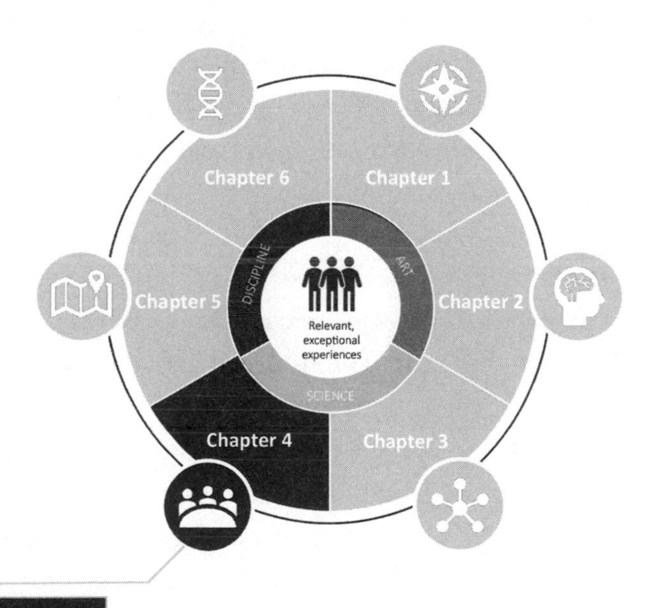

Aligning your asset and positional advantages with your corporate capabilities will power greater value capture from price premiums, cost and capital efficiencies, and strategic growth.

LEARN THE FUNDAMENTALS

My fascination with numbers blossomed in my childhood. In elementary school, I was enamored with practicing my times tables. I appreciated the simplicity and constancy of the numbers; I could always rely on the figures to multiply to the same answer. My appreciation of the unwavering black-and-whiteness of numbers carried into middle school, and algebra quickly became my favorite class. Unlike other courses, laced with subjective interpretations, biases, and unknowns, math was pure and absolute. I found it exhilarating to solve for *x* or *y* or to apply a linear equation to uncover the answer to a perplexing word problem.

I began to put my number knowledge to work outside of the classroom in childhood business schemes. When I was thirteen, I purchased sodas from the store and sold them to classmates on the school bus at a four-times markup. I carefully tracked my venture's inflows and outflows in a ledger book I concealed in my nightstand. Striving to maximize my earning potential, I boosted my price and began purchasing off-brand soda to cut costs. Unfortunately, upon discovering my soda business, my bus driver abolished my operations. I had to settle for selling gum to classmates, a more manageable scheme, as packs of gum were more discreet and easier to transport.

My understanding of numbers and my fascination with financials burgeoned into college and graduate degrees and eventually my career. I continued to consult numbers for answers, especially when working in businesses. Prior to launching my consulting firm, I stumbled across key financial insights that transformed my thinking and fueled my passion for the integration of strategy and finance.

One of my clients was earning revenue of $10 billion through global credit card processing and payment solutions. The company was bogged down with over $20 billion of debt resulting from its private equity buyout the year prior to the Great Recession. To cover its $2 billion interest payments and excessive operating costs amid the economic downturn and decline in consumer spending, the company focused on executing a strategy to combat its smaller, nimbler competitors who were stealing market share with lower fees and superior technology. My client sketched out plans to reduce complexity, cut costs, minimize debt, and improve cash flow. Leadership defined initiatives and targets and generated reports to monitor progress.

While the intention was legitimate, the leaders designed incomplete, convoluted reports to track strategy and financial performance. The reports were a complex tangle of numbers, filled with rows of data that the managers were unable to interpret. High-level employees who were responsible for monitoring the data and making critical, million-dollar changes based on the information were bewildered by the numbers. They were consumed by data paralysis.

Although the company earnestly committed to bold strategic moves, performance continued to backslide. The strategic decisions, detached from financial insights, were not strong enough to overcome the client's rivals who were disrupting the business with more innovative structures and offers. The client's failure to implement its strategy due to a financial knowledge gap revealed two business realities:

1. leaders often struggle to discern the story behind the numbers, and
2. there exists a prevalent disconnect between strategy and finance across businesses in every industry.

Working with this client inspired the genesis for many of my ideas and convictions about strategic financial leadership and the importance of marrying strategy and finance. Companies that design and implement strategies without data fly blind. While strategy is often a gray, cryptic puzzle, financials provide a clear-cut diagnostic. Numbers offer a single element of strategic certainty. They tell a story and provide clarity around business's variabilities.

Financials reveal insight into strategic operations, indicating areas of strength and weakness and guiding you on where to focus and how to proceed. Oftentimes, however, financials are obscured by misunderstanding and misinterpretation, limiting a company's ability to leverage financial insights to make positive change. Throughout my career, I have met with thousands of business professionals and am continuously surprised by how many accomplished, intelligent businesspeople lack a foundational understanding of value.

They don't know how to approach the numbers and look only at the *value creation* aspect of strategic success. They assume that if they conceive an innovative solution that tackles a customer problem while delivering an excellent CX, their businesses will grow and prosper. This mindset is not incorrect; creation is a critical input into the value equation. Understanding customers and building from advantages is the requisite first step in designing and executing a successful strategy.

However, this mindset is incomplete. I discussed how organizational performance often falls short in the *value capture* side of the equation. While strategy affords wiggle room and demands creativity, it also requires black-and-white financial thinking. There are good decisions that make financial sense, and there are poor decisions that ignore or overlook monetary implications. Leaders will hash out mission, vision, and value statements, mistakenly believing that their work is complete. While these statements serve a purpose and are valuable in certain instances, unless a strategy is financially grounded, it lacks the specificity and economic feasibility required for successful implementation and adjustment. Strategy without finance is dead.

Your strategy can be innovative, provide significant value to customers, and effectively leverage your advantages, but if it doesn't align with your financial goals and support your company in gaining a competitive advantage, it's unsustainable. To be effectual, you must support your strategy with broad and deep, short- and long-term data-based analysis. A great strategist accepts the uncertainty of business and takes risks while integrating and interpreting the numbers to reinforce decisions. The best business leaders aggregate, read, and elucidate strategic diagnostics by uncovering the story embedded in the numbers. In this chapter, we will dive deeper into the principles of value capture and introduce financial levers that leaders can apply to realize an outsized share of economic profits.

ASCEND THE ECONOMIC PROFIT CURVE

Misapplication of strategy due to misunderstanding of competitive advantage plagues companies across the board. I have conducted many strategy sessions and applied countless financial analyses to measure organizational effectiveness in a variety of industries. My work unveils a pervasive, underlying theme—too many companies don't understand how to strategically maximize financial value.

To illustrate this point for a single industry, I analyzed a representative sample of 363 industrial and nonresidential construction companies ranging from $1 million to over $1 billion in revenue located throughout the United States. I then computed economic profit earned by each firm and segmented the results in deciles (e.g., bottom 10 percent, as illustrated in Figure 4.1). The companies in the tenth decile, or top 10 percent, earn 64 percent of all economic profit, and the top 20 percent earn nearly 83 percent of all economic profit, fulfilling the Pareto Principle, or the 80/20 rule.

This economic profit curve exists in all industries and has been leveraged by numerous strategy consultants and companies in attempts to answer the age-old question: Why do some companies thrive while others die? McKinsey & Company expounds on the economic profit curve defining the ten levers that explain the "up-drift and down-drift" in corporate performance.[1]

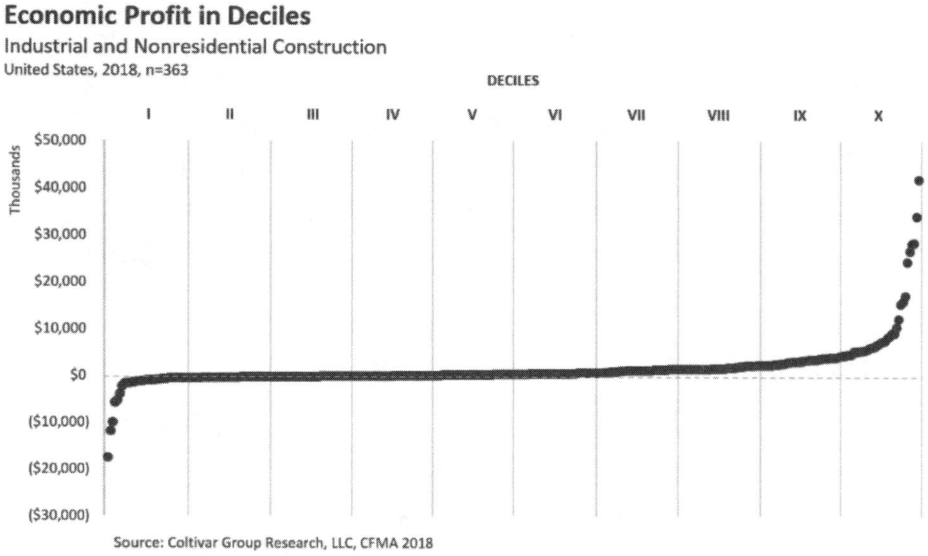

Economic Profit in Deciles
Industrial and Nonresidential Construction
United States, 2018, n=363

DECILES
I II III IV V VI VII VIII IX X

Thousands
$50,000
$40,000
$30,000
$20,000
$10,000
$0
($10,000)
($20,000)
($30,000)

Source: Coltivar Group Research, LLC, CFMA 2018

Figure 4.1: Top-performing companies earn economic profits disproportionate to average- and low-performing organizations. Economic profit follows the Pareto Principle, commonly referred to as the 80/20 rule, which states that 80 percent of the outcomes are produced by 20 percent of the causes.

The company's book, *Strategy Beyond the Hockey Stick*, focuses on the concept of progressing into higher quintiles and beating the market by making specific, targeted strategic moves. For example, the book defines the M&A ventures, approaches to resource allocation, and capital expenditures (CAPEX) investments that have historically propelled companies into higher deciles along the curve.[2]

While I believe the economic profit curve serves a distinct

purpose, it is limited in two key ways that many theories and applications overlook:

1. Financial decisions such as increasing revenue fueled by debt could perhaps move a company from one decile to another, but these decisions may also have an adverse effect. For example, what about those companies that took the same approach and went bankrupt? This relates to survivorship bias, the logical error of concentrating on people or things that pass some selection process and overlooking those that did not. Yes, revenue growth fueled by leverage could perhaps lead to higher economic profits and advancement along the economic profit curve; however, this assumption disregards other soft factors such as culture or leadership, which also greatly impact strategy. What if management is incompetent or fails to focus effort on strategic action? Referring solely to financial drivers to correlate movement along the economic profit curve may lead to biased, erroneous conclusions.
2. Past performance is no guarantee of future results. Looking backward to determine the steps a company took to capture a greater share of economic profits may be helpful; however, it is incomplete to base strategy on this information alone.

Rather than employing the economic profit curve to prescribe a blanket course of action based on historical data, we can leverage it as proof that too many companies chase ineffective strategies. If 20 percent of companies secure over 80 percent of the profits, then 80 percent of companies are missing the mark: applying a weak, ineffective framework; relying on biased focus and flawed design; or lacking the strategic discipline to get things done. These companies struggle to outsize. The greatest outcome that a poor strategy can produce is short-term nominal improvement leaving many

REVENUE DOES NOT EQUAL PROFIT

When looking at the economic profit curve, most people believe that companies with the most revenue will make it to the top deciles because of size, regardless of whether these companies earn a low profit on a percentage basis. Conversely, my research reveals that size is rarely a determinant of decile. In fact, half of the companies in the highest two deciles only earned roughly 14 percent of the revenue in the corresponding categories. Albeit important for scale, size is not typically a predictor of profit. I have seen too many leaders falsely assume that growing the top line in the short term will result in margin improvement over the long term. As I describe later in this chapter, this approach can be difficult and dangerous.

---

companies confined to the dog-eat-dog environment of the lower deciles, where rivals contend for leftover scraps of industry profit. These companies struggle to advance and are constantly battling the looming threat of bankruptcy. As displayed in Figure 4.2, remaining in business becomes tougher and less likely as the years progress.

In many instances, faulty strategy doesn't just limit companies to lower deciles; it eliminates them completely. Kiewit, an established, multibillion-dollar construction firm, conducted an internal study comparing the top 500 construction companies in 1965 to the top 500 in 2015. Chris Dill, vice president of the Kiewit Technology Group, stated, "What we found was startling; 450 of 500 who were on the list in 1965 were gone in 2015."[3]

The road to bankruptcy is built over time, fabricated by a string of strategic mistakes. Rather than building advantages out of client-centricity and data-driven analysis, many companies construct strategies based on industry trends, macroeconomic forecasts, or operational improvement agendas. While these are important ingredients to the strategy design, in isolation, these components are unlikely to produce the momentum required to break through the partition into the higher deciles.

Outsizing occurs through a combination of incremental improvement and big, bold moves when warranted. While it's highly improbable that a company that is stuck in the first or second decile and is flirting with bankruptcy will make a dramatic overnight leap to the tenth decile, outsizing requires time and patience. Don't be discouraged if your company is competing in a lower decile. Set realistic goals; build implementable, data-based strategies; take calculated risks; and fight to the top of that decile. By committing to outsizing and intelligently leveraging advantages and financial information, firms can make great strides to advance along the economic profit curve within a given decile. Whether you're operating on the left or right end of the economic profit curve, your focus should be on winning within your decile, earning your fair share of economic profit, and steadily advancing up the ladder.

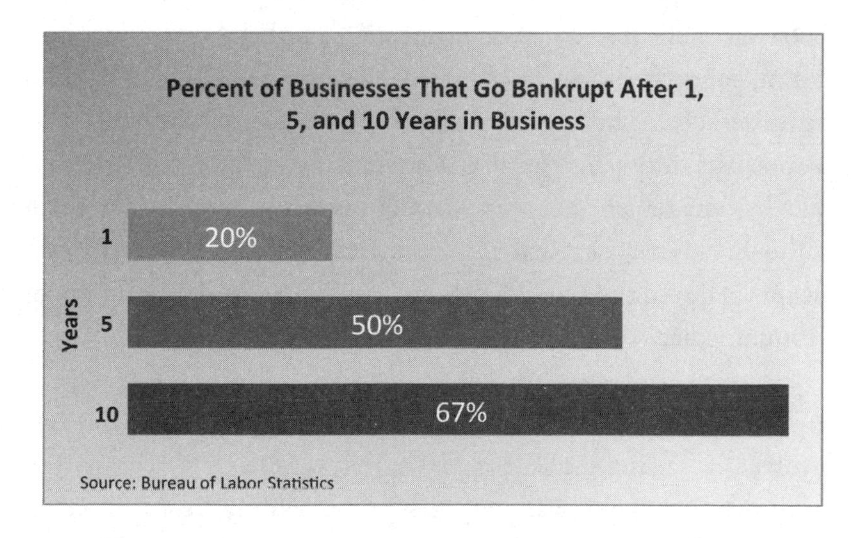

Figure 4.2: The threat of bankruptcy increases over the course of a company's life. Approximately 33 percent of companies survive past the ten-year mark.

ASSEMBLE A BETTER BUSINESS MODEL

In 1998, amid the craziness of the dot-com boom, poetry critic Ernst Malmsten and former fashion model Kajsa Leander conceived of Boo.com, one of the first fashion e-retailers, a web platform where the founders envisaged wealthy global sophisticates flocking to buy their clothes. When the business launched in October 1999, it employed four hundred people across eight offices. It was an expensive venture, funded with nearly $94 million. Like many other dot-com companies, though it had not yet proven its economic model, it was expected to generate a lucrative ROI. Before the site even went live, *Fortune* magazine deemed it "one of Europe's coolest companies."[4]

Boo.com's launch, however, was a bust. Sales lagged far below expectations. Though publications and investors alike had proclaimed its potential, it was unable to capture the value necessary to remain afloat. The e-retailer's spending far exceeded its earnings: Boo.com expended nearly $200 million in its short six months of operation but earned just $230,000 in its final two months.[5]

Investors poured money into the brand and its seasoned owners. The concept of Boo.com was promising; since the company's liquidation, online fashion retail has reigned supreme. Why did Boo.com fail miserably? The owners struggled to translate the site's value proposition into value capture. The financial projections were half-baked. Management believed it could occupy a much larger corner of the global market much faster than it was able to. Therefore, the owners believed they could quickly offset the expensive groundwork with immediate revenue.

However, the company's return on capital was lower than its cost of capital. Management had vastly underestimated the costs involved in raising global brand awareness. They spent four times more than originally planned in the time leading up to Boo.com's launch.[6] Sluggish sales and diminished margins quickly engulfed the company. Before admitting defeat, the owners requested an additional $30 million from investors to keep the brand alive. However, after witnessing the beginnings of the dot-com bust, the skeptical investors refused. The business model didn't make economic sense.

Boo.com was not the first and certainly won't be the last company to make large strategic bets without vetting financial returns. The recent rise of Bitcoin and other cryptocurrencies has emulated the mysterious and tumultuous rise and fall of the dot-com bubble. When the Bitcoin market exchange opened in March 2010, the price of a single coin was $.008.[7] In December of 2017, the price of a Bitcoin surged to over $19,000.[8] The value has since dropped by 50 percent over the course of 2018.[9]

Cryptocurrencies, like Bitcoin, enable peer-to-peer transactions without the interference of a third party. Bitcoin's value proposition is built on its low transaction fees, untaxed purchases, user anonymity, and increased security. Few fully understand what Bitcoin does, however, and no one can absolutely predict the fate of cryptocurrency. Bitcoin investors were recently quoted on their motivations, explaining, "I just did it kind of blindly."[10] Only time will tell whether this little-known asset will yield the desired return.

At the end of the day, the goal of any company (or asset) must be to generate a financial return and uphold a commitment to shareholders. As Milton Friedman stated, "There is one and only one social responsibility to business—to use its resources and engage in activities designed to increase its profits."[11] While I believe that successful companies are bound to a variety of social responsibilities outside of profit maximization, I agree that companies cannot commit to any further duties without proper capitalization. Companies that lack financial security are restricted from pursuing other ventures and, eventually, from remaining in business.

Therefore, strategy is inherently tied to financials. A business model must power value capture. Without such advantages, companies are doomed to compete on price. These companies become stranded in the lower deciles.

How can one ensure that the business model paves the way for outsized value capture? As discussed in the previous chapter, a company must resolve how to effectively leverage advantages to build a competitive advantage. I introduced the where-to-compete and how-to-compete decisions that provide inputs into the three value-capture strategies: price premium, cost and capital efficiency, and growth. In this chapter, I conduct a deeper analysis on what it means to capture value and how to do it to promote long-term financial strength.

EARN A PRICE PREMIUM

Simply put, companies command a price premium by charging more than competitors. This approach demands customer-centric understanding. Consider the following questions:

- Why are customers willing to pay more for your products or services?
- What additional value are you delivering that warrants a price increase?

In many instances, price premiums can stem from effective positioning strategies. There are a few ways in which proper positioning can lead to a price premium. One approach is to establish a first-mover advantage to cement a higher price point for goods or services. First movers set prices and consumer expectations. First movers also secure reign of the market before competitors can catch up, building brand presence and eliminating pricing pressure at least temporarily.

I consulted for a large general contractor that began exploring P3 (private-public partnership) projects years before many of its competitors. P3 entails complicated contracts, a unique equity structure, and complex work agreements; therefore, it involves a learning curve and certain level of risk for inexperienced firms. The concept of P3 has existed for centuries, initially rising in popularity as a viable contracting model in the UK. The North American construction market was largely unexposed to these projects. This contractor, however, employed a few people who were familiar with the structure and operations of P3 agreements, and the contractor jumped at the opportunity to bid on P3 projects.

The decision to move into this new space turned out to be extremely profitable. Where the average net operating margin for a general contractor on most federal projects fell between 1 and 2 percent at the time, the company was earning margins in the low double digits for its work on the P3 projects. The company's price premium endured for a few years; however, as competitors gained education and experience in the P3 realm, the barriers to entry that preserved this brand's price premium, such as knowledge and certification, began to diminish. Within a few years, the contractor had to return to the drawing board to devise a new value-capture strategy as fees compressed in the P3 arena.

Construction is among many industries where creating barriers to entry can help companies capture a temporary yet sizeable price premium. As shown in Figure 4.3, all products and services travel along a commoditization curve, illustrating the rise and fall of demand from launch to maturity. Breakthroughs in technology ride one of the most aggressive commoditization curves. For example, in the last decade, renewable energy has taken center stage in construction due to regulatory requirements and economic and environmental benefits. When renewable energy was first introduced, engineering, procurement, and construction (EPC) firms building solar and wind projects were reaping large returns, upwards of 20 percent on the projects. However, the situation has changed. Today, more competitors are operating in the space, industry fees have compressed, and margins have shrunk to single digits over the years.[12]

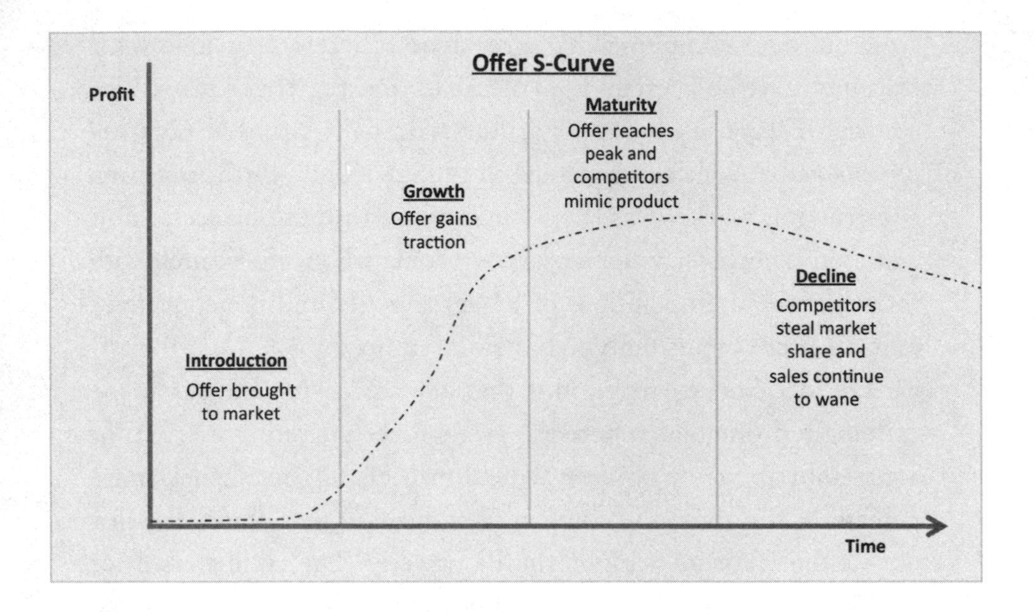

Figure 4.3: Innovations ride along a commoditization curve, where they gain traction, yield revenue and margin growth, and then experience revenue leakage and profit erosion as new competitors and novel innovations enter the space.

Another prominent example has been the dynamic commoditization curve of the big-screen TV. I laugh when I think back to my first flat-screen TV mounted to my living room wall. It was a Sony forty-inch TV that I bought in the early 2000s for $3,000. My basement houses a much larger, far superior TV that I bought a decade later for a fraction of the price. The full-featured fifty-inch plasma-screen TV debuted in early 2000 with a price tag of roughly $20,000. By 2005, the price of the same TV was a mere $5,000, and it has since continued to drop by roughly 25 percent per year.[13] The first movers had the know-how, manufacturing, distribution, and marketing capabilities to capitalize on hefty margins. However, as competitors began to catch up, the product commoditized, and profits deflated. The early-mover advantage provided only short-term bankability.

Other companies have commanded price premiums through effectively demonstrating how the value of products and services exceed the price. For example, in the early 2000s, Goodyear Tires introduced Assurance tires with extended tread life. These tires were superior quality and more expensive to manufacture, forcing Goodyear to charge a higher price. However, the company's customers were largely uninformed about tire quality; therefore, they were inclined toward the lower-end tires. Goodyear's innovation fell flat due to a lack of market understanding.

In response to meager sales, Goodyear leveraged its marketing and branding as a platform to educate customers. Rather than sharing engineering jargon to justify the tire prices, it shifted its pricing model to correspond with the average lifespan of the tires. The expected number of miles per tire directly corresponded with the price per tire. The customers' ability to cling to this tangible value proposition resulted in their willingness to pay the premium for high quality and durability.[14]

Over time, companies like Goodyear drive brand differentiation and loyalty by providing superior, proven products and services. Some brand prestige, however, extends beyond quality and taps into social acceptance. In chapter 2, I described how a Lamborghini appeals to a unique customer type's emotional needs. Luxury brands successfully engage customers' desires for psychological fulfillment beyond functionality. In 2015, Louis Vuitton released a City Steamer Crocodile bag that retailed for $55,500.[15] It's unlikely that the quality of the purse drastically outshined one that cost $5,000. Rather, the steep price premium is indicative of the iconic fashion brand's exclusivity.

While price premiums can be very lucrative, they are not lasting. Competitors eventually develop or invest in the talent, capabilities, and requisites to compete. Brand equity for even the most prestigious companies can fluctuate and wane over time as new entrants

The Goodyear example represents an important pricing lesson that many of my clients have struggled with. When value exceeds price, people buy. Sales teams especially wrestle with this concept. Employees will complain about lost sales opportunities and overly price-sensitive customers, sulking in the low win ratios on new sales. However, their experiences are just symptoms of a bigger problem—price to value. Companies typically provide discounts and lower prices to push their products and services. It's easier to sell on price. However, if your company is dealing with depressed win ratios, the likely issue is that you are not effectively demonstrating the true value to the end user. You must show how you provide a solution that helps customers progress to their end goals.

---

secure consumer attention. For example, Louis Vuitton has recently experienced brand fade as revenue drops in China, formerly one of the company's largest-consuming economies.[16]

Price premiums enable value capture, but they are usually limited and fleeting. Barriers to entry eventually erode or change, and companies must reposition to maintain a competitive advantage.

Additionally, you can only raise prices so high before surpassing the point of equilibrium and losing buyers. While increasing prices may allow you to earn higher profits, doing so at the cost of alienating your customers will bear expensive consequences. Eventually the law of economics dictates that margins will dwindle, and you will soon be competing in a zero-sum game. To safeguard against a losing positioning strategy, it's important to balance your strategy with pursuits in the other two value-capture categories as well.

OUTSIZE COST AND CAPITAL EFFICIENCY

The second way to capture value is by lowering your cost structure through cost and capital efficiencies. This approach necessitates operational insights as you assess how you can enhance efficiency by redesigning processes, restructuring operations, and even reimagining your business model to be agile and customer-centric.

The most accessible, inexpensive way to capture a cost and capital efficiency is to conduct a simple process audit. I frequently work with management who complain of high labor costs and squeezed margins. A few years ago, I was working with a large B2B company that employed a sizeable sales force. Leadership explained that while the company had enough bodies to sell, expenses were creeping up, and the sales team wasn't performing to expectations. The company's issue was rooted in its ineffective deployment methodology. Sales accounts were sprinkled throughout the US with little rhyme or reason behind the deployment structure. As a result, salespeople were spending much of their time in the air, moving between customers instead of selling to them. Sales expenses accumulated, and the company's bottom line suffered.

To alleviate the negative implications of the half-baked approach, the client had to completely revamp its deployment strategy, starting with its segmentation methodology. Leadership began by conducting an in-depth analysis of its customers and potential customers and grouped them by characteristics that defined these companies' needs. Then, to improve travel efficiency, the company categorized customer accounts by geographic region. The geographic territory alignment saved the company thousands of dollars on travel expenses and increased the sales team's client-facing time. Refining the segmentation strategy enhanced the employees' sales pitches, as they were able to better identify and speak to specific customer challenges. This organizational shift freed up thousands of dollars while simultaneously growing sales and improving employee satisfaction.

This process redesign cost the company little in time and money and made a large impact. In some instances, however, developing cost and capital efficiencies requires a more significant investment. One increasingly common approach to combat rising labor costs and ease the burden of the labor shortage is to automate processes. Automation has transformed manufacturing, proving its ability to slash labor costs while boosting productivity.

In 2012, Amazon invested $775 million in Kiva robots that the company uses in fulfillment centers to move items and deliver them to human workers. These robots have effectively reduced operating expenses by 22 percent.[17] As Amazon continues to introduce these robots into its hundred-plus fulfillment centers, the company is set to save upwards of $2.5 billion. Technology and automation also drive productivity, therefore improving throughput, a critical efficiency metric. The automobile industry, one of the first trades to pioneer robotics, has experienced a 16 percent increase in production from the use of advanced robotics.[18]

In addition to AI, a slew of technologies aimed at efficiency and cost reduction have permeated a wide variety of industries, driving down cost structures and ramping up productivity. Oftentimes, companies are stuck in a cycle of leveraging archaic, poorly designed, or paper-heavy processes that disable information sharing and increase

THROUGHPUT

Throughput is a productivity metric that refers to the amount of work a company puts in place over a specific period. The numerator typically consists of a derivative of a profit margin metric (e.g., project gross margin, margin per manager, etc.), and the denominator is derived from some variant of time (per month, week, hour).

complexity. Digital collaboration tools, online software, and services that enhance project management, workflow, and communication have carved out a sizeable market that is anticipated to grow to over $6 billion by 2020.[19] These applications, when properly implemented, empower companies to break down communication barriers, generate greater project transparency, custom-design efficient workflows, and effectively allocate resources. The result is operational improvement and value capture. Shown in Figure 4.4, as a company transitions to the new operating model, it fuels growth with continuous innovation and efficiency and is rewarded with long-term value capture.

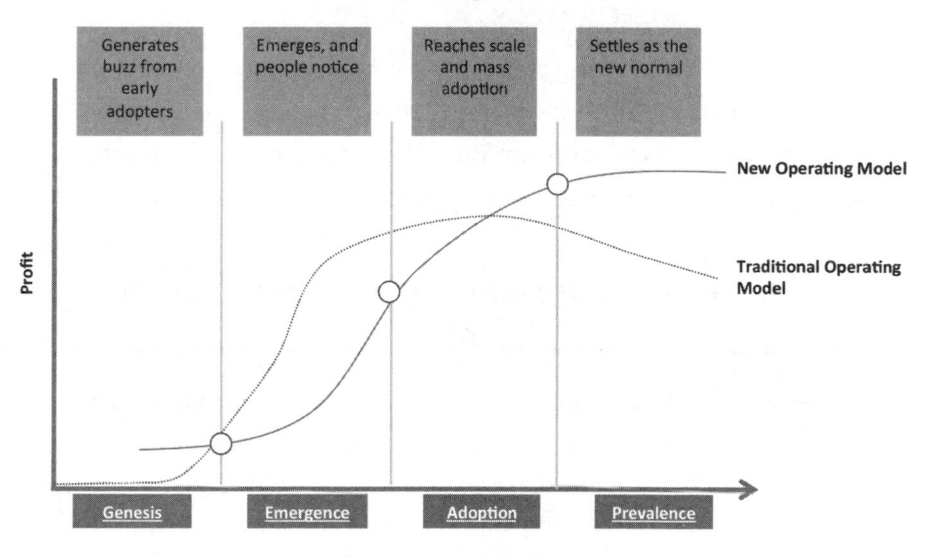

Figure 4.4: Companies are introducing new operating models that elevate performance and profit, lengthening the period of profit capture and deflecting the impact of commoditization.

Some companies are moving beyond updating the business model with innovations and are completely reinventing the way that business is done. The introduction of technology, automation, and

IoT has blurred business model lines and encouraged companies to question conventional operations. Organizational trailblazers examine the business model and ask themselves, "How can we provide the ideal customer with better service for less?"

In chapter 2, "Power Customer Centricity," I touched on the craze of collaborative consumption, explaining how space and budgeting requirements have erected a sharing economy. While the sharing economy was originally targeted at millennials and low- to middle-income households, there has been a recent influx of brands aimed at luxury sharing.

Following in Uber's footsteps, app Jetsmarter highlights its revised business model, proclaiming on its homepage, "Yesterday's flyers settled for expensive brokers, inefficient jet cards, and crowded airport terminals. We've created a fresh alternative."[20] The company allows you to browse and book seats on existing shared flights, enabling you to choose the aircraft, desired location, and number of seats. Jetsmarter does not own or operate any of its aircraft. Rather,

ADDITIONAL COST AND CAPITAL EFFICIENCIES

Economies of Scale: As companies increase production, the cost per unit declines due to a larger spread of overhead costs and cost discounts for bulk orders from suppliers.

Like in the Boo.com example, the agile business model must generate quick turnaround between spending money and earning revenue. By increasing the rate of speed to value, companies capture more value.

Additionally, agile companies are better at adapting to demand changes. By avoiding excess fixed costs, companies can easily shift cost structure to fit operational needs. Agile companies are excellent at matching capacity to demand.

for a pay-as-you-go rate or annual membership fee, it connects you with global flights, concierge, and other luxury-partner benefits. The company attracts jet owners by filling their planes and receives a generous commission in return. Jetsmarter rakes in revenue while avoiding the capital outlay of long-term ownership, leading to a scalable and efficient business model.

Regardless of your approach, cost and capital efficiencies should be customer-centric. When auditing your company, it's important to consider throughput and eliminate the bottlenecks that customers don't care about. As I mentioned in chapter 2, executing an outstanding CX requires companies to invest in activities that effectively address customers' wants and needs. Standardize the activities that don't enhance the customer experience to reduce the cost structure. Doing so will provide an upside to both the customer and the company, resulting in additional money in both wallets.

Regardless of your approach, securing an efficiency advantage is key in capturing value. By enhancing throughput while reducing expenses, your company procures an outsized competitive advantage, accelerating along the economic profit curve into higher deciles.

BALANCING CORPORATE PRIORITIES

Tradeoffs are inherent to strategy. Tension often boils when companies attempt to reconcile growth with margin enhancement. When executing on growth plans, remember there is smart growth and stupid growth. Accelerated growth outside of core capabilities can lead to severe financial challenges, including bankruptcy. To circumvent detrimental growth strategies, avoid focusing on revenue and market share metrics in isolation, and instead review your comprehensive progress, considering contribution margin as a key success factor.

OUTSIZE YOUR GROWTH

The third way to capture value is by convincing customers to power strategic growth. Growth can be sourced from the following four alternative growth strategies defined in the Ansoff Matrix, a framework that helps companies analyze and plan for future growth.

1. **Market penetration: Focus on selling more of your existing products in your existing market to increase market share.** Market penetration, one of the most popular growth strategies, allows companies to leverage brand equity in an existing space, eliminating some of the challenges of new customer acquisition. Market-penetration strategies often include promotions, price reduction, marketing expansion, terms enhancement, or distribution channel development.

Various market-penetration approaches have been employed by companies of all sizes to gain or regain traction in a specific market. For example, in 2011, the global recession was at its peak, wreaking havoc on the job market and reshaping consumer spending habits. Cutbacks on everyday items were especially widespread, driving even some of the more established household brands to the brink of bankruptcy. As inexpensive grocery store private labels rose in popularity, premium household brands struggled to maintain market share.

Despite its entrenched legacy as an American food authority, Kraft Heinz was facing financial difficulty as earnings slowly began to parallel the shrinking household budgets. By mid-2013, year-over-year quarterly growth declined by 5 percent.[21] The company knew that it had to restore market share to sustain normal operations.

In 2014, the company decided to execute a market-penetration strategy, launching its first pan-European sales campaign in nearly a decade, which proclaimed, "It has to be Heinz."[22] The commercials flashed through a series of images customized for each market. In the UK, the ad featured a bacon sandwich, whereas the ads for Spain and France showed chicken filets. The campaign strove to remind the world that regardless of where you are or what you're eating, "it has to be Heinz."

While this campaign may not have been revolutionary, it was unique for its space. Table sauce promotion is typically limited to simple, inexpensive brand reminders. Heinz took a risk on this multimillion-dollar market-penetration strategy, one that paid off for the brand. Roughly one year post-launch, year-over-year quarterly growth surged by 136 percent.[23] This promotion convinced global customers to bypass the competition and seek out Heinz ketchup.

While controlled market penetration can be effective, overly aggressive tactics can be dangerous. For example, coming out of the recession, I worked with a service company that quadrupled its revenue in only four years. The company drastically increased its market share by becoming the low-price leader in its field (notice that I did not say low *cost*). While the company's cost structure mirrored its rivals in its competitive set, it enacted an assertive growth strategy, slashing prices to secure more business from its existing market. The company experienced immediate, significant growth, stealing customers from competitors with its low-price guarantee.

However, the company was quickly swept up in the excitement of expansion, and the swift, low-margin growth eventually caught up to it. In addition to process breakdown and dizzying turnover due to an overburdened, weary staff, the service company's margins plummeted. The market-penetration strategy had an inverse effect on the bottom line, and the company was swimming in debt and overhead, fighting imminent insolvency.

A market-penetration strategy can be a fast and effective approach to growth; however, it's important that you don't sacrifice your other business objectives while chasing revenue.

To determine whether a market expansion strategy is right for your company, consider the following questions:

- Is my company struggling to compete in its current market?
- Do I feel that my company has tapped the full potential of its existing markets?
- Do my company's offers, resources, and capabilities align with the needs of other markets?

---

2. **Market expansion: Sell current products in a new market.** A company typically pursues a market expansion strategy once it has maximized sales in its existing channels. Beyond securing a price premium, market expansion is one of the most impactful levers of value capture. A robust where-to-compete strategy is critical to consistent long-term growth.

Market expansion often involves geographic expansion. When successfully executed, extending internationally yields a slew of benefits, increasing your company reach to untapped markets where your products or services are in high demand. A global footprint can build brand exposure and, over time, develop goodwill.

Additionally, a strong multimarket presence can boost overall revenue while smoothing out demand spikes. For example, in 2017, Nike's North American wholesale revenue slumped.[24] The athletic footwear and apparel company saved itself from shareholder scrutiny, however, because while domestic demand dwindled, sales in China escalated, growing by nearly 10 percent from 2016. The brand's global presence and market diversity enabled it to offset the negative impact of the domestic demand shift.

Market expansion can be a highly valuable, long-term approach to growth; however, it is one of the most complicated growth options. When pursuing this strategy, ensure that you're deeply aware of these points:

- **Who you will be selling to.** Immerse yourself and your organization in the unique needs, interests, and characteristics of the customer type in this market. Additionally, consider the inherent tradeoffs that could impact your current customers. As I mentioned in chapter 2, you want to avoid straying too far from your ideal customer so as not to dilute your value proposition. Seek out customer and market synergies when considering new places to play.
- **What you will be doing.** Focus on your core how-to-compete and where-to-compete advantages. Don't jump into a market where you're limited in delivering a superior customer experience.
- **Who you will be competing against.** Before deciding on the market, conduct an in-depth analysis to evaluate opportunity. Study your competition. What has made them successful? What new innovations are they bringing to market? How saturated is this market? Why will customers want to buy from your company over the competition?

Understand the intricacies of competing in this new space, weigh the risks, and move forward in executing your value-capture strategy.

3. **Product development: Sell new, updated, or augmented products in an existing market.** As in a market-penetration strategy, in a product-development strategy you are selling to an existing customer base; therefore, you can leverage

your reputation and brand awareness to drive more rapid results. You may opt for a product-development strategy if your current offerings have lost their allure or you identify new or changing market needs and wants. Product development may come in the following forms:

- **Product line extension.** New products in an existing product category with a shared brand name. For example, Lay's potato chips represent one of the clearest and most successful examples of a product line extension. Frito-Lay introduced offshoots of the original chip that launched its success, expanding its offerings with a wide variation of textures (Original, Wavy) and flavors (Sour Cream & Onion, Flamin' Hot, Barbecue). The brand has even invited consumer participation in its product line extension, hosting Lay's flavor contests with recent winners adding flavors like Smoked Gouda and Honey, Everything Bagel with Cream Cheese, and Crispy Taco to the lineup.[25]
- **Brand extension.** New products in a new product category under the same brand name. Dove successfully made the shift from a soap company to a powerhouse in the shampoo, deodorant, and body wash industries. It leveraged its established brand presence to launch new household products, growing from a $200 million company to a multibillion-dollar company.[26]

Product development is an effective way to sell more to existing customers and adapt to changing consumer demands. However, before pursuing this strategy, it's important to ensure that new offerings align with or complement existing offerings; a product that appears disconnected from your overall strategy will confuse consumers and could end up damaging your overall brand. Ensure that your offerings align with your core advantages.

Additionally, be careful not to cannibalize existing offerings with the introduction of new products. For example, Dove's introduction of body wash was a deliberate strategy that produced lucrative growth. However, this brand extension cannibalized some of its bar soap sales. Dove's tradeoff was calculated and worthwhile, but in some cases, new products can dismantle companies' legacy products. Before investing in new products, conduct an analysis to confirm that the tradeoff is worth it.

4. **Diversification: Carve out a new space by selling new products to new markets.** This is the riskiest of the alternative growth strategies, as the organization does not have a product or established market to rely on. While the payoff can be great, companies must agree to be bold and enter the unknown; when dealing with diversification, financial projections are uncertain.

Diversification can be related or unrelated. Coca-Cola pursued a related diversification strategy with its $4.1 billion acquisition of Glacéau, the parent company of Vitamin Water. In response to the consumer shift toward health, Coca-Cola sought out a new, related product to offer a different but associated audience.

Unrelated diversification transports a company outside its box to add new product lines or penetrate new markets. Apple unlocked a powerful diversification strategy with the launch of iTunes in 2003. Though file sharing gained popularity in the 1990s, iTunes was the first of its kind to offer legal à la carte song downloads, formulating a flexible CX that quickly captured the world's attention. Before setting out, the path was fuzzy, but Apple's gutsy, pioneering move into this new space has since provided the tech company with revenue from over twenty-five billion song downloads and approximately 60 percent of the digital-music market share.[27]

Before committing to a diversification strategy, it's important to understand the following:

- **Potential risks and rewards.** I worked with a high-energy CEO who was adamant about developing a market for his latest innovation. He set aside money and firm resources into launching this endeavor at the expense of his main business. Not only did the new product not produce the anticipated attention, but it siphoned valuable time away from the firm's core customers. In addition to losing money, this venture cost the CEO customer loyalty. His brain was so focused on the reward that he failed to consider the risks.
- **Access to capital.** Launching a new venture can be very expensive. You must validate that you have locked down the funds necessary to effectively and fully pursue your diversification strategy.

As you go forth and outsize your growth, keep in mind that the business model is the mechanism for value capture and must make financial sense. Whether you position your company to capitalize on a price premium, focus on reducing your cost structure, or drive sustainable growth, strive to achieve long-term, healthy improvement. Holistic value capture will propel you along the economic profit curve, powering your company to beat the market.

DISCERN PROFIT FROM VALUE

Researchers maintain that it requires roughly six years to build a profitable line of business.[28] As leaders build these businesses, most will tell you they want their companies to endure for the long haul, often citing centuries as their goal. And yet, while companies operate in this (albeit quickly changing) long-term time frame, leaders often adopt a short-sighted view of financial management. They apply a simplistic perspective to address complex strategy.

People often misunderstand the meaning of competitive advantage, and many also confuse the meaning of value. A common pitfall that batters businesses is the common belief that accounting profit is a sweeping measure of financial success. Leaders often adopt a myopic view of value. They are misguided by the conventional mindset that growth is paramount, accounting profit is the ultimate end, and short-term decisions outweigh long-term planning. This leads to short-term thinking where employees act haphazardly at the expense of long-term value capture.

Accounting Profit

People often use the term *profit* to refer to accounting profit, not economic profit. Accounting profit and economic profit are not synonymous. The essence of outsizing is to grow *economic* profit. However, because accounting profit is the more familiar metric and the simplest of the economic levers to calculate, many default to applying it as the sole diagnostic to measure the value of their companies.

Accounting profit, often referred to as EBIDTA (earnings before interest, depreciation, taxes, and amortization), NOPAT (net operating profit after taxes), or net income, does not represent the flow of money. Accounting methodologies surrounding depreciation, amortization, impairment, provisions, valuation, and accruals can mask the true economic performance of a company. Though economic profit provides an objective measure of value, most professionals cling to accounting profit, a metric that can be manipulated through these "window dressing" techniques to reflect a distorted financial image. Many businesses find out the hard way that accounting profit doesn't necessarily indicate outsized value.

I advised a service company that celebrated a successful year when accounting profits doubled year-over-year from 3 to 6 percent of revenue, respectively. In response to the margin improvement, the company gave itself a pat on the back and paid out large bonuses, thinking it had mastered a sound strategy to gain a competitive advantage over rivals. However, further evaluation revealed that the company was merely enlisting a set of generic platitudes (e.g., "be the best service provider in the northwest, attract the top talent by being the most desirable place to work, grow revenue and the bottom line by a minimum of 20 percent for the next three years") to manage the business. Analysis divulged that the significant jump in profit was attributed to a market force rather than the company's strategy (or lack thereof). The industry was facing a severe labor shortage, providing companies with an opportunity to secure a price premium from the high demand and low supply of the talent pool. The leaders were celebrating success without understanding the source of the company's financial achievement.

Additionally, although the company had boosted its margins, it was still performing below the rest of its competitive set. Managers welcomed the positive surge in EBIDTA without questioning how they had earned it or how the rest of the industry was faring. The leaders' simplistic, accounting-profit-focused approach toward financial management encouraged a complacent strategy and ignored opportunity costs associated with alternative actions that could have been taken to maximize the company's return on capital. Unbeknownst to the company, it was leaving millions of dollars of profit on the table as it underperformed its peers in both margin and capital management.

Don't get me wrong. It's important to measure accounting profit. Without accounting profit, you can't calculate economic profit. Accounting profit measures the total monetary revenue less costs. It provides a quick snapshot of how much you're bringing in versus

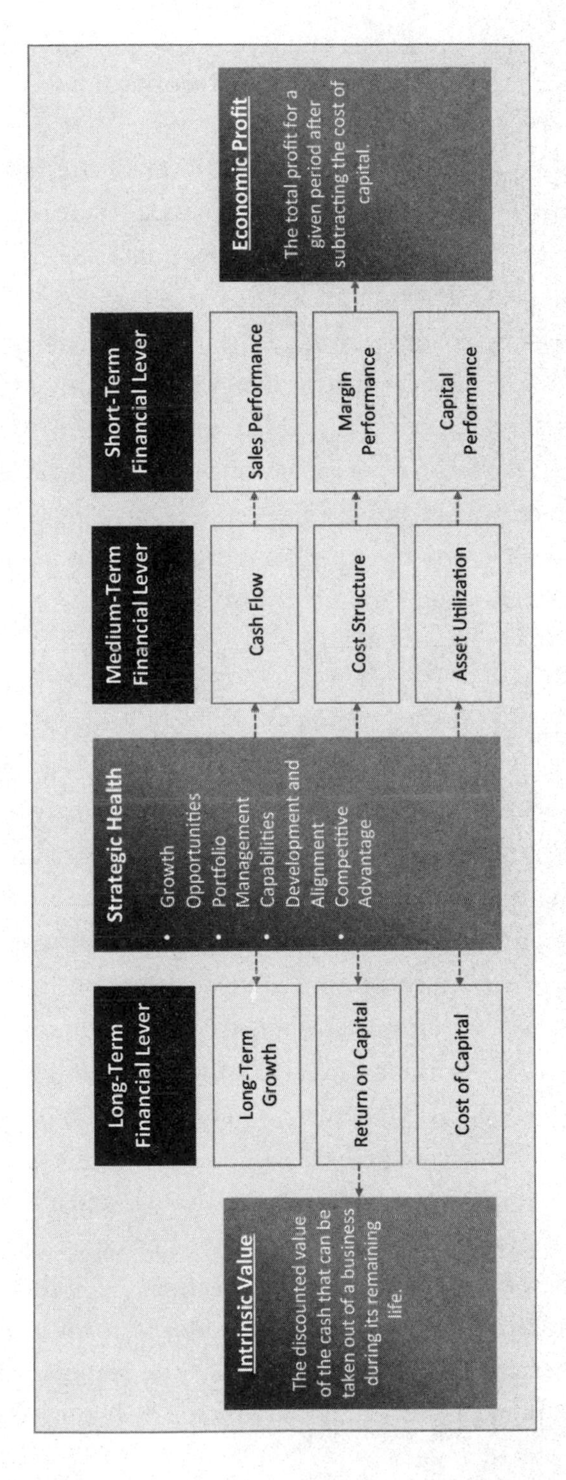

Figure 4.5: Measures of value

what's going out. However, accounting profit cannot measure value when examined independently.

Accounting profit tells only one chapter of the financial story. As shown in Figure 4.5, margin performance is but one short-term financial lever. Accounting profit ignores noncash charges, changes in working capital, and capital expenditures.

To effectively manage your company's financial performance and drive value capture, you must integrate medium- and long-term financial levers into your analysis. To outsize your profit, you must supplement your short-term accounting-profit-centric view with an eye to economic profit and intrinsic value. Outsizing calls us to look at our businesses from multiple perspectives to paint a holistic picture of our financial and strategic performance.

Economic Profit

Economic profit provides a slightly longer-term perspective of your financials than accounting profit. In earlier chapters, I discussed how tradeoffs are a key tenet of strategy. Economic profit acknowledges the opportunity costs of making such tradeoffs by measuring the net operating profit less taxes after subtracting the cost of capital.

A company may earn $10 million (M) in net profit after tax and celebrate its success. However, when accounting for its cost of capital [(fixed assets + working capital) x weighted average cost of capital), or ($150M + 50M) x 9 percent = $18M], the company is actually losing $8M.

I was working with a manufacturer that earned a healthy profit but was struggling with cash flow. When I engaged this client, the CEO was bewildered about how the company could earn a profit, pay out employee bonuses, and still underperform in the market. Upon further analysis, I discovered that the leaders were making large-scale financial decisions based on an incomplete financial

ECONOMIC PROFIT CAVEAT

This measurement works well for asset-rich businesses, but it is less relevant to companies with light assets, such as technology firms.

---

analysis. They were overlooking the capital cost for financing fixed assets and working capital requirements. Revising the calculations to account for the manufacturer's high cost of capital unearthed the fact that the company's economic value had been diminishing over the last few years. Without knowing the economic profit, the leaders were blind to the true economic reality of the business, costing the manufacturer money in bonuses that employees hadn't truly earned.

Intrinsic Value

Accounting profit feeds into economic profit, which over time fuels the third and longest-term financial lever, intrinsic value. Commenting on the importance of the long view, Warren Buffet said, "In the short term, the market is a popularity contest; in the long term, it is a weighing machine."[29] Intrinsic value, on the left side of the formula, provides the longest-term view of firm value. It is defined as the discounted value of cash that can be taken out of a business during its remaining life. To convert intrinsic value into mathematical form, companies can apply the constant growth model:

Firm Value = Free Cash Flow x [(1 + Growth Rate)/(Cost of Capital – Growth Rate)]

This long-term financial lever offers the only logical approach to evaluate the attractiveness of investments and assess the true value of a business. It discloses the true financial situation, making it difficult for companies to camouflage financial performance. It is more comprehensive than other metrics, integrating long-term growth, return on capital, and cost of capital into the calculation. Intrinsic value sticks to the fundamentals that investors focus on when evaluating whether to buy. Rather than paying for the promise of EBIDTA, profit, or revenue, they're buying a business for the cash it generates.

INCREASING INTRINSIC VALUE

Get more cash: A company increases its amount of available cash through improving its operating, investing, and financing decisions. It can do this through price premiums, cost and capital efficiencies, and/or smart growth. Getting more cash increases your margins.

Get cash faster: Getting cash faster boosts firm value because of the time value of money. A company gets cash faster by optimizing the collection process. Companies can alter payment terms, offer prepayment discounts, or change the way customers pay using electronic fund transfer or credit cards to expedite payments.

Lower the discount rate: The weighted average cost of capital is the discount rate used to calculate the present value of cash as part of intrinsic value. Firms can lower the discount rate by substituting debt for equity (the cost of debt is lower than the cost of equity) or negotiating lower interest rates on debt by improving credit worthiness. One word of caution: you must be careful when adjusting your capital structure, as piling more debt on top of an already-leveraged company could be extremely burdensome and risky.

If we plug some numbers into the Intrinsic Firm Value Equation, 3 percent growth based on historical GDP and a hypothetical cost of capital of 12 percent, we end up with [(1 + 0.03)/(0.12 – 0.03)], which equals 11.4 x free cash flow (FCF). This means that every $1.00 increase in FCF will result in an $11.40 increase in value for the firm. According to this model, we can increase firm value in three different ways: by getting more cash, getting cash faster, and lowering the discount rate.

Cash flow is integral to operations. While accounting profit is the starting point for cash flow, it won't pay your suppliers or employees. Beyond maintaining normal operations, cash flow is critical to powering growth, investments, research, and innovation. An intense focus on cash flow and increasing intrinsic value has allowed some of the world's largest companies to get ahead.

Amazon, for example, has excelled at increasing its intrinsic value, securing cash faster than many of its competitors. Once customers place an order, Amazon receives cash. However, Amazon has weeks with the cash on hand before having to pay its suppliers. By optimizing the cash conversion cycle, composed of days of inventory plus days of sales outstanding minus the number of days it takes a company to pay its suppliers, Amazon has bankrolled the company's dynamic growth with a negative working capital cycle.[30]

Other big brands like Apple have also dominated in this space. Apple's "resilient and recurring" free cash flow of roughly $59 billion per year generates a 7 percent yield.[31] In 2018, Apple set a record with $285.1 billion of cash on hand.[32] The company intends to spend this sum of money largely on capital expenditures and advanced manufacturing investments.

Ultimately, your company requires a combination of metrics to assess value. Writing your company's strategy requires you to also read its financial story, and the only way to do so is to adopt both a short- and long-term view of its economic performance.

True financial strength unites a competitive advantage (higher-than-industry-average profit) with ongoing free-cash-flow yield. By understanding and integrating the three key financial indicators, you will ensure that you are taking the right steps toward maximizing your value via your strategic decisions.

BOOST YOUR FINANCIAL IQ

This plethora of financial material may throw your brain into information overload. As I describe the importance of marrying strategy and finance, the economic profit curve, and how to increase value, you may be overwhelmed by the amount of financial information. However, one does not have to be a financial wizard to get strategy right and outsize profitability.

Leadership is about growing and making progress, not about being perfect. Wherever you are in your financial and strategic journey, the important thing is that you understand the financial fundamentals and begin to chip away at some of business's uncertainty. Success will stem from integrating these principles into your strategic view, from acknowledging the importance of long-term economic feasibility over short-term growth and profit.

Committing yourself and your colleagues to learn is the first step. I have worked in companies where managers divulge their financial limitations and are apathetic about learning new financial tools. When they say something like, "I am not in finance or accounting. Why do I need to understand how this works?" I usually respond with three points:

1. **Businesses don't make profits—people do.** People own the overarching strategy and day-to-day decisions that ultimately generate outsized profits. People are the ones driving financial success for their companies, so it's

Arriving at Free Cash Flow	Example Functions of Influence
Revenue	Business Development, Sales, Customer Service, Research & Development (R&D), Account Management
Cost of Goods Sold	Project Management, Customer Service, Human Resources (HR), Engineering & Manufacturing, Operations
Gross Margin	Estimating & Pricing, Sales, Finance, Marketing
(Selling, General, & Administrative Expenses)	Management, Administrative Staff, IT Support, Sales, HR, R&D
EBITDA (*Earnings Before Interest, Tax, Depreciation, and Amortization*)	
(Depreciation & Amortization)	Accounting, Management
EBIT	
(Taxes)	Accounting, Management
NOPAT (*Net Operating Profit After Tax*)	
+ Depreciation & Amortization	
- Capital Expenditures	Management, Equipment Management, Engineering & Manufacturing, R&D, Operations
+/-△ Net Working Capital	Management, Relationship Management, A/R & A/P Staff, Operations, Account Management

FCF *(Free Cash Flow)*

Figure 4.6: Everyone in the business impacts free cash flow.

important for employees at all levels to understand the financial fundamentals.

2. **A company is a financial machine.** Cash is the fuel to run the machine, and it's impacted by every individual and decision in the business. If you don't understand how your actions produce a monetary domino effect throughout the organization, you are blind to the value you are driving for the company. (See Figure 4.6.) If you can't contribute to conversations about your company's or project's financial performance, you are less likely to be promoted to more strategic, value-based roles. Regardless of your position, it's important for every employee to have a core understanding of value-based management, financial statement analysis, and forecasting to advance as a strategic leader.

3. **The new economy demands that we progress and advance our skill sets.** Automation is leading to an increased demand in skills that machines can't do. It is reshaping jobs and challenging employees to further differentiate themselves. A recent report proclaimed, "More occupations will change than be automated away."[33] Employees are now being called on for more specialized work and complex tasks. For example, most airport check-in desks are now automated. However, airline employee count has remained unchanged. Rather, the employees are now dedicated to solving customer problems and increasing efficiency to improve CX.[34] Automation is making waves in all industries. Journalists' work is changing as they focus less on transcribing interviews and more on applying their creative skill sets to produce more articles.[35] New roles reliant on interpersonal skills and cognitive thinking are emerging as a result of automation. Who would have conceived of social media managers or app developers two decades ago?

In our new economy, we must progress our abilities beyond that of machines and strive to be more creative, curious, innovative, and solution-driven.

TRANSFORM THE ROLE OF THE CFO

The future of work doesn't just demand that nonfinance employees expand their capabilities and boost their acumen; it also compels financial leaders to adapt and learn. The future of finance requires daring leaders with diverse skill sets. CFOs' success will be increasingly measured by the amount of value they cultivate and capture. Outsizing the efficacy of the financial function and tying it to strategy requires CFOs and other financial leaders to apply both technical and business expertise.

Technical Skills

A financial leader must first possess the technical skills to drive business value. While CFOs are already allocating less time to manually collecting data and configuring spreadsheets, they must procure the technical skill sets to do the following:

- **Manage reporting software and interpret reports.** Accounting processes are digitizing at a rapid pace. As accounting software continues to branch into different functions and integrate new types of information, today's CFOs must understand how data entry points flow into a variety of systems that culminate in an end report. Then, they must understand where distinct sets of information are derived from, analyze the data in real time, and tell the story behind the numbers. Correctly interpreting the numbers drives strategic success, enabling leaders to identify and attack strategic problems.

- **Conduct in-depth analysis and financial modeling.** One of the first changes I made as a CFO was dividing the accounting department into FP&A (financial planning and analysis) and finance and accounting. I appointed a VP in charge of each of these functions. While finance focuses on the historical information, FP&A molds the raw data into projections. CFOs must be able to oversee both historical and future-focused analysis and relay the findings of both types of analysis in a simple, actionable manner. It all comes down to analyzing data to drive a price premium or reduce costs through efficiencies.
- **Adopt and operate emerging digital tools.** I want to emphasize this final topic, because it has been the largest point of contention that I have encountered while training experienced CFOs. In the new economy, rather than viewing technology and automation as stealing away jobs, successful financial leaders consider how these innovations can augment their capacity and optimize the financial function. A slew of digital options are reinventing how financial professionals do their jobs, enabling employees to move from compliance and transaction-based work to analysis, risk mitigation, and strategic improvement. Emerging technologies such as advanced analytics, in-memory computing, cognitive computing, and artificial intelligence are transforming business. Other disruptive technologies such as cloud computing and automation have contributed to the ease and security of financial processes. This technology has led to exponential growth in data. Cloud computing allows CFOs to incorporate far more information when making critical business decisions: How risky is this client? What are the likely outcomes of engaging in business with this client? By adopting these innovations, CFOs can focus greater time on

driving value creation through applying intellectual assets and human capital.

In addition to the technical financial skills such as financial planning and analysis, CFOs must embrace these technological innovations to increase productivity, drive cost reduction, and mitigate error.

The role of the CFO isn't just changing; it's expanding. CFOs in the modern economy also play the role of the strategist.

Business Skills

CFOs bridge the gap between art and science. They support decisions with data and fact, leading companies down a financially sound path constructed with value-capture activities.

CFOs are firm leaders who are responsible for influencing and impacting their companies to enhance holistic operations. They must be able to do the following:

1. **Establish organizational awareness and oversight.** Financial leaders must understand and analyze operations, seeking areas for cost reduction, productivity improvement, and even training opportunities. The CFO is the CEO's right-hand man or woman. This role sets the tone of the organization and strategy; therefore, it's important that the CFO is exposed to all business activity. CFOs must understand the intricacies of operations, including R&D, purchasing, marketing, and sales from both a financial and strategic perspective.
2. **Maintain a macro, market perspective.** A company's market share, competitive advantage, and cash flow vacillate due to a variety of external competitor, consumer, social, and political forces. It's critical that as a CFO evaluates the economic feasibility of a company's next move or seeks opportunities

to grow the bottom line, they are deeply aware of the market environment. How will a recent competitor acquisition influence the demand for a specific product? What is the anticipated impact of a new, innovative supplier?

3. **Think and plan strategically.** CFOs are essential contributors to the strategy. While their skills are often leveraged to confirm or critique a proposed strategy, they are increasingly involved in the strategy design. They must see the bigger picture. In the new economy, a CFO must know the steps to outsizing a strategy, understanding the art form, and validating decisions with data. CFOs often hold access to the executive purse strings, so it's important that they can analyze decisions and make tradeoffs to ensure that capital is making the largest positive impact.

CFOs can bring a financial discipline to support and extend the above strategy process by addressing questions such as these:

- Are the financial goals of the company viable?
- What products and markets deliver the greatest promise for revenue or margin growth?
- How should the company organize and structure the financing of key investments to generate competitive advantage?
- What structures (e.g., business models; legal and tax entities; onshore, offshore, or outsourcing talent models) and processes (e.g., automation, build vs. buy, networking, and so on) enable competitive advantage and deliver superior market valuation and returns?
- What financial and management reporting enables management to effectively execute and deliver the strategy?

4. **Lead a team to execution.** CFOs wield financial discipline. Effective financial leaders deeply and technically understand financial implications and can simplify the information and translate it for nonfinancial colleagues. They motivate everyone—from the CEO to frontline employees—to take action and build confidence in organizational decisions by explaining the ROI. They show employees *how* each individual captures and creates value for the business.

Leaders of the future sit at the intersection between strategy and finance. Tomorrow's prominent employees are well-rounded, open-minded, and strong-willed. As our economy and marketplace continue to change, bold financial leaders don't allow market forces to shrink demand, diminish margins, and desiccate cash flow; they shape the future of their businesses by leveraging versatile skill sets and knowing the fundamentals of value. CFOs are assuming a more strategic role in their organizations. In a survey of the top finance executives across Europe, the Middle East, and Africa, 57 percent of respondents said their biggest responsibility will be to support senior decision-makers in strategic analysis.[36]

By understanding how to convert customer-centric advantages into value capture, leaders can maximize the value of their businesses. Doing so presents tremendous benefits for all stakeholders, including

- more growth opportunities,
- better compensation,
- increased financial security,
- higher employee engagement and retention,
- outsized brand equity, and

- improved overall experience for employees and customers alike.

However, value is not created in a vacuum. In the next chapter, we will bring the principles of outsizing value together as we explore techniques to unlock the potential of your talent and build a culture that allows value maximizers to thrive.

5

UNLOCK THE POTENTIAL OF YOUR TALENT

A culture is the summation of its people's competencies that enable a company to thrive. You can drive value capture and creation through recruiting, hiring, training and retaining value maximizers, enabling teams, and celebrating success.

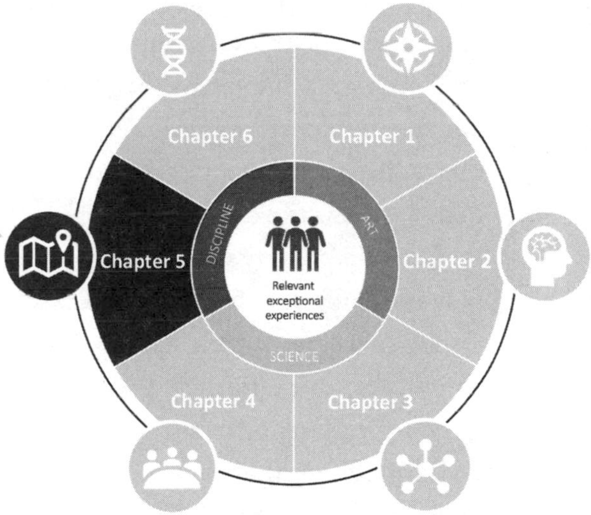

Chapter 6
Chapter 1
Chapter 5
Chapter 2
Chapter 4
Chapter 3
DISCIPLINE
ART
SCIENCE
Relevant exceptional experiences

Some time ago, I encountered a quote by J. Paul Getty, a big-time industrialist in the early 1900s, that read, "The employer generally gets the employees he [or she] deserves."[1] I reflected on this assertion, mulling over the wide assortment of leaders that I have worked with and for in my life.

Leadership comes in many flavors. Some leaders are strong-willed and autocratic; some are open-minded and democratic; some employ laissez-faire, employee-centric leadership styles; and most fall somewhere in the middle. Great leaders apply situational decision-making, adopting a blend of approaches to best serve the circumstances. Regardless of leadership style, effective employees gravitate to influential, humble, and tactful managers and executives. While anomalies are woven into life's patchwork of experiences, it's almost always the great employers who attract great employees.

Strong leaders hire, develop, and retain the best and brightest. Conversely, poor leaders hire disengaged, unreliable employees. I have seen some ineffective leaders charm high performers into a job, but the high performers either flee after a short period of time, or they collapse their standards and performance to that of their peers. People follow the examples others set for them.

Extending Getty's statement, I would add that employers get not only the employees but also the *results* that they deserve. Strong leadership transfers passion, understanding, and purpose to dedicated employees who ultimately execute the strategy. People accomplish the value-capture activities that cement a company's success.

Throughout this book, I have defined how to design and implement a client-centric, future-oriented, and advantage-driven strategy to achieve outsized results. While I have alluded to employees' chief importance to strategic success, I felt it necessary to dedicate an entire chapter to those who power performance. Employees are the integral strategic puzzle piece. They fuel your results and breathe life into your organizational purpose. They are the masterminds behind the numbers, enabling your company to harness a price premium, reduce your cost structure, and grow top-line earnings.

We are experiencing a global labor and skills gap, increasing workforce diversity, and a shift to millennial leadership. By 2020, employers in Western nations predict a shortage of eighteen million college-educated workers.[2] Between 2017 and 2018, job postings for diversity and inclusion positions increased by almost 20 percent.[3] Fifty-six million millennials now compose the biggest chunk of the workforce.[4]

The future of work is quickly changing, and the opportunity belongs to those who can keep up. Companies must adjust their strategies to unleash the potential of our constrained talent pool. Strategic achievement requires you to effectively enable your biggest organizational resource. This chapter will show how an overarching culture contributes to an individual's satisfaction and development, team performance, and organizational output, defining how to

- build a strong culture,
- identify and motivate company leaders,
- develop employees to unlock their potential, and
- establish strong teams to carry companies to success.

Empowering your people will promote near-term and lasting results for your business. By fostering a motivating culture that guards against complacency, your organization will reinvent itself with new talent who share your timeless values. Your legacy will live on in the people you develop.

FOSTER CULTURAL INGENUITY

Empowering employees starts with culture. A culture is the summation of its people's competencies that enables a company to capture value. It's a system of shared beliefs and values that guide behavioral norms and group conduct. Culture must be the initial and primary focus, because it entwines your whole people strategy. Employees can't fully learn, grow, and produce in a pernicious work environment. Over time, even the brightest, most promising people wither in a contemptuous culture.

Chapter 1 examined the cultures of Uber and Amazon as negative examples, but most companies don't face as acute or conspicuous issues as these megabrands. The bulk of cultural concerns are buried deep within organizations. Many leaders overlook cultural negativity because the culture may not be actively or outwardly causing issues. Many employees carry out their daily lives apathetic to the company culture.

However, I have always preached that if a culture isn't *positive*, it can have a *negative* impact. A mundane environment inhibits companies from maximizing the engagement and potential of employees. Settling for an average culture limits full value capture. If employees are indifferent to the company culture, then they're likely disinterested in their jobs. Low engagement and commitment in the short-term culminate in lackluster CX and costly attrition over time.

In many cases, barely-there cultures stifle employee morale and ingenuity. These cultures don't encourage employees to form relationships with their colleagues and integrate work into the rest of their lives. If work is merely something that allows your employees to fund their lives outside of the office, then you'll be hard-pressed to inspire the passion necessary to drive forward ambitious initiatives. Muted culture coaxes employees to get their work done, quelling creativity and employee bonding.

To drive competitive advantage, company culture must be distinct. As competitive saturation and commoditization overwhelm the market, strong culture can be a differentiator for customers and employees alike. For example, in an industry slammed for rude employees and atrocious customer service, Southwest Airlines has excelled in forming a culture that unites employees around common goals and values. In fact, the airline explains that three key values are instilled in every employee: "a warrior spirit, a servant's heart, and a fun-luving attitude."[5] Southwest encourages employees to enjoy themselves at work. Employees receive standardized training but are "[given] permission to go that extra mile to make customers happy, empowering them to do what they need to meet that vision."[6] Southwest's approach is validated by its voluntary turnover rate of less than 2 percent.

As Southwest has proven, sometimes companies reap better results when they encourage employees to be themselves, have fun, experiment, and learn. In *Delivering Value*, I discussed the importance of establishing Big Rules (Big R's) and little rules (little r's) in business. This concept was introduced to me by leadership expert and president of Competitive Edge, John Berkley, who led an outdoor leadership-training program I completed for the MBA program at Duke University. John explained that Big R's constitute the essential, unbreakable rules central to the core of a company, whereas the little r's are phantom rules created by mental constructs. Big R's and little r's are highly pertinent in a business setting. I modified John's framework to adapt to a business place where leaders institute unnecessary little r's that are carried through generations of employees and become ingrained in organizational processes.

If employees decided that a more efficient way to increase their personal income was to lie about commissions, they would be breaking a Big R and would be reprimanded and likely dismissed. The Big R's set the hard boundaries, eliminating any gray area.

Little r's are inessential, often restrictive rules that are deep-rooted in company practices because leaders have implemented them, or they are ingrained simply out of habit. For example, a little r might be how an employee is expected to greet someone on a phone.

The problem with being too planned, deliberate, and rule-based—too focused on little r's—is that you may miss out on some fruitful discoveries. Many companies' greatest innovations have stemmed from experimentation. A company that restricts employees' freedom to explore and experience successes and failures first-hand prevents employee development and limits innovation.

I read of a recent example of the impact of liberation from little r's in brothers Chip and Dan Heath's book *The Power of Moments.* The authors depict a story about some employees at the Ritz Carlton who break the script to deliver an exceptional experience to a customer.[7] The hotel calls the mother of an upset son after he forgets his favorite stuffed animal at the resort. To comfort the distressed child, the staff captures pictures of the animal enjoying a luxurious vacation. They share images of the soft toy lounging on a lawn chair, getting a massage, and driving a golf cart. Though it was not company protocol for the staff to do anything of the sort, by giving the employees the autonomy to creatively respond to the situation, fifteen minutes and a little inspiration created a magical CX. The employees' efforts produced a lifelong customer while building up brand recognition and exposure from millions of social media views.

Cultural flexibility also sheds light on your company's personality. The fierce battle for talent will increasingly require you to distinguish your company from competitors. I vividly recall finishing my master's in accounting, earning my CPA, and applying to work in assurance for the Big Four Accounting firms: Deloitte, PwC, Ernst & Young, and KPMG. I expected to interview at a variety of firms and be able to quickly identify my future work "home." However, as I attended countless recruiting events, the firms blurred together in my mind. At every dinner, happy hour, or Rockies game, I engaged in forgettable conversations and answered the same questions repeatedly. Nothing about these cultures wowed me. The companies appeared inauthentic, as if the leaders were parading employees around for a two-week performance to charm the candidates they thought they wanted.

When employees are seeking new jobs, they are assessing where they will spend roughly one-third of their lives. Because of this, it's imperative that they get a glimpse of the genuine corporate character. Showing your true colors and values through your policies, performance, and peers will be as effective a detractor to those who don't fit as it will be a magnet to your ideal candidates.

Since my values revolve around learning and growth, I have always promoted a culture that supports education and development. I seek out employees who respect boundaries but also desire freedom and exploration. When hiring employees, it's important to understand the values they are seeking in their employers and determine how your culture can maximize the performance of these individuals.

My ideal colleagues are hungry for knowledge and constantly strive to outsize their improvement. Therefore, whether I am running a company or leading a business unit, I must foster a culture focused on continuous growth. Because I've established a supportive culture that champions experience and experimentation, employees also have more fun. Here are some approaches that have fueled my quest in forming a learning environment:

1. **Let your customers be your guide.** Nearly all my best business ideas have been inspired by clients. Spending time with customers and getting to know them is integral to optimizing the customer experience. Rather than asking simple questions such as, "What can we do differently to better serve

you?" ask in-depth questions to nail down specific loves and hates surrounding the overall CX. For example, "What is one thing we could do superbly that would motivate you to rave about us to your friends and family?" The first question may lead to unspecific, trivial feedback, as clients will inform you about myriad fragmented insights that could improve their experiences. The latter stimulates a true learning environment, as clients share their big winning ideas. By building a customer-centric culture, your employees will follow suit, asking the tough questions to solicit the information necessary to make real and lasting change.

2. **Stir things up.** Keep people on their toes by changing the pace of work. When is the last time your accounting team visited a customer's jobsite, manufacturing plant, or call center? Consider the other functions of your business as well. Does everyone in your company regularly connect with customers and seek ways to improve the overall experience? If not, get out there. Surprise your team with a group field trip to learn something new, move outside of the office, and build relationships with peers, take clients out to lunch, or volunteer on an assembly line to uncover the nuances of others' jobs. By keeping every day fresh, employees will grow and be excited to discover what's next.

3. **Expand employee horizons.** When I first launched my business, a few of the new hires had not been to New York City. I wanted them to see a major business metropolis in motion. The employees geared up for a typical business trip—conference rooms, pressed formalwear, and all-day meetings. Instead, I planned a trip completely devoid of work. We went to a Yankees game, saw *Wicked* on Broadway,

ate pasta in Little Italy, and rented bikes in Central Park. I believe that effective employees are well-rounded, and it's important to see the world outside of the office.

4. **Launch an office book club.** Launching an office book club was another successful cultural endeavor. While we initially focused on business books, every club member had the opportunity to suggest a title. I was exposed to wonderful books that I would never normally pick up, and I believe my colleagues would say the same.

5. **Don't overcomplicate it.** Too often, companies throw exorbitant amounts of paperwork, unnecessary meetings, phone calls, and emails at employees. They convolute processes and overburden employee schedules, resulting in long work hours and, eventually, resentment. One of the best pieces of business advice I have gotten is to keep it simple. Focus on what matters. Embody essentialism. Before every meeting, ask yourself, "Does this meeting warrant the time it has been allocated? Is there something more valuable to my employees' growth that they could be doing rather than sitting in this meeting?" While the occasional meeting is helpful and necessary, a jam-packed meeting schedule can quickly spiral out of control. One way to manage your time is to cut meeting times in half. Oftentimes, a logistical meeting set for one hour can be effectively condensed to thirty minutes and accomplish the same objectives. If you keep it simple and save time for the important matters, employees have more time to connect with one another, try new things, and think strategically.

CULTIVATE VALUE MAXIMIZERS

While the whole—the culture and company—is greater than the sum of its parts, it's important to understand employees at an individual level and identify their contributions to the overarching culture. A culture is a medley of different viewpoints, personalities, and skill sets. A cohesive culture should never overpower or change the individual; it should elicit the unique strengths of each person and harmoniously blend these capabilities into a powerful, unified front.

Your strategy relies on this blend of capabilities. A homogenous culture breeds groupthink and boredom. Diversity powers innovation and enables you to fill the many necessary roles in a business with the appropriate individuals.

For example, let's insert people into the value-capture equation:

Price Premium: Marketing and branding minds enable your business to demand a price premium.

Cost advantage: Savvy operational folk may help you reduce your cost of capital by creating new efficiencies and eliminating redundancies.

Top-line growth: Sales personnel are responsible for generating business, growing your top line.

These three value-capture activities require wildly different skill sets. If you have only salespeople, you will continue to grow revenue but might poorly manage expenses or cash flow, ultimately leading to your company's demise. If the company is composed solely of marketing and branding employees, who will run the show and deliver the products and services?

Your business is dependent on a distinct combination of strengths. Employees serve their unique purposes. Because every position is necessary, companies should not focus on employees based on certain skill sets—for example, the engineers over the marketers or the marketers over the sales personnel. Rather, it's important to emphasize the employee's level of performance and quality of work. We should concentrate on the value each employee generates for the business. Title, level, and job description are only labels. At the end of the day, we should consider what an employee brings to the business that enables our company to charge more, cut costs, or contribute to growth. Within every business function there exist some standout stars who power value capture.

These high performers, or value maximizers, as I refer to them, are the driving force in your organization. They make the greatest strategic impact on your business. A recent study on employee productivity shows the Pareto Principle in action, yet again, defining the level of output by level of performer:

- The top 1 percent of employees account for 10 percent of organizational output.
- The top 5 percent account for 25 percent of organizational output.
- The top 20 percent account for 80 percent of organizational output.[8]

A study of more than six hundred thousand researchers, entertainers, politicians, and athletes found that high performers are 400 percent more productive than average ones.[9] In addition, simply adding a top-performing employee to a team boosts the effectiveness of the other team members by 5 to 15 percent.[10] Value maximizers are clearly critical to your strategy, but how do you find them? Are they hired or trained?

When I attended an executive education program at Dartmouth, I had the pleasure of learning from Professor Sydney Finkelstein, the author of *Superbosses*, a book that explores common characteristics and shared people strategies that legendary leaders like Ralph Lauren, Larry Ellison, and George Lucas applied with great success. Finkelstein integrates years of research and hundreds of interviews to uncover unique similarities between some of the world's greatest leaders.[11]

One common characteristic that these leaders share is their unconventional approach toward hiring. Rather than strictly pursuing Ivy League graduates and promoting them up the chain of organizational command, Superbosses employ unorthodox recruiting methods, finding star employees in unlikely places. For example, Ralph Lauren once laid eyes on a future employee at a restaurant in New York. He was captivated by her style. Without seeing her resume or credentials, Lauren hired the young woman, who ended up working in the brand's design department for four years.[12]

Great leaders, like Lauren, seek out candidates based on attributes beyond what's on paper. Finkelstein explains how Superbosses hunt for individuals who exhibit specific traits—intelligence, creativity, and flexibility—rather than evaluating new hires based on experience or capabilities. Superbosses emphasize talent over position and are willing to adjust roles to best suit the strengths of those they want to hire. They understand that skills can be taught; personality and attitude cannot.

Finding a purpose-driven value maximizer often requires you to read between the lines and follow your gut. I experimented with hiring for attributes when recruiting for a marketing internship after launching my consulting firm, Coltivar Group. I sent out requests for candidates to many local universities and received piles of resumes within a week. Most of these candidates were qualified business students who had relevant work or internship experience. I conducted multiple interviews with viable candidates but wanted to remain patient until I found the right person for the job.

The resume of a candidate who appeared unqualified on paper caught my eye. She was earning a music degree, had taken only a few business classes, and from the description, had few applicable skills. However, I was intrigued by her degree (there is a strong correlation between musical abilities and math skills and cognition) and was impressed by her high GPA.

I brought Sarah in for an interview and, despite her lack of experience, hired her for the job. Her excitement to learn and motivation shined through during our conversation, and she grew to be one of my value maximizers. Following the six-month internship, I hired her on full time as a consultant. The company grew and thrived during her employment, as she brought in new work, crafted winning strategies for clients, and facilitated leadership workshops. She even helped me write and publish my first book, *Delivering Value*.

Conversely, I have also mistakenly hired individuals solely based on skill set. As my company's growth surged, I was in desperate need of some help. I wanted someone on board who knew the ropes and, I wrongly assumed, would require little training. I hired a few managers with extensive corporate experience and quickly realized my expensive mistake. Because these employees were experienced, they came with a higher price tag. Additionally, they had established ways of working and were less open-minded and willing to learn a new approach.

Don't get me wrong; experience is enormously valuable. You want employees who will bring a multitude of learned know-how to the table. But experience cannot replace attitude. If my ideal culture centers around learning and growth, then my employees, too, must embody these values.

Another common company blunder is focusing solely on senior employees or employees in what are deemed "important" positions. In fact, on average, companies allocate far more to training senior leaders than they do to mid-level managers or contributors.[13] I am not condemning this approach toward budget allocation. As people progress in an organization, dedicating their time and effort, they earn additional incentives like focused training.

However, a heavy focus on senior leadership becomes problematic when it detracts attention from other areas of the business. Every position in the company is vital to its success, and companies are vastly underspending on training. Companies allocate less than 1 percent of revenue to training.[14] Building a scalable business requires new, less-experienced employees to successfully step into the shoes of their superiors. Significant training opportunities help ease this transition. Additionally, every role contributes to the strategy. Whether employees are responsible for taking notes or making multimillion-dollar investment decisions, they should be trained to be the best in their roles.

Just as strong talent can stem from unlikely places, great ideas may bubble up from unexpected pockets of the organization. Value maximizers are dispersed throughout an organization. The unlikely story of a very successful inventor demonstrates the importance of nurturing all your employees, regardless of their titles.

Richard Montañez was one of eleven children who grew up in a migrant labor camp outside of Los Angeles. A native Spanish speaker, Montañez struggled to learn English, dropped out of high school, and worked in an assortment of odd jobs at a poultry factory, car wash, and gardening service.[15] He took pride in his work and was grateful for every opportunity. When Montañez was told about a janitorial opening at Frito-Lay, he jumped at the chance, bearing in mind his grandpa's adage, "There's no such thing as just a janitor."

In addition to honing his janitorial duties, Montañez dabbled in other parts of the business.[16] He followed salespeople to appointments and devoted a portion of his days to immersing himself in Frito-Lay's operations and products. One sales meeting in a predominantly Latino neighborhood caught Montañez's attention. He realized that the brand didn't cater to Latinos, one of its biggest customer bases. As he wandered the neighborhood pondering the brand's lack of diversity, eating some local chili-covered *elote*, he was struck with an idea: covering Cheetos in chili powder.

This thought sparked Montañez's wild ride through the ranks of one of the world's largest companies. Montañez began by personally testing the product, covering uncoated Cheetos in chili powder. Following family and coworkers' widespread enthusiasm over the product, he decided to elevate his concoction to senior leadership. The CEO, Roger Enrico, heard Montañez's pitch, sampled the product, and Flamin' Hot Cheetos hit shelves shortly thereafter.[17] Flamin' Hot Cheetos continues to dominate snack sales, and Montañez has since played a variety of rolls in the company, including executive vice president.[18]

Montañez stands as a testament to the importance of emboldening employees at all levels of the organization. Had Enrico refused to listen to a janitor's product pitch, Frito-Lay would have missed out not only on a lucrative product but also on the opportunity to diversify its brand. In tandem with a strong culture that supports every individual, you must promote a platform that enables all types of value maximizers to meet their potential. Who knows how your next great idea will sprout?

TRAIN FOR RESULTS

Speaker, author, and pastor John Maxwell said, "A word of encouragement from a teacher to a [person] can change a life. A word of encouragement from a leader can inspire a person to reach [his or] her potential."[19] I have been lucky to have learned from a handful of talented, encouraging teachers throughout my life who helped me maximize my value. I reflect on the influence that my middle school history teacher, Ms. Weidner, had on my life. With animation and passion, she recounted the stories of our country's vibrant past, transferring her zeal for American history to the bulk of the seventh-grade class. Her enthusiasm was electrifying, and many of her teachings made an impact on my life today. For example, the American Revolution remains one of my favorite topics to read about, and Boston, with its deep historical roots, claims its status in my heart as one of my favorite cities.

My high school wrestling coach, Mr. Ottmann, taught me the value of hard work. He filled the void of a father in my life, inspiring me to work harder, care more, and persevere. On and off the wrestling mat, Mr. Ottmann pushed me to seek opportunities to refine my techniques, strengthen my discipline, and build a unified team. These attributes of hard work and persistence are deeply embedded in me and manifest themselves both in personal and professional settings. Wrestling requires intense self-discipline and physical tenacity, and I leverage the same grit when turning around a company; managing cultural, growth-based issues; or resolving client conflicts.

My life and career have been influenced by nontraditional teachers and coaches as well. My Grandpa Clifford instilled in me a passion for continuous learning and growth. A reflective and thoughtful man, he carried around a pocket-size notebook where he would scribble down his thoughts. The pages were brimming with insights, creative ideas, and questions. He was curious, hungry for knowledge, and emphasized the importance of stepping back to quietly observe and think. Amid the chaos of the workweek and familiar obligations, I reserve the early morning for alone time. I will wake up as early as 4 a.m. to run, allowing my brain to generate new ideas in the tranquil hours before dawn.

Great leaders and teachers have enlivened my thinking and ignited my passion for education. While I have been fortunate to have access to outstanding teachers and coaches, some people are not as lucky. This is a major strategic problem, as the deeper purpose of strategy and outsizing is to drive people and organizations to meet their full potential and achieve more than they ever thought possible. Fully empowered employees have the skills and support to navigate the changing workplace terrain; however, most employees don't receive adequate training to propel them to this next level of performance. More than 30 percent of workers report that they haven't done anything to develop their skills in the last year.[20] The training deficit is especially prevalent for workers ages twenty-four and younger, as businesses spend only 3 percent of the total training budget on these employees.[21] Those who do devote the time to training often don't achieve their desired results.

Business training, in particular, tends to fall short. Studies have shown that only 10 percent of corporate training is effective.[22] Leaders express dissatisfaction with results and frustration with employees for failing to progress. Though there are multifarious issues with corporate training, one of the most prevalent problems is its lack of diverse teaching methods.

I have attended countless company and association training sessions inundated with PowerPoint slides, charts, graphs, and manuals. Even in the case of high-quality presentations, banging employees over the head with boatloads of content does not make the concepts more applicable. If people only have a single, flat perspective of the material, their understanding is limited. Traditional training is transforming. In our hypercompetitive environment, it's important to enable employees with cutting-edge tools and methods not only to better equip them for their work in your organization but to engage and retain them.

In recent years, many training programs have moved online. eLearning provides the flexibility for participants to learn at their own pace while attending courses at their convenience. It can also be extremely cost effective. However, I recommend supplementing online training programs with in-person sessions. A blended approach gives attendees the opportunity to engage in social, experiential learning alongside online sessions. While it's possible to stimulate the neocortex with content-based learning on the web, many have reaped the benefits of incorporating experiential learning practices in their development programs.

Everyone possesses a distinct learning style; therefore, the most effective training blends different learning approaches. Experiential learning is a learner-centered approach that engages participants in hands-on activities. In this approach, the "teacher takes the role of the guide on the side rather than the sage on the stage," empowering learners to tackle challenges, co-create with colleagues, and reflect on their experiences.[23] This approach brings concepts into action, spanning the divide between theory and practice.

Active learning powers greater memory retention and topic comprehension. Applying a mix of different techniques promotes understanding of the holistic subject matter; thus, it's important to engage participants in active learning where they can make mistakes in a controlled environment.

I have witnessed the impact of experiential learning in my Coltivar Institute programs. For example, I hosted multiple corporate Strategic Financial Leadership Academies (SFLs), where multilevel, finance-focused value maximizers gathered for a blended learning experience. Prior to designing my first SFL, I defined my objective: to provide a collaborative, engaging yearlong program where top leaders grow and transform into financial innovators. Before initiating each session, I requested that participants define their intentions for the course. Reviewing their objectives helped me center the material and discussions to assure that everyone was training with a clear purpose in mind.

Cohorts met in person for three two-day-long sessions where they experienced a mix of lecture and individual and group activities.

To imbue active learning principles, participants designed corporate strategies and populated and presented a tool I will discuss in depth in the next chapter—IARs, or initiatives, actions, results—for feedback. This blend of reading, hearing, saying, and seeing ingrained the main ideas and accelerated these leaders' growth.

During the interim remote work periods, participants were immersed in e-learning sessions and coaching phone calls and collaborated in small groups on yearlong work-related assignments. One executive developed a speed advantage that catered to time-constrained clients. Another crafted a plan to pursue complex projects in the industrial space, a high-margin, high-opportunity segment. Through her financial analysis, one leader persuaded her company to invest heavily in mobile project management software and data analytics to improve the CX.

Completing the related company initiatives cemented the course's concepts and transformed savvy executives into strategic financial innovators. The leaders were able to pilot their proposed strategies and measure results in a controlled environment before implementing the initiatives in the organization. In addition to honing their financial skills, the leaders took away another key learning from the program—the understanding that organizational success relies on adaptive leaders who can grow into value maximizers to unleash the potential of their talent and build client-centric advantages.

Following my first SFL, a student revealed how the experiential learning shifted her thinking and built confidence in her abilities. She described how while she was an adept student, she had never felt confident in applying new ideas or concepts that challenged the status quo in the workplace. Her biggest stumbling block was her struggle to unveil the true story behind the financial reports. She was competent at reading and interpreting the income statement and balance sheet, but she had little understanding of the flow of money in and out of the business. She feared that asking questions at her job would belittle her knowledge and experience. After all, she had financial responsibility for her business unit, so prior to this program, she avoided integrating any new concepts into her line of work.

She explained how the SFL encouraged her to dig into real-world problems in a controlled, supportive environment. She returned from the program more self-assured and successfully continued to apply many of the SFL lessons in her business to improve margins through better pricing strategies and cost controls. What was once a millstone turned into a milestone. Her superiors took note and commended her on her innovative problem-solving.

While this woman gained tremendous value from the experiential learning components, the training was effective for different people for different reasons. Participants' feedback varied on what each person considered the most impactful activity. Some greatly appreciated the lectures, others were more engaged in the off-site group work, and another subset enjoyed the team-building and problem-solving activities.

While the SFL was a success, I developed the program through years of trial and error. Since launching employee-training programs, my teaching style has transformed. When starting out, I relied almost entirely on PowerPoint presentations as my sole instructional tool. However, our limbic systems, the area of our brains responsible for emotion and memory, are stimulated through repetition and continuous stretching. Building competencies and filling leadership positions call us to move beyond the transmission of theory and provide hands-on industry- or function-specific tools and processes that can be practiced and implemented to immediately drive value.

After attending and leading numerous training and development programs, I suggest that sessions incorporate a wide variety of teaching techniques and mediums to engage a greater number of participants. I put these principles into action when leading a strategy course for business students at the University of Denver. Rather than designing a lecture-based course, I incorporated case studies, hands-on activities and competitions, and digital simulations to test real-time applications.

It's important to tailor your content to your audience and situation. For example, this might entail providing millennials with cell-phone e-learnings, printing booklets to appeal to kinesthetic learners who want to manually capture information, or integrating report-outs for those who absorb information through teaching. It's important to define what you want to teach employees and then observe how they learn.

Ultimately, training should go beyond maximizing employees' skill sets specific to your organization. A well-designed training program ignites employees' passion to learn and outsizes their impact in your business (and outside of it). Unlocking your talent's full potential requires more than teaching them techniques and frameworks to implement in your business. The goal shouldn't just be to help participants learn something new but to become something new.

Results and Feedback

Knowing how employees learn requires their input. Gaining the most honest and pertinent feedback entails a three-pronged approach:

1. **Immediate feedback.** Following every session, amass employee thoughts and insights. I recommend incorporating a mix of reactionary, close-ended questions (e.g., rate the effectiveness of this training on a scale of 1–10) and some open-ended questions (What was the most valuable aspect of this training for you, and why? What was the least enjoyable aspect of this training for you, and why?).

2. **Periodic third-party review.** Every so often, it's helpful to seek an external perspective. Whether it's on a quarterly or annual basis, I recommend hiring a third party to support you in gathering and applying feedback. This mediator will provide an unbiased evaluation of your results and help tailor future programs to maximize effectiveness.
3. **Monitoring results.** In addition to employee feedback, reflect on your overall progress toward achieving your desired results. Everyone learns at a different pace, therefore the noticeable benefits of training appear after time and iteration. Don't immediately discount your efforts, but do ensure that you're regularly monitoring your progress. If you see little advancement over time or if your results grow stagnant, you should consider switching gears. Gathering additional employee feedback or coalescing responses from prior sessions can help you structure new courses to better serve your overall goals.

When designing and updating training programs, keep in mind that effective employee development isn't monotonous, inflexible, or closed-minded. Over time, employees will likely forget the detailed content presented in a session. But they will remember the relationships they built and the challenges they overcame. They will recall how they approached a problem and prevailed. After all, as we inch closer to the future of work, the most important thing you can do for your employees is teach them how to think.

ENABLE TEAMS

One of my favorite places on earth is New York City. Family and friends joke that if I ever disappear, they know they'll find me in the Big Apple. I love how the city buzzes with vibrant commerce and culture, renowned for its world-class dining and entertainment. Beyond the city's cosmopolitan allure, however, I am captivated by New York's rich history, its buildings and streets steeped in centuries of stories.

Among my favorite sites is the architectural masterpiece the Brooklyn Bridge. While the structure is iconic and commanding, the story behind it deepens my fascination with this bridge. In the 1860s, German engineer John Roebling conceived the bold idea of building a suspension bridge to link the two boroughs of Manhattan and Brooklyn.[24] Critics denounced his vision, labeling it dangerous and impossible. However, Roebling was determined to proceed and partnered up with his son Washington to help manage the project. Tragically, just before construction in 1869, Roebling was fatally injured while taking some final compass readings across the East River. Washington assumed the position of chief engineer, committed to finishing this feat and honoring his father.

During the process, however, Washington became ill with decompression sickness, an ailment that affected many of the bridge's workers, which devastated his health and rendered him partially paralyzed. Resolute in completing the project, Roebling developed a secret code of communication with his wife, Emily, tapping his fingers to provide her instructions.[25] Emily was up to the challenge, taking over as chief engineer. She immersed herself in the project, studying the materials, cable construction, stress analyses, and calculating catenary curves through her husband's teachings.[26]

In 1883, this unlikely team successfully erected the Brooklyn Bridge, the world's first steel-wire suspension bridge. The fourteen-year project was costly, taking twenty-seven lives and consuming roughly $500 million in today's dollars. While the project was fraught with obstacles, the bridge now stands as one of construction's most tremendous achievements and a testament to the power of collaboration. This great architectural accomplishment was truly a team effort—between father and son, husband and wife, and the hundreds of engineers who helped transform this bold vision into reality.

The triumphant story of the Brooklyn Bridge remains one of my favorites. It is not a run-of-the-mill inspirational narrative; it's filled with enormous, tragic obstacles. But it demonstrates an intense dedication to a cause and the willingness to unite in the face of hardship to achieve a shared goal.

While challenges in the office may not rival the perils faced by the Brooklyn Bridge team, solving any complex problem is most effectively achieved by leveraging the skills and abilities of a strong team. Designing and implementing a robust strategy is extremely difficult. The importance of value maximizers extends beyond their individual contribution to your strategy. Value maximizers are also team players who elevate the efficacy of the group. Just as the Brooklyn Bridge had a set of devoted leaders who were ardent about completing the project, assigning strategic ownership in a company drives forward a team of employees dedicated to organizing themselves and their colleagues around an overarching purpose.

Because strategy can become convoluted and messy, you need your best players aligned and committed to see it through. I advocate that companies build specialized strategic teams called S-teams. S-teams are comprised of five to ten value maximizers with different skills and experience who work interdependently to achieve a common goal. They are the strategic tissue of a company. The structure of an S-team enables the following:

- **Open communication.** From a logistical standpoint, it's easier to organize smaller groups to meet more frequently. Therefore, you achieve a regular meeting cadence to perpetuate an ongoing fountain of ideas. The deliberate size of an S-team also provides a greater opportunity for everyone's voice to be heard.

- **Decision-making.** Too-large teams decelerate decision-making. Because you don't want S-team duties to overwhelm value maximizers or interfere with their other responsibilities, it's important to optimize group productivity.
- **Creativity.** S-team members hail from all levels and across business units and departments of the organization, so each value maximizer brings a different perspective to the table. The unique ideas and opinions of each member combine to generate innovative, holistic solutions.
- **Accountability.** Within the S-team, individuals are assigned to manage the workflow. Every S-team member commits to a distinct role and set of responsibilities. All members are dependent upon each other's work and check each other's progress, forming an automatic accountability structure.

The role of the S-team is to own the initiatives, not necessarily complete the work. The team is responsible for delegating strategic duties and connecting the organization around a shared mindset. The S-team disaggregates the rest of the organization into sub-teams that support distinct value-capture initiatives such as project, client, or quality teams.

TEAM SIZE

The optimum team size is estimated to be between five and ten people. This team structure has been implemented by many effective institutions from the Navy Seals to Amazon, where Jeff Bezos famously instated the rule to "never have a meeting where two pizzas can't feed the entire group."[27]

Matrixed organizations possess multiple S-teams. For example, I helped establish an S-team structure for a multibillion-dollar company with business units dispersed throughout the US. While in some instances matrixed organizations can maximize resource allocation and improve workplace communication, the client was suffering from the common side effects of this operational structure. Rampant confusion around who reported to whom stifled accountability and ownership. Additionally, the geographic separation and contrasting projects in each location made it difficult to entrust strategic responsibility to a single S-team. Rather, we dedicated an S-team to each business unit. These S-teams associated on broader organizational topics to ensure that they kept an eye on the bigger picture. Within each business unit, however, the teams would assemble a web of interlocking sub-teams to deliver on specific strategic and client IARs.

The results were palpable. This once-disjointed company with misaligned initiatives was reinvigorated with a clearer sense of purpose and a more defined direction. The S-team structure eliminated much of the organizational confusion and served as a vehicle for results-oriented execution. Employee engagement increased as the S-team communicated the conviction behind the cause, the purpose for the organization's existence, and built a strategy that outlined the roadmap for success. The silos that once fostered a sense of competition and isolation crumbled in the face of collaboration.

While the company reaped substantial benefits from the new team-oriented structure, prior to achieving these results, the group endured an arduous adjustment period. At first, leadership grappled with who to appoint to the S-team. One of the business units designated seventeen members to the S-team. Each meeting ended in stalemate, as the overabundance of ideas and opinions decelerated decision-making. The cumbersome team couldn't decide on initiatives and next steps. Additionally, over time, certain members deprioritized their S-team obligations. The lack of engagement further halted progression.

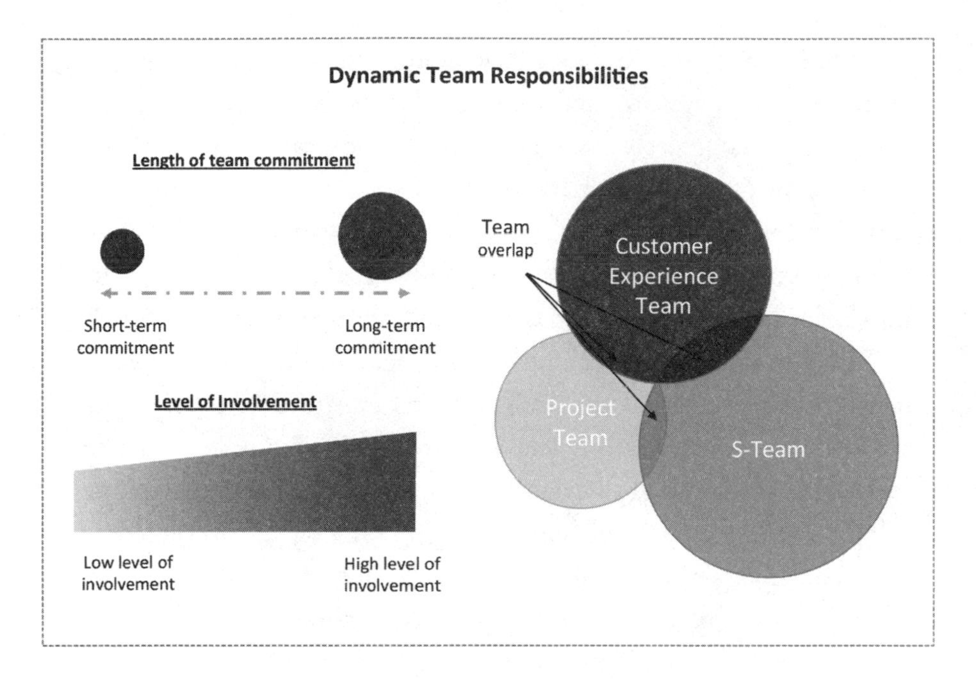

Figure 5.1: In the average company, most people balance the responsibilities of multiple teams simultaneously. These teams are dynamic, continuously shifting the membership level of involvement and time of commitment. The goal is to maximize overlap between team duties to optimize resource usage and not overwhelm members.

Teamwork, while imperative to success, is not easy, especially since most people are balancing the responsibilities of multiple teams simultaneously while managing their own workloads and responsibilities (see Figure 5.1). Have you ever worked in an ineffective and unproductive team? A Harvard study revealed that nearly 75 percent of cross-functional teams are dysfunctional.[28] Fostering great teamwork is hard, and the changing work environment is shifting team circumstances, presenting additional obstacles for companies that don't adapt. Teams today are more diverse, scattered, dynamic, and digital than ever. Success hinges on a team's ability to modify its structure and communication to fit the new context.

While tools and technology have helped bridge the gap between dispersed teammates, written language has its limitations. Research has shown that merely 7 percent of communication is conveyed through words. Body language accounts for roughly 55 percent of communication, and tone conveys 38 percent of what we say.[29] When team communication largely lacks the nonverbal elements, the likelihood of misunderstanding and misinterpretation drastically increases.

To mitigate misunderstanding and lack of alignment, remote team members must *over*communicate to ensure that their points are correctly interpreted. If you are discussing a complex topic or feel that someone might be confusing your point, schedule a phone call (or if possible, an in-person meet up). Don't try to sort out complicated conversations via email. If you do need to send a message, ensure that you're being clear and providing context; always assume that people understand less about the topic in question.

Additionally, remote communication methods like emails or phone meetings can lead to longer lag time between conversations. To maintain momentum, set communication norms and expectations when forming the group. You might enact a twenty-four-hour response policy or set up a regular weekly meeting. It's important to be even more organized and attentive when working with a scattered team. Working in a remote team doesn't reduce your effectiveness or chances of success if you're aware of and actively managing the challenges.

Another team consideration is increased workplace diversity. The workplace has transformed into a vibrant patchwork of perspectives and experiences, as teams are composed of employees of different races, ethnicities, genders, ages, and religions, as well as different

- ways of working;
- means of work coordination, such as direct supervision, standardization, and mutual adjustment; and

CEO: CHIEF EMAIL OFFICER

It is easy to fall into the default mode of emailing. Although appropriate in some circumstances, email can be construed as disingenuous. I have heard stories about leaders who opted for convenience at the price of camaraderie. For example, a CEO was deemed "chief email officer" for his habit of blasting out emails to his direct reports rather than walking down the hall to speak with them face-to-face. Another CFO worked for a company for five years and set foot in only one of the company's ten offices. Especially when in a leadership position, it's critical to be *present*, *engaged*, and *interested* in your colleagues. As leaders in a digital world, we must remember that sometimes the most effective means of communication are nondigital.

- learning styles, including principles-based and applications-based learning.

I had the opportunity to work in diverse teams at Ernst & Young (EY). In nearly all instances, our diverse teams learned from each other, thoroughly evaluated and considered one another's viewpoints, and drove innovation and creativity. Research confirms the importance of diversity, citing that companies that rank in the top quartile of executive-board diversity are 35 percent likelier to outperform the industry median.[30]

Working in diverse teams at EY was crucial during the early stages of our projects as we developed our work plans. Because every team member had a different background and perspective, we each brought unique opinions and solutions to the table. It was effective to vet a wide range of ideas, and through respectful disagreement, we devised an innovative approach to the project that none of us could have manufactured independently. However, once the work started and deadlines loomed, our polite disagreement morphed into a total lack of consensus. The more our plans dawdled behind schedule, the less we saw eye-to-eye.

My experience demonstrated that while diversity is imperative to overall organizational success, diverse teams should be deliberately leveraged. Research suggests that diversity is critical in driving innovation and idea-generation; however, higher-diversity teams are "often disrupted by inherent social conflict and decision-making deficits."[31] While diverse teams should be formed to facilitate the discovery and exploration of ideas, team harmony is the biggest indicator of success in implementation. Homogeneous teams should be used during execution or in a time crunch; employees who share the same views will stand in solidarity and move toward agreement much faster.

While team circumstances may be changing, great teamwork is founded on the same abiding principles. Research shows that successful teams, regardless of composition or location, share similar characteristics:

1. **They hear each other out.** Each member strikes an even balance between speaking and listening.[32]
2. **They work as a collective unit.** Members connect directly with each other; they don't rely on the team lead to relay all communication.
3. **They explore outside of the group.** Members are not constantly, fully immersed in the team; they work outside the team to explore their thoughts and bring back information to the group.
4. **They represent deep diversity.** Members are cognitively diverse or embody "deep diversity," which focuses on diversity of personalities, attitudes, and beliefs.[33]

Most importantly, teams unite around a shared vision and persevere until they achieve their goals. Like with the Brooklyn Bridge team, all teams should challenge the individuals to strive for more than they ever thought possible. Strong collaboration lifts each person to higher levels of performance and lasting success.

CELEBRATE VICTORY

The strongest teams persevere in the face of adversity. The best leaders challenge employees to flirt with failure and stretch their boundaries. Influential cultures encourage employees to continuously learn, grow, and improve. They push people to outsize their efforts and, in turn, maximize their results. In addition to challenging employees, high-performing companies celebrate success. Effective leaders acknowledge and reward employees' hard work.

When was the last time you carved out time to celebrate your achievements? I am not only referring to achieving a large, long-term goal. I am talking about the small wins that are too often overlooked and dominated by the daily commotion of the workplace.

While it may be easy to move past what seems like an inconsequential achievement, celebrating the small victories can lead to the accomplishment of overarching objectives. Organizational, team, and individual success is imperative to employees' excitement, motivation, and stamina. Celebration unleashes endorphins that reinforce positive behavior.

Research demonstrates how employees strategically buy in when they take time to reflect on results. *The Harvard Business Review* defines the progress principle in this way: "Of all the things that can boost emotions, motivation, and perceptions during a workday, the single most important is making progress in meaningful work."[34] When you boil down the data, it shows how the worst workdays are prompted by setbacks, and the best, most productive workdays are triggered by any progress made by the individual or the team.

Work doesn't have to be revolutionary or transformative to be meaningful. Part of celebrating success is showing employees how their efforts contribute to a milestone. I will repeat that any role or person has the potential to greatly impact strategy, and these efforts, however big or small, should be commended.

In our modern work environment, it's easy to get burned out. I initiate *Outsizing* by introducing the new levers of influence and opportunity that will impact how we create, deliver, and capture value and our market at large. As we tiptoe into unprecedented territory, we will experience unforeseen challenges and setbacks, making for some of our worst days. But we also have the power to increase the vitality of our businesses by making celebration a habit.

There are many ways to celebrate employees' achievements:

- **Handwritten thank-you notes.** Celebrations don't have to be grandiose or expensive. Never underestimate the power of a thoughtful thank-you note.
- **Company lunch.** Honor a team or individual with a small party.
- **Public recognition.** Whether it be via a company-wide announcement, newsletter, or through social media, give an appreciated employee a shout-out. This will set a tone and motivate the rest of the employees to receive similar praise.
- **Compensation.** If an employee is a key player in your organization, appreciate them with bonuses and salary increases. Ensure that their pay matches the level of value they drive in your company.

Philosopher Alfred North Whitehead said, "No one who achieves success does so without acknowledging the help of others. The wise and confident acknowledge this help with gratitude."[35] As you move forward in designing and implementing a winning strategy, remember the importance of your people and remind them of their impact regularly. Go forth into the new market with understanding and gratitude.

6

FORGE PATTERNS

Outsizing strategy requires companies to move beyond designing and talking about strategy to making it a habit. By creating an ongoing strategy process that aligns initiatives and actions, companies can build the patterns of success to achieve outsized results.

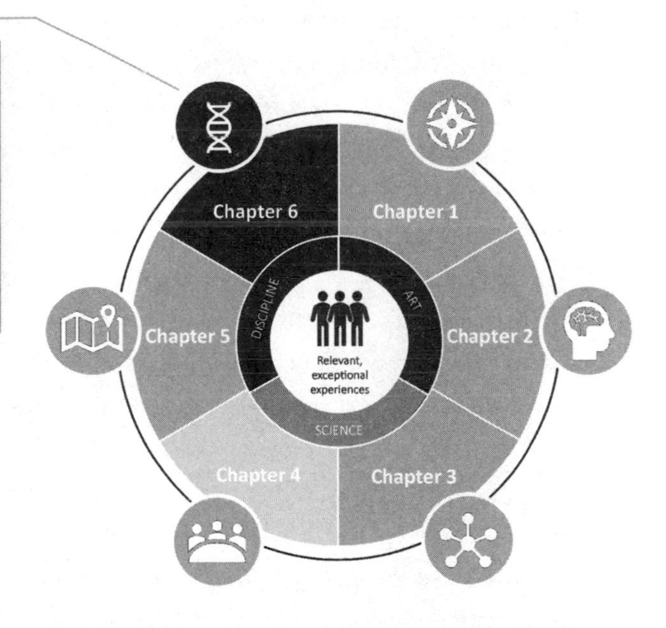

So far in *Outsizing*, we have examined how the shifting economy has transformed value drivers and how companies can capitalize on innovations in the new environment. We have discussed how to devise a winning strategy that delivers an excellent CX to the ideal customer while capturing outsized financial value for your business. We have learned how to develop individuals and teams and motivate employees to lead. Thus far, we have focused heavily on conception and design, on the science and art of strategy. In this final chapter, we shift our attention to the discipline of strategy, defining how to forge the patterns of leading organizations.

As I stated in the introduction, a competitive advantage cannot be sustained. Therefore, strategy can't be a one-off effort in your company. You must continuously revisit your how-to-compete and where-to-compete decisions to ensure that your business is built from advantages that customers truly care about. Customers and the market don't stand still, so your strategy can't either. Strategic efficacy is achieved through consistency and cumulative improvement.

Throughout this book, I emphasize that strategy is hard. It requires leaders who are used to being right to take bets on scenarios where there is no one correct answer. It demands that companies make critical tradeoffs that focus on the great over the good. Strategy involves questioning biases, failing in order to grow, changing perspective, and adjusting actions along the way. It calls for a balance between steadiness and routine and agility and adaptability.

In the face of these challenges, many companies give up. Leaders abandon true strategy to focus on filling operational voids. They prioritize short-term reward over long-term success. They simply don't "do" strategic planning because they have never realized the benefits.

I won't lie to you; strategy is at times daunting and disheartening. But the strongest, most successful organizations persevere to see their strategies come to fruition. These companies establish strategic patterns and internalize the process. By doing so, they streamline and simplify strategy. Rather than bow out, strategic leaders double down. Ingraining strategy as a habit enables proactivity rather than reactivity. This doesn't mean that strategy should be easy; if a strategy is easy, leaders should worry because competitors can copy it. Creating and acting on an outsized strategy requires significant effort. However, design and implementation are facilitated by making strategy habitual.

In this chapter, I explain the patterns of success, providing a framework to support implementation. IARs—initiatives, actions, results—are a simple, effective tool I designed to help organizations (and individuals) execute on strategic plans. This chapter ties a metaphorical bow around the different concepts you have learned so far. Establishing strategic discipline will enable your organization to

- build strategic patterns to drive simplicity and ease in planning and implementation,
- define long-term initiatives focused on building advantages for the organization and delivering value to the customer,
- align your actions to initiatives, and
- measure progress and adjust.

ESTABLISH YOUR INITIATIVES, ACTIONS, RESULTS

Since the beginning of time, the human brain has evolved through innate pattern recognition. At a basic level, we use patterns to establish order in a chaotic world. As kids, we learn to tell time, identifying the pattern of seconds, minutes, hours, days, and years. We construct language by recognizing and reorganizing combinations of sounds and words. As we age, we draw on existing and emerging patterns to build our worlds. For example, I avoid driving between the hours of 8 and 9 a.m. because of the horrible traffic pattern in my city. I book flights on Tuesdays, because in my experience, you get the best deals early in the week.

Over time, patterns transform into our automatic behaviors. Eating breakfast, brushing my teeth, telling my wife and kids goodbye, and starting my car to head to work all occur with minimal deliberate thought or action. My morning routine is assembled by patterns. A recent study by MIT asserted, "Neuroscientists have found that certain neurons in the brain are responsible for grouping behaviors together into a single habitual routine."[1] These habits are entrenched in us, so much so that breaking out of these patterns becomes hard to do.

While some perceive patterns as sticking us in a rut, they are critical to our efficiency. Patterns simplify our lives. Can you imagine how much time and mental energy it would take to dissect each step of our mundane tasks? For example, brushing your teeth would require your brain to think through finding your toothbrush and toothpaste, picking up your brush, squeezing on toothpaste, wetting the bristles in the sink, setting a timer to brush your teeth, and remembering how to circle the brush to clean your teeth. Life without patterns becomes complicated.

Strategy, too, can become complex and distracted when it lacks patterns. I see a lot of leaders overthink the strategic process. They arrange a big annual leadership retreat with a throng of peripheral prerequisites:

- Host the event somewhere remote, quiet, and comfortable.
- Involve every leader in the company.
- Schedule the discussion for eight hours with a long lunch break.
- Arrange for a speaker to present for ninety minutes at the end of the day.

- Provide the team exactly forty-five minutes outside of the strategy session for small talk and to learn about each other's lives.

These involved strategy sessions often result in convoluted, unrealistic outputs. The team typically conceives a complicated strategy with an excess of strategic "priorities." Leaders will return from these retreats with four-hundred-page slide decks crowded with recommendations. They will promote their top one hundred strategic initiatives to the rest of the company. The problem with overdone strategy is that complexity rejects patterns. It burdens growth and buries purpose. To return to the concept of essentialism, when people try to do too much, they often fail to do anything well.

That's why with strategy, as in life, simplicity is key. Leonardo da Vinci famously stated that "simplicity is the ultimate sophistication."[2] Patterns can play an integral role in driving order and clarity around the strategy process. By establishing norms and habits around how we design, implement, and measure strategy, we simplify our efforts. Strategic thinking shouldn't only occur at a swanky leadership retreat in Vail, Colorado. Strategy must be a way of life for your company.

Your patterns must support your goals. When coaching leaders, I often ask them how the patterns of their days align with their goals in life. There are often huge disparities between how they prioritize their actions, the patterns of their days, and their objectives. For example, a man may say he prioritizes losing weight, but his eating patterns prove otherwise. A woman yearns to build stronger relationships outside of work and pursue a work-life balance, but her working patterns, arriving at the office at 7 a.m. and leaving around 9 p.m., squeeze out any personal time.

Similarly, organizations say they prioritize strategy. But they address it haphazardly. In fact, my research of nearly two thousand executives revealed that 56 percent of companies conduct strategic planning only once a year, and 16 percent avoid it altogether. Their patterns defy their objectives. When patterns and desired results contradict one another, confusion and frustration set in.

One key way to forge strategy as a pattern in your organization is through repetition. IARs are a framework to facilitate strategic goal setting and effort alignment. They enlist a straightforward, continual process to guide your team in defining the following:

- **The Strategic problem.** The most pressing challenge your company is facing.
- **Initiatives.** The objectives of your strategy.
- **Actions.** The steps you enact to achieve your initiatives.
- **Results.** The desired outcomes of your strategy.

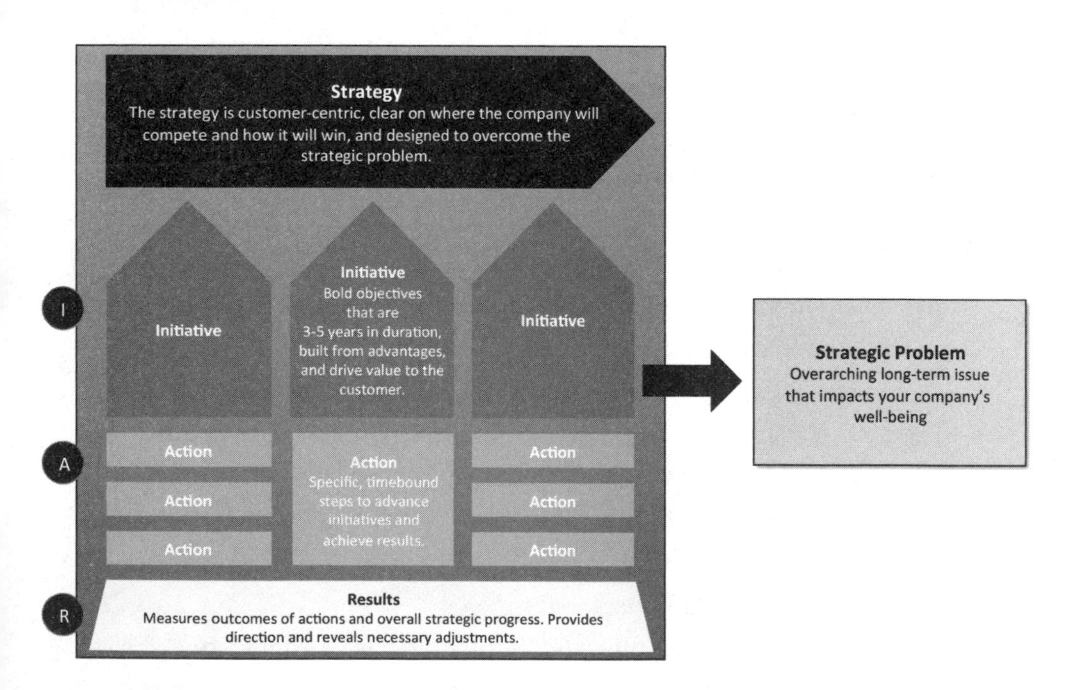

Figure 6.1: All components of IARs must align with one another and work together to solve the strategic problem.

By helping companies simply define the what, how, and why of strategy, IARs serve as the mechanism by which organizations solve strategic problems through the execution of their strategies.

IDENTIFY THE STRATEGIC PROBLEM

Before establishing IARs, it's important to step back and understand the problem you are hoping to solve with your strategy. The strategic problem should be viewed as the number-one issue your organization is facing that will impact its long-term success. In other words, solving this one strategic problem allows you to offset a series of interrelated problems.

Take the taxi industry's strategic problem as an example. It's no secret that ride-share giants like Uber and Lyft have wreaked havoc on the taxicab industry. In 2014, taxis commanded 37 percent of the business traveler market. As of Q1 2018, the taxi industry's market share declined to a scant 6 percent.[3] In some parts of the country, taxi revenue has declined as much as 65 percent since the introduction of Uber.[4]

Ride-sharing apps have had a dramatic and devastating impact on the taxi industry, including on its drivers. Tragically, in 2018, six taxi driver suicides were linked to their increasing debt and inability to cover the cost of their medallions amid the fierce competition of Uber and Lyft.[5] Despite the crushing consequences of the disruption to the industry, it has been sluggish to react. The industry's primary strategy has been to focus outward, filing lawsuits and hiring petitioners.[6] Taxi firms united at the court, claiming that Uber's initial operations were "illegal and predatory."[7]

The taxi industry's flimsy defense strategy could be due in part to its inability to define its true strategic problem. Taxi companies first targeted the ride-share apps themselves as the strategic problem, thinking, "If only we can get rid of Uber and Lyft, things will go

Type	Strategic Problem
Growth	Growth in our business has slowed while the overall market is performing well. If this continues, we may lose market share to our competitors.
Industry	Profit margins continue to shrink in one of our competitive segments due to increases in costs and competitive rivalry. If these trends persist, our financial position may be threatened.
Customers	Our customer retention rate continues to decrease despite our efforts to offer a superior service. As a result, our market share is also decreasing while our customer acquisition cost is increasing.
Employees	Employee engagement and retention is at an all-time low, and we are struggling to produce a quality product and meet deadlines. If we cannot keep and attract top talent, we may continue to lose key customers.
Costs	Our overhead costs are increasing due to rising organizational complexity, and customers are not willing to pay higher prices for our service. If we cannot right-size our overhead, we will struggle to earn an attractive return.

Figure 6.2: The strategic problem is the overarching long-term issue your company is facing that is inhibiting it from maximizing its potential.

back to normal." To confront the challenge, taxis poured energy and resources into expensive, minimally successful litigation.

Taxi companies failed to understand that the apps had already made a lasting impact on customers. The disruptors had paved the way for an improved transportation CX, and whether it be with Uber, Lyft, or other newcomers, customers would continue to seek an elevated experience. Taxis had long been protected as the only player in the game. They didn't have to understand customers or compete on price. Now, in the new economy, taxis are the expensive option that requires riders to stand curbside in the freezing cold in hopes of finding an open car. Taxis are the frill-free choice where riders must rifle through their belongings to pay at the end of a ride.

In response to Uber and Lyft, the taxi industry should have reframed the strategic problem and considered how they could maintain or grow market share amid the disruption of a ride-share economy while enhancing the overall experience for the customer. Rather than blaming the competition, these companies should

INITIATIVE DURATION EXCEPTIONS

Although I state that initiatives should range from three to five years in duration, there are exceptions to this rule. The more uncertain your business is, the shorter the duration of your initiative. If you're in crisis mode facing imminent bankruptcy, initiatives will be very short term. In this instance, you may only have one initiative that's not strategic or focused on building advantages. In times of crisis, an initiative might be as straightforward as "sell more work" or "improve cash flow." If your organization is in startup mode, time spent on the I's will likely be shorter in duration and shift as needs evolve and you uncover your customers' true value drivers.

have approached the problem with a customer-centric strategy. By understanding the true problem, taxi firms could have looked at the situation with a fresh perspective and contemplated how they could form a strategy so convenient and customer oriented that they make Uber and Lyft obsolete.

In the case of the taxicab, the industry took a myopic approach to the strategic problem, attacking the innovators rather than seeking ways to out-innovate. When defining the strategic problem, it's important to step back and look at your organization and the market from a high level. When leaders are sidetracked by the operational details, their strategies often meander down the wrong path.

For example, I had one client who was struggling to procure and retain talent. Upon asking the CEO about his biggest strategic problem, he responded, "Our primary strategic problem is our lack of an HR specialist. The role is currently empty. The last one we had was no good. That's why we can't find talent. If we fill this role with a talented employee, then our related problems will be solved."

While the client needed a high-performing HR specialist to assist with the hiring and retention strategies, framing the void of this single role as the overarching strategic problem was inaccurate. If the client's first assumption was true—that the lack of an HR specialist was the chief strategic issue—then the company's strategy would be as simple as hiring an HR specialist. Rather, the strategic problem went beyond that.

Realistically, the client struggled with cultural turmoil, offered comparatively low compensation, and maintained a rigid, stratified organizational structure. The true strategic problem revolved around the client's inability to recruit and engage talent across the board. This talent issue instigated other issues, such as excessive turnover costs, low client satisfaction due to delays, and the inability to grow. By approaching the talent problem holistically, the client could address numerous issues simultaneously.

This CEO, like many leaders, struggled to identify the root cause of his company's strategic problem. Whenever I guide leaders in defining their companies' strategic problem, I challenge them to dig deep to the essence of the issue by continuously asking why. For example, someone might say, "Our problem is that we don't make enough money." This could be true, but this statement alone won't drive an actionable strategy. So, I follow up by asking why. "Our market is saturated." Why? "A lot of new competitors have entered the space, so our margins are flatlining." In this instance, the strategic problem isn't about not making enough money. That's a side effect of the true industry-related challenge. While "not making enough money" is an issue that has myriad potential solutions, the industry-specific strategic problem narrows down the list to the root of the cause, helping the company clearly see the initiatives. The client could expand its footprint into new geographic markets to protect its financial position. Or it could diversify its offerings to capture a new chunk of the market.

The strategic problem is bound to shift and evolve over time, reflecting changes to your organization and environment. However, even as it's updated, it will remain a specific, big-picture problem that guides your strategy. Accurately defining your strategic problem will enable you to create and implement IARs that will serve as the antidote to this issue.

Initiatives

Once you have defined your strategic problem, you can determine the initiatives you will pursue to solve this challenge. Initiatives typically span three to five years in duration and should be focused on building advantages for the organization and delivering value to the customer. The initiative should make the highest possible contribution to building those advantages. If the return is substantial and potentially game-changing, you are heading in the right direction. If not, you may want to re-evaluate the initiative you are considering.

Perhaps the most challenging aspect of defining initiatives is limiting them to the true essentials that will move the dial. As a rule of thumb, clients should focus on only two to three initiatives at any given time. Because solving the overarching strategic problem mitigates other tangential problems, emphasizing the few mission-critical initiatives in your strategy will make a sweeping impact. As I mentioned in chapter 1, focusing on the critical and ignoring the trivial enables enhanced efficiency and effectiveness.

So how do you narrow down your list to the key endeavors your business should emphasize?

- **Tollgate #1: The initiative positively impacts the customer.** Earlier, I discussed how companies should funnel time and resources into activities that drive value for the customer. Initiatives are no different. Since your company can only focus on a few at a time, you must ensure that you're emphasizing initiatives that build advantages for your ideal customer.
- **Tollgate #2: The initiative captures value for the company.** Fulfilling this initiative should not only delight customers but should also drive a competitive advantage for your business by enabling you to capture a price premium, cost efficiency, or growth opportunity.

Companies that design initiatives with these criteria in mind stand out in their respective industries. For example, there are vast strategic disparities between fast-food restaurants. In the wake of an economic recovery, a shift toward health and wellness, and the emergence of fast casual, the fast-food industry has had to overhaul its strategy. Some restaurants have prevailed in defining valuable customer-centric initiatives. For example, Chick-fil-A has striven to deliver value to its customer types. Its initiatives center around making high-quality food more convenient and the fast-food experience more enjoyable. By prioritizing speed and efficiency, Chick-fil-A captivates its customer type "In a Hurry" while driving down its cost structure and increasing throughput, the revenue it generates, and the profit it earns per hour. Chick-fil-A has succeeded through its outward-looking initiatives, claiming the title of the "hottest fast-food chain in the country" with growth that's "almost too astounding to believe."[8]

On the other hand, Burger King continues to flounder. This is not due to a lack of effort. The fast-food chain has reinvented its menu, upped its advertising budget, and completed some large-scale acquisitions like its 2017 purchase of Popeyes Louisiana Kitchen.[9] However, Burger King's initiatives are company-centric. Customers don't want companies to thrust more advertisements in their face. They don't care about whether their favorite restaurant becomes a fast-food conglomerate. I am not saying that acquisitions and marketing are unimportant. They are strategic moves that can make a big impact on a business. However, unless the strategy is underpinned by customer-centric initiatives, companies will fail to reap the full value of executing on other pursuits.

In addition to customer centricity, ensure that you're focusing on the initiatives that will make an impact. Correctly defining the strategic problem will promote the creation of initiatives that attack this problem and therefore drive an ROI. However, a company may have relevant, customer-centric initiatives that still fail to maximize the strategic potential of the business. Initiatives should be evaluated by the amount of probable value capture. In other words, when it comes to initiatives, it's about the size of the prize.

Let's say that a company's strategic problem is cost related, described as increasing overhead costs due to organizational complexity, and that customers are unwilling to pay higher prices for their

Initiative Characteristics and Considerations	
Client-Centric	Initiatives should **build advantages** that customers care about and contribute to **exceptional experiences** while adding **value.**
Duration	Initiatives are **long-term** and typically take **3-5 years** to fulfill.
Contribution	The initiative should make the **highest possible contribution** toward the purpose of the organization and the development of advantages.
High-Level	Initiatives are general and realized through the completion of **multiple, ongoing** steps.
Alignment	Initiatives are in alignment with and **support the overall business unit** and **corporate strategic plan.**
Size of the Prize	Consider the **ROI** if the initiative is successfully realized. The **reward** should significantly outweigh the risk and effort.

Figure 6.3: Initiative guidelines

services. An organization might believe that an initiative to right-size overhead would be to reduce headcount in all departments. While this cost-cutting initiative could be customer-centric in theory, enabling the company to maintain or reduce prices while retaining its margins, the impact of laying off a portion of the workforce won't likely have a reverberating impact on the bottom line. Cutting 10 percent of the staff will save the company marginal salary expenses for the year. However, this initiative could backfire, dragging down morale, overburdening employees, and reducing throughput.

An ambitious, more impactful initiative would be to restructure the entire organization to be more streamlined and efficient. Shift from a bureaucratic structure to a flatter organization or combine profit centers to maximize resources and reduce redundancies. In this case, the initiative can accomplish the goal of cutting costs by reducing unnecessary oversight and complexity. Rather than hiring layers of management, the company could enable its existing workforce with training and tools. By elevating more employees into leadership roles and giving them the power to make decisions without tiers of review, an organization can enhance transparency, increase agility, and drive efficiency. Successfully implementing a reorganization to be more streamlined would provide a more substantial benefit to the bottom line for years to come.

Once initiatives are defined, your company will want to assign ownership. The initiative owner is accountable for achieving the key result(s) of the initiative. This does not mean the owner is the only person exerting effort or bearing responsibility. In most cases, the initiative owner works closely with select individuals or a small team to direct and perform the action steps that will allow the organization to build advantages and capture value.

Designing customer-centric initiatives that capture value is crucial to strategic execution. However, the meat of execution occurs as you work toward actualizing these initiatives.

Actions

Typically it's easy for leaders to conceive initiatives but difficult for them to define the actions necessary to achieve their desired results. This is where you must be careful, because one of the most prevalent and poisonous issues that halts strategic execution is the misalignment between efforts and results. Once a company defines its initiatives, it must coordinate its efforts with its top priorities. If a company's actions don't support its end results, then it's working hard to no avail.

I like to relate misaligned strategic initiatives and actions to a misguided marathon strategy. If I want to qualify for the Boston Marathon, I need to maintain a seven-minute twenty-five-second mile pace for roughly 26.2 miles. The time is my desired result. To achieve the result, I produce a long list of related activities that support my goal:

- I can purchase the best apparel, shoes, and nutritional supplements.
- I can gain access to a nearby gym.
- I can set my alarm for 4 a.m. to complete morning runs before work.
- I can read every article in *Runner's World* magazine.
- I can give up refined sugar and commit to drinking more water.

I can fulfill all these relevant subgoals, investing significant time, money, and effort. Yet I can still be unsuccessful. Unless I am running with the purpose of shaving my time down to my desired result, tracking my progress, and adjusting to ensure success, my efforts are for naught. If I read every article in *Runner's World* but never lace up my running shoes, my chances of qualifying are extremely slim. At the end of the day, I can try diligently, but unless I am focused on the right things, I will fail to achieve my results.

Do you ever feel as if you are putting in a lot of effort but aren't seeing your desired results? I frequently encounter executives who are frustrated with lackluster performance. Confused and discouraged, they will ask me, "Do you know how many hours I have worked this year? I have put in the time, so why am I not seeing the outcomes?" I gently remind these leaders that success isn't directly tied to the hours they work. Yes, achievement requires hard work, but to see results, you must be spending your time on the right things.

Our workdays are crowded with distraction. As leaders, we are pulled in a million directions, and unless we clearly define the critical actions, we risk spending significant time and money on irrelevant fluff. It's when we are busiest—when we struggle to pull ourselves away from our overwhelming workloads—that we must step back and gain a big-picture perspective. We must ask ourselves, Is my energy on this project worth it? Is there a more valuable way I should be spending my time? Michael Porter said it best: "The essence of strategy is choosing what *not* to do."[10]

IARs help you focus your energy and resources on what is essential to your business. By successfully completing steps one and two, defining your company's strategic problem and the initiatives to solve it, you are poised to describe the actions that will power your business forward in fulfilling its strategy. Actions, as defined by the IARs framework, are specific, actionable, time-bound, realistic, and manageable steps that empower you to proactively and strategically execute your strategy. A series of actions compose an action plan that serves as a hypothesis that your organization will test and refine to achieve the desired results.

In addition to being one of the most important components, action steps are the most commonly overlooked strategic ingredient. Companies will define grand schemes, laying out initiatives that are big, bold, and vague. Execution is the biggest challenge facing organizations, often because people have defined where they want to go but don't know how to get there.

For example, let's assume that a company's initiative is to build a network of trusted industry partners, and the COO, Joe Smith, owns the execution. This initiative allows the organization to develop a capability advantage and a stronger network while delivering value to the customer through an expanded group of industry partners who can serve as qualified referrals. Joe knows that to succeed on this initiative, his company must focus on building and nurturing industry relationships. However, doing this effectively will require the company to establish governance around managing relationships and tracking interactions. Joe determines that the very first action step is for the company to invest in a customer-relationship management tool (CRM).

Since this will be the company's first time using a CRM, it's important to research an assortment of choices and find the best one. When clarifying the action of finding a CRM, ensure that it fits all the following characteristics described in Figure 6.4:

BUILDING A NETWORK OF TRUSTED INDUSTRY PARTNERS

In addition to identifying a CRM to invest in, Joe might define some other relevant action steps as follows:

1. Join a national industry association with more than five thousand members by 7/31.
2. Put in place a network referral program and sign up five partners by 9/30.
3. Collaborate on a webinar with an industry partner by 12/31.

- **Specific and Actionable.** It could be written as "Research and identify a CRM tool to track industry partner relationships." Additionally, you may provide notes to enhance clarity. For example, "this CRM should have the capability to record dates of interaction, include message links, and assign targeted follow-up contact. The cost should fall within a specified budget." By making the action clear and applicable, Joe can assign someone the duty of completing it.

However, when delegating actions, ensure that you're not giving too much detail or explicitly telling the person *how* to complete it. As WWII General George S. Patton advised, "Don't tell people how to do things. Tell them what to do and let them surprise you with their results."[11] Great leaders provide crystal-clear clarity around what you should do (the initiative) and what they expect (the results). They do not, however, micromanage the how, because they understand that there are different ways to accomplish the same goal.

For example, a person may be assigned the initiative to schedule a trip to New York. The action could entail traveling by car, plane, or train to arrive by the stated date. Depending on the distance, weather, and traffic, one option will supersede the others. The person responsible for execution should have the power to test the hypothesis and determine the best course of action.

- **Time bound.** Deadlines help create momentum, ensure that you're focusing on your priorities, give your team a sense of accomplishment when they are met, and allow leaders to hold people accountable to a time-bound plan. For the initiative "find a CRM," the action might be defined as "research and identify a CRM tool to track industry partner relationships by October 31."

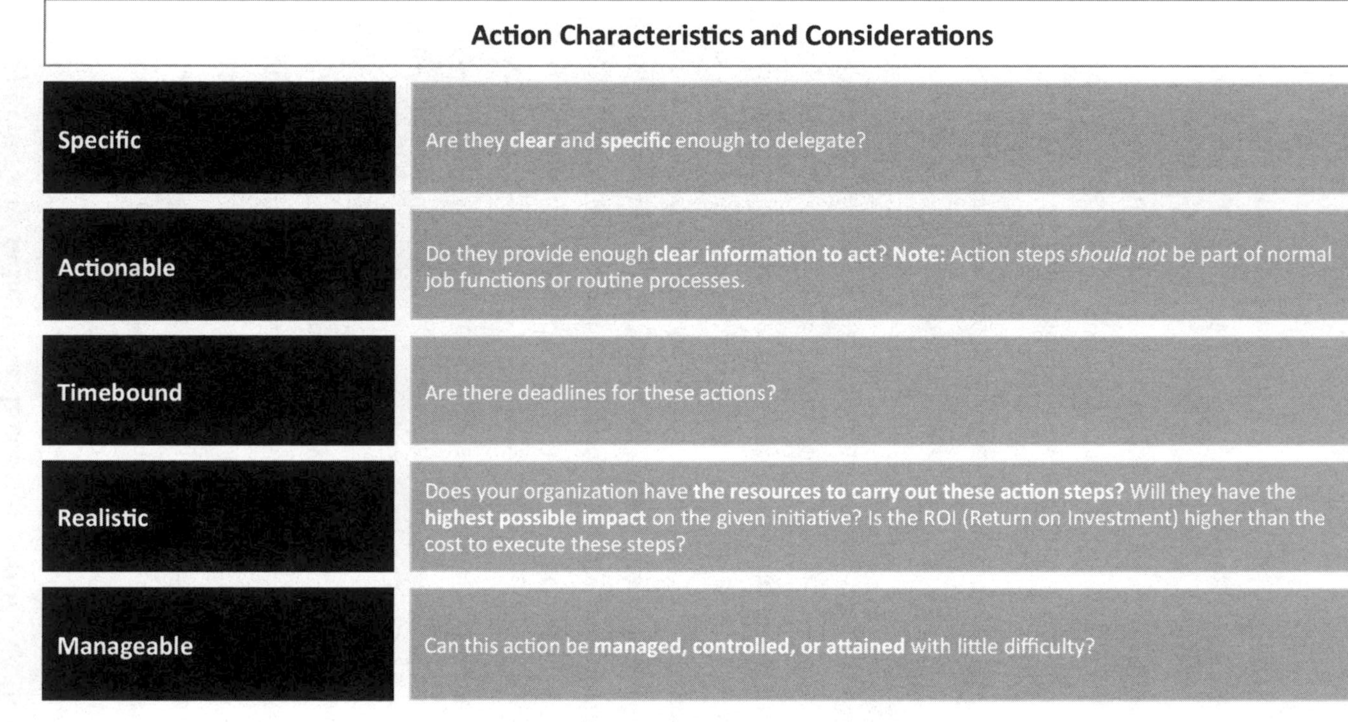

Figure 6.4: Action guidelines

- **Realistic.** You must also decide whether the action is reasonable. From an individual perspective, does the employee have the capacity to complete this within the expected time frame (considering that these actions are outside the scope of their daily duties)? Additionally, do you have the budget to invest in any CRM? Do you have the resources to implement the CRM?

It would be unrealistic for Joe to create an action that required every employee to dedicate fifteen hours a week to serve in a leadership position in an association. First off, I would argue that no company should devote its entire team to the same objective, and very few employees would (or should) have fifteen hours a week to spare. Additionally, getting voted into a leadership position in an association takes time and dedication. Those in leadership roles are most often selected from a pool of active longtime members. Though the accomplishment of this action would likely drive your firm toward achieving its broader initiative, it's setting employees up for failure. Ensure that your expectations are realistic.

- **Manageable.** Finally, are the actions executable? Does the person responsible have what is needed to manage implementation? By subscribing to the first four criteria, your team should be able to manage the action to produce the desired results.

While action steps are tactical in nature, they should not be routine items on a to-do list or contained within a job description. Action steps must be strategic and produce the largest possible return with the least amount of effort or resources. (See Figure 6.5.) Remember, much of your strategic success relies on doing the best you can given capital, time, and resource constraints. Therefore, when defining actions, be realistic, but also dare to be bold.

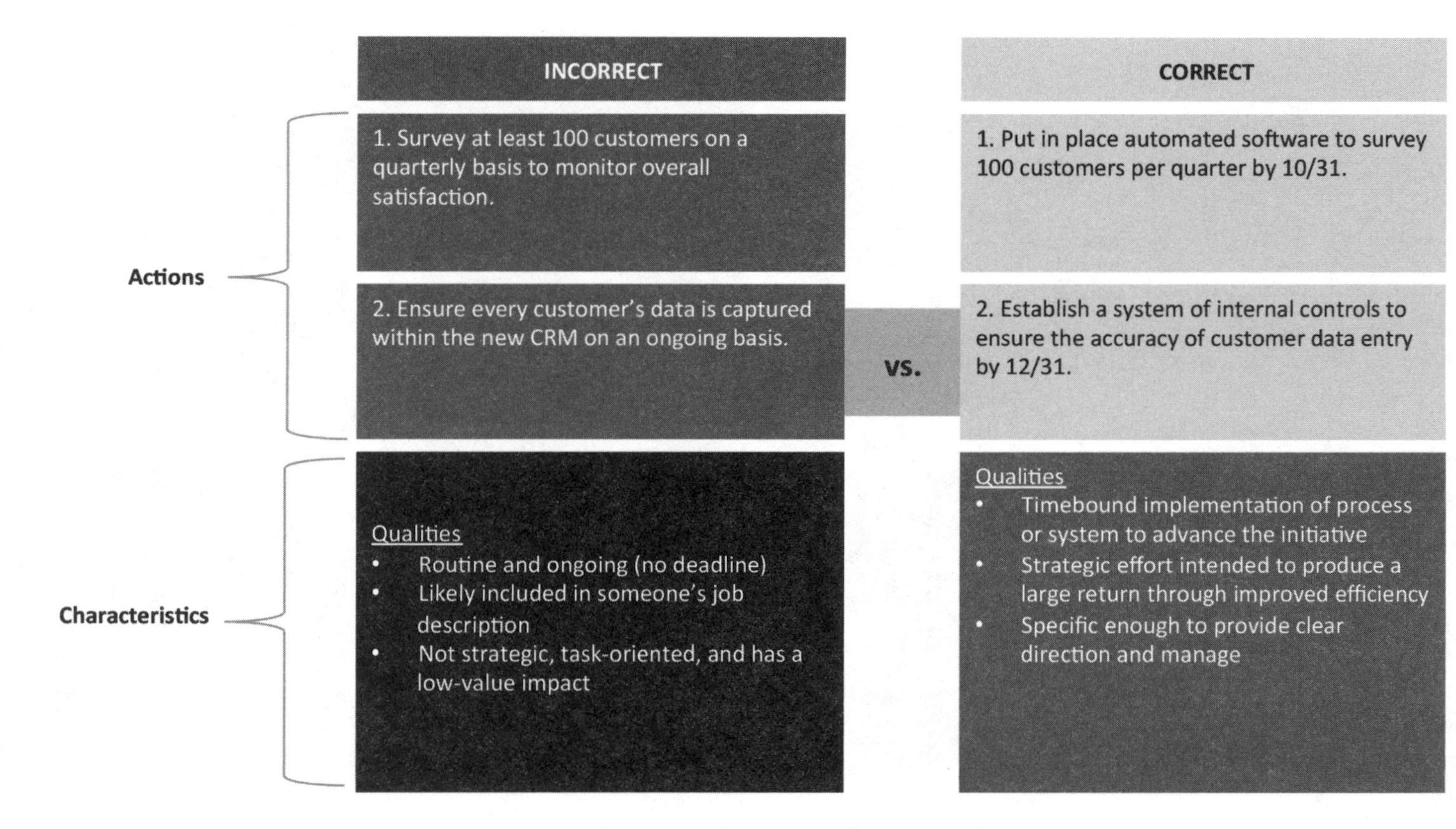

Figure 6.5: The subtle differences in the written actions can make a large impact. Ensure that actions are written as specific, time-bound, and strategic assignments.

Additionally, remember that it is the culmination of action steps into an action plan that drives results. Just as advantages are built from a web of interlocking activities, initiatives are fulfilled by an assortment of supportive, relevant actions. Returning to the example of Chick-fil-A, let's consider the mix of audacious actions that have fueled two of the restaurant's top initiatives: enhance the fast-food CX and make fast food as convenient as possible. Chick-fil-A has outperformed the competition and actualized results by committing to the following action plans:

- **Design and roll out hands-on training and engagement programs to enable employees.** Chick-fil-A has fully embraced the notion that happy employees equal happy customers. The fast-food chain does not skimp on employee development. In fact, Chick-fil-A claims to invest more in training its employees than any other chain restaurant.[12] It hires actors to run simulations on a variety of scenarios, so employees know how to react in any situation that comes their way.[13] In addition to training employees on how to go the extra mile to be happy and helpful to customers, Chick-fil-A employees are engaged and accommodating because they're treated well. The restaurants are closed on Sundays to promote work-life balance for employees.[14] Chick-fil-A also makes employees feel valued by offering perks like college tuition assistance. It has donated more than $61 million to college scholarships since launching its program.[15]

  The results of these actions are clear. Chick-fil-A has received numerous accolades, including the vote for the most polite restaurant chain.[16] Chick-fil-A's targeted actions claimed the brand the title of America's Best Fast-Food Chain, topping the list for its outstanding customer satisfaction and financial performance.[17]

- **Prioritize innovations to increase efficiency.** In addition to customer centricity, Chick-fil-A is at the forefront of innovation in the fast-food industry. It has married its two initiatives by focusing on innovations that the customer cares about. Chick-fil-A's dedication to efficiency and effectiveness are evident as it has pioneered many industry breakthroughs. It was one of the first restaurants to outfit its stores with dual drive-thru lanes, increasing the volume of business and the speed of service, driving up throughput levels. The chain continuously seeks opportunities to fulfill its initiatives, recently opening an Innovation Center in Georgia Tech's Technology Square, where the restaurant works with "faculty and students to explore design, innovation, and development projects."[18]

  Furthermore, Chick-fil-A employees take curbside orders via tablet, accelerating the order process while providing face-to-face contact for the customer. This improves accuracy—Chick-fil-A has the second highest order accuracy of any drive-thru, coming in at 95 percent—while strengthening the CX. Although this ordering phenomenon is catching on at other chains, it was first developed by Chick-fil-A operators and team members.[19]

Chick-fil-A's deliberate, concentrated action plans have enabled it to develop unique advantages. It has gained a capability advantage, partnering with the top minds in innovation to devise inventive ways to modernize fast food that also enhance the customer experience. It has focused on positioning advantages in the design of its physical stores (by adding dual drive-thru lanes, laying out restaurants to enhance traffic flow, and adding family-friendly play areas) and through geographical positioning. Since more than half of the restaurant's business comes through the drive-thru lane, Chick-fil-A has focused primarily on setting up shop in high-traffic areas.[20]

Keep in mind that while Chick-Fil-A has excelled at developing and implementing action plans, it likely took the restaurant a few tries to get it right. Strategy is a hypothesis that requires regular adjustment. With IARs, we hypothesize on the initiative based on what customers value. We validate this hypothesis through our actions. As we will discuss in the next section, we test the efficacy of our strategies through our results.

Sometimes our actions don't advance our initiatives. Maybe we are seeking to invest in technology to simplify key processes, and one of our actions is to attend five technology demos by March 1. We might successfully complete the action, participating in five technology demos—however, they could be on the wrong topic or for products that don't help us meet our needs. The intent of our actions may be good and yet still fail to produce the anticipated or desired outcomes.

When we find that despite our best efforts, our actions and initiatives misalign, it's important to quickly adjust. Adopting Eric Ries's Build-Measure-Learn methodology from his book *The Lean Startup*, success is dependent on our ability to quickly put the action in motion, understand its impact, and adjust to improve the results.[21] In the case of the misaligned marathon strategy, it'd be much more helpful to test my speed weeks before the race and realize that my actions weren't supporting my goal. By measuring early, I'm given the opportunity to update my approach. If I don't measure my progress leading up to the race, I will show up completely unprepared to run twenty-six miles. That's a painful mistake, literally.

When it comes to actions, it's all about experimentation. Simple adjustments can make a big impression. Oftentimes, adding ancillary actions, shifting ownership, and mixing up the sequence of activities can lead to sizeable improvements. Knowing whether and when to shift your actions requires you to consistently assess your progress.

Results

Former CEO of IBM Lou Gerstner stated, "People do what you inspect. Not what you expect."[22] I learned this lesson early in my career. As a young twenty-something, I was completely romanced by the excitement of entrepreneurship after having recently launched my landscape architecture business. I set up shop on the cusp of the economic boom and quickly expanded my company to capitalize on the market opportunity.

I was feeling on top of the world. Customers were lining up to work with my company, and I had a diverse and talented staff upholding my strong brand. While my first taste of entrepreneurship was captivating (I went on to form and operate three more companies), I was also working like a dog, putting in eighty-hour workweeks to keep up with demand. I jumped at my first opportunity to take a two-week vacation, leaving the company reins in the hands of one of my top managers. We were currently working on a large high-end project, but this manager had worked for me for a few years, and I trusted him. I gave him little instruction—he knew the business as well as I did—and was off to relax on a beach in Mexico and forget about work for a while.

I returned frustrated with my employees for their lack of progress. While I was away, the high-end project suffered from operational issues that led to cost overruns and schedule delays. The client was upset, as the project team missed an important deadline after installing the wrong material and having to backtrack. By communicating with the field supervisor, this manager could have ensured that specifications were followed, the customer was receiving timely updates, and profit fade was minimized.

Upon my return, I was most upset with my manager, whom I had entrusted to assume operations. And while the manager and the team deserved some of the blame, I, too, was responsible. While at the time I was confused and agitated, the experience taught me a valuable lesson: strong leaders follow up.

I should have been explicit in stating my expectations. What did I count on my managers and employees to do while I was away? More importantly, how would I ensure they held up their end of the bargain? I failed to create an accountability structure. Had I informed the team of my goals for this project prior to leaving, they would have had clear, measurable outcomes that could be inspected upon my return. For example, by reinforcing the deadline, explaining the quality expectations, and describing the client's need to feel involved, I could have ensured the crew clearly understood my expectations. Not only would this have benefitted me by holding my team responsible for my outcomes, but it also would have helped them. Rather than being frustrated and shaking my finger at my employees, I could have provided targeted feedback on how they could improve.

Can you think of a time when you earnestly committed to doing something but other priorities took precedence? We have all fallen prey to breaking a commitment. I am sure my team began the week with strong intentions, but without clear guidelines or motivations, they allowed other things to get in the way of completing their work.

An accountability deficit hampers strategic execution, and unfortunately, this issue is immensely common. Just 9 percent of managers say they can rely on their colleagues across different functions and business units all the time.[23] People are immediately motivated to carry out a new strategy and work toward achieving an initiative. However, time and fatigue fade ambition, and before you know it, you're back at square one. I am not saying that leaders shouldn't trust their colleagues to see through their responsibilities. I am simply stressing that achieving organizational goals requires you to build in accountability, and the simplest way to do so is through measuring your results.

While I didn't want to call the tool IRAs (and opted instead for IARs), in fact, defining the R—results—is truly the second step in the process. Once you have established the I—initiative—it's important to determine what you want to get out of it. Having a clear-cut outcome in mind will help you focus your efforts.

Your R's should be defined specifically and comprehensively. For example, if "drive sustainable growth in key markets" is your initiative, "increase revenue by 50 percent" is too general a result. Placing the emphasis on merely increasing revenue doesn't focus on the holistic health of the business. Vaguely defined results can lead to unintended consequences. Note that this R doesn't specify where the revenue will come from or how you will get it.

You could lower the price of your product 20 percent below competitors', stealing away their customers, therefore drastically growing your revenue. However, this move could have severe margin ramifications. If your R is to grow revenue by 50 percent while maintaining margin, you still risk your team engaging in detrimental, company-centric behavior such as overcharging customers or irritating them with aggressive sales tactics. Achieving your results should never alienate customers. A more comprehensive approach would be worded as, "Increase revenue by >10 percent and maintain customer retention at >85 percent while earning a minimum margin of 50 percent."

Incorporating qualitative data may help you further enhance the integrity of the result. People resort to quantitative measures because they're unambiguous. Often my clients refer to simple financial metrics like revenue and profit to judge success. However, adding in qualitative measures is more comprehensive and ensures that a high-quality product or service is delivered along with a great customer experience. In the example above, in addition to measuring customer retention, you might investigate customer satisfaction via open-ended questionnaires, consumer case studies, or anonymous audits.

Additionally, as you write your results, ensure initiative owners and the employees that they delegate have the power to influence the result. If you're expecting the owners to accomplish a result as sweeping as increasing overall firm revenue, they must be in a position with access to a variety of resources to make this happen. They must have a budget and be able to call on sales, marketing, product, and service personnel with definitive actions directed at growing the business. If achieving this metric is outside their control, it's not an accountability structure; it's a punishment.

Furthermore, results should measure outcomes, not actions. When I encourage employees to "track their R's," they often respond with statistics to monitor their actions. Let's say that "get new clients" is their initiative, and their actions are outreach oriented: sign up potential clients for the newsletter subscription by December 31 and call potential customers to set up meetings by February 28. Most people resort to building their R's around their A's; for example, recruit at least a hundred new subscribers to the newsletter and call five hundred potential customers.

The problem is that achieving these results does not guarantee that the company will get new clients. The employees could far exceed their R's, adding three hundred newsletter subscribers and calling a thousand potential customer contacts. And they could obtain zero new clients. If the action isn't driving the initiative, then the company is focusing employees on the wrong topic. In this instance, the result should be tied directly to the company's ability to drive sustainable growth. It should assess metrics around new client acquisition. Remember that results are relative, meaning that they should relate to and measure the overall strategy.

Linking your results to your initiatives helps you course correct. To be both consistent and adaptive, you must understand *where*

TRAILING TWELVE MONTHS (TTM)

As you assess your progress, ensure that you're looking at outcomes normalized over a twelve-month period. For example, if you want to compare your revenue before implementing the action, don't take the most recent month; take the revenue spread over a twelve-month period. TTM eliminates seasonality and other anomalies in the data to ensure you have an accurate view of your results.

---

and *how* to shift your strategy when you're not seeing your desired results. I advise clients to be patient with I's and impatient with A's. Initiatives are longer-term and based on ideal customer values. These do not waver frequently and should be fully pursued. Actions, on the other hand, should be flexible. If you are not achieving the key result after persistent effort, consider modifying your action items to improve your return on investment.

When writing your key results, consider the following questions:

- Why am I pursuing the specified strategic initiative and supporting action steps?
- What am I hoping to gain from them?

As you answer these questions, as with defining the strategic problem, dare to dig deeper and respond to the *why*. For example, when Chick-fil-A was designing the dual drive-thru lanes, it might have started with wanting to increase the number of current drive-thru customers from twenty to thirty people per hour. The surface-level result revolves around increasing capacity. Why is growing capacity important? Chick-fil-A might determine that growing capacity allows them to serve more customers per hour, therefore boosting their hourly throughput. Rather than measuring the number of customers, the result should evaluate the hike in throughput (drive-thru revenue per hour). Then Chick-fil-A can more easily analyze the anticipated ROI of the action to determine whether to move forward. In this instance, they could calculate a cost-benefit analysis for the action: "It costs $100,000 to outfit each restaurant with a drive-thru lane. Our throughput increase is expected to put an extra $50 per hour in our pockets, amounting to a nearly $220,000 total increase over the year."

ROI isn't simply just speculation before investing in an action. It should also serve as a strong measure of success. As described in Figure 6.6, it's important to garner both pre- and post-implementation data to analyze your progress. For example, if I want to inspect how effectively my team has executed on the initiative "develop leadership capabilities in our value maximizers," we would want to understand the baseline of these employees' capabilities to start. Our desired result might be for teams to rate their supervisors' managerial effectiveness at an average of a 5 out of 7 on the employee-engagement survey. To see if our training program is working, we must know the supervisors' average ratings before and after training implementation. The delta will explain whether we are meeting our results.

Finally, when crafting a list of measurable results, ensure that no two overlap. If two of your metrics share a strong correlation, then you're measuring one unnecessarily, creating complexity. Recall that the IARs process is intended to simplify and streamline strategy, so measuring results should be an effortless pattern in your organization. If two of your results tell the same or a very similar story, for example, employee retention and employee engagement, pick the one that tells the story the clearest and is the easiest to populate.

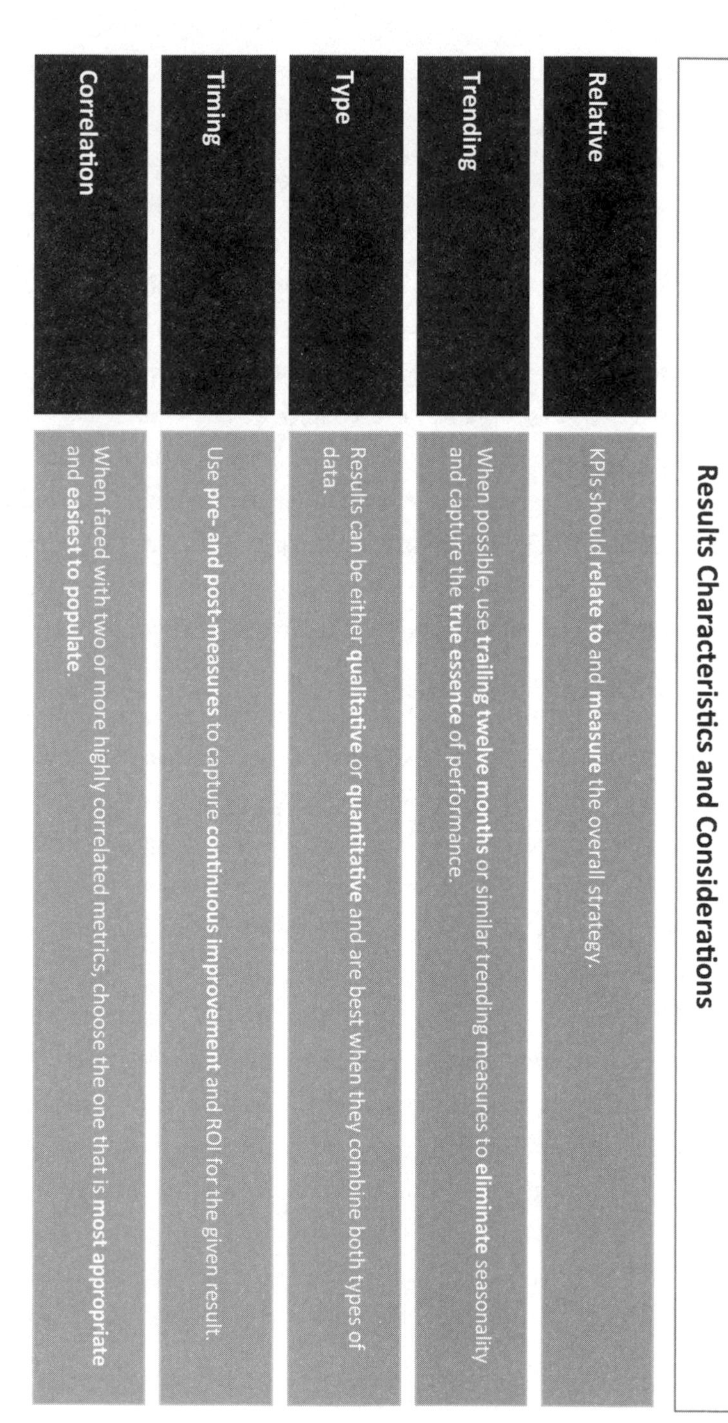

Figure 6.6: Results guidelines

IMPLEMENT THE IARS SYSTEM

Now that you know how to define and execute on initiatives, actions, and results, you're ready for the other half of the accountability structure, the meeting architecture. Continual assessment and a consistent reporting structure are imperative to IARs. Measuring results and communicating adjustments are achieved through two meeting structures: the strategy review meeting (SRM) and strategic integration meeting (SIM).

The Strategy Review Meeting

The SRM is designed to provide organizational leaders with a proven methodology for monitoring the progress of strategy implementation. By using the SRM process to track strategy and hold your team accountable, you significantly increase the odds of executional success. The SRM is a bi-weekly or monthly meeting where initiative owners report on their initiative and the progression of the action items. Based on the owner's report, the initiative receives a rating on a scale of green (good), yellow (fair), or red (poor) to describe the level of progress toward achieving the results. Even if the result is not yet attained, the improvement of the initiative may still merit a green score because it is on track. All initiatives and actions are discussed during this meeting, and depending on their rating and the owner's recommendations, next steps are determined and delegated. The S-team (introduced in the last chapter) is responsible for executing the strategy of their specific business unit or department; therefore, this group of value maximizers leads the SRM.

Strategic Integration Meeting

The SIM unites the company's strategy with its financials. Unlike the SRM, which involves reviewing actions toward results, the SIM is designed to evaluate financial performance, monitor the fulfillment of key results, and integrate internal and external issues in the organizational environment. SIMs are conducted monthly, following financial close once financials are released. Finance sends the financial statements twenty-four hours in advance to all participants. In addition to trailing statements, they will prepare rolling, forward-looking metrics that tie to the strategy. Participants then review and come to the meeting ready to discuss them. As actions are modified to advance the initiatives of the strategy, rolling forecasts are updated respectively. If a strategy is not allowing a company to capture an above-industry-average economic return (or at a minimum, a return higher than its cost of capital, as discussed in chapter 4), then the plan should be reassessed. The bulk of the meeting deliberation should revolve around the challenges or issues that have arisen in the last period. Participants assemble data and analysis on their relevant challenges prior to the meeting. The discussion should serve as a forum for executives to share resources, make decisions, and commit to specific actions to advance the overall strategy. Participants include leaders who have the ultimate responsibility for the financial and operational performance of their business units or departments.

Measuring results makes your organization answerable to its goals. It is the final puzzle piece in fulfilling your IARs. By instilling the patterns of strategic design and execution, defining the overall objectives and the actions to achieve them, and measuring and adjusting based on your progress, strategy becomes less *hard* and more habitual. Ingraining these fundamentals as a habit will make your business stronger, more resilient, and more judicious. As Aristotle wrote, "Quality is not an act. It is a habit."[24]

CONCLUSION

If you found a shortcut in life, would you take it? In our fast-paced world, companies have built empires on the promise of immediate results. Countless books proclaim that they share the keys to getting rich quick, losing ten pounds in a week, or feeling happy and confident today. These headlines call to the emotional parts of our brains that crave instant gratification. In our businesses and personal lives, we want to see results quickly.

However, can shortcuts ever deliver on their promise? One of the most legendary shortcuts is the Hastings Cutoff. In May of 1846, the families of James Reed and George and Jacob Donner fled Missouri with a large wagon party to settle in California.[1] Their travels over the Sierra Nevada mountains were constricted to a 120-day window of time before arctic-like conditions made the rugged terrain impassable. If the group left too early in the spring, bad weather and immature grass could have left them (and their cattle) stranded and starving. Therefore, the fleeting travel time frame left little room for error.

It wasn't long after leaving Missouri that the group confronted challenges. The trip was dragging and physically exhausting for all. The trails were caked in mud and fragmented in some areas. However, the assurance of a better life in California beckoned the pilgrims onward, and the wagon train advanced, reaching Wyoming in June. There in Fort Laramie, roughly two months into their travel, Langsford W. Hastings approached the families with news of a "new and better road to California."[2] Falling prey to the promise of a shortcut, the group abandoned their original plan to follow the Oregon Trail to instead pursue the Hastings Cutoff, heading southwest through the Great Salt Lake Desert.[3]

Though a returning traveler warned the families against the cutoff, they were tempted by the hope of shaving down their trip time. If successful, the Hastings Cutoff would save the group three hundred miles, amounting to roughly a month of travel. They strayed from their strategic course and planned on reconnecting with the others at the California Trail on the far side of the Sierras.

The eighty-seven travelers and twenty-three wagons in the Donner-Reed group struggled southwest and forged a trail through the rugged Wasatch Mountains. As they traveled through the blistering heat south of the Great Salt Lake Desert and through the soggy surface of the salt flats, they experienced significant delays and expended an incredible amount of energy. The alternative route cost the group an additional month to reach the Sierra Nevada Mountains. In early November, as the party struggled up the eastern slope in a desperate attempt to beat the first snows, they were caught in a horrific winter storm just one day short of the summit and the downhill path into California.

After roughly two months trapped in the mountains at the east end of Truckee Lake, now named Donner Lake, California, the group's food supply ran low. By the middle of February, nearly half of the group died from starvation and illness. Out of desperation, many resorted to eating their animals and even deceased group members. Thirteen-year-old survivor Virginia Reed finally reached California after enduring unimaginable hardships of hunger and terror. She sent a letter to her cousin in the Midwest that recounted her experiences of her sufferings and concluded with the advice, "cutoffs, and hurry along as fast as you can."[4]

As you continue along your journey, bear Reed's words in mind. There are very few, if any, shortcuts in business or in life. Leading businesses and successful individuals make it to the top with hard work, dedication, passion, and discipline. Robust strategies are formed through experience.

When leaders focus on finding shortcuts instead of answers, they sacrifice learning opportunities. Shortcuts provide surface-level answers to in-depth problems. They discourage immersion in the key practices that turn a good business into a great one—understanding customers, devising exceptional experiences, building advantages, developing talent, and fulfilling initiatives. As with the tragic Donner-Reed story, shortcuts often lead you away from your goals.

Because there is no one right answer with strategy, there is no shortcut. Strategic success is not a point in time. Rather, it's a journey to understanding. No company knows what will strike a chord with customers. None can predict what the market will or won't do. When it comes to strategy, the "secret" to success is different for every company. Uncovering it requires experimentation, exploration, and examination.

To Reed's second point, "hurry along as fast as you can," I wanted to emphasize that strategy doesn't wait. Putting off a strategy until everything is perfect and aligned in your company will cause you to miss out on great opportunities. Winning in our modern environment requires your business to be agile and expeditious.

I wish I could tell you that there was an *easy* way out, that with my three-step process you could craft a winning strategy for a business that runs itself while you sit on the beach three hundred days a year. But I can't.

Strategy is work. No great strategies emerge from a lack of thought and effort. They are hard to design and even harder to implement.

While strategy isn't easy, there are best practices to make it more efficacious. I hope that *Outsizing: Strategies to Grow Your Business, Profits, and Potential* provides you with tangible takeaways and timeless information that help you drive closer to your objectives. I intend for this text to serve as a guidebook, creating clarity and structure around an otherwise ambiguous process.

Your business is on the edge of a great adventure. This strategic tool kit will assist you on your trek. As you enter the market with a bold, well-designed strategy, move swiftly and confidently. Design and implement customer-centric advantages to capture value. Engross your business in the science and art of strategy. Outsize your actions and expand your vision. Wholeheartedly pursue your intentions, block out distraction, and leverage your inherent gifts to achieve success that brings satisfaction and fulfillment. And don't take shortcuts.

NOTES

INTRODUCTION

1. Ron Carucci, "Executives Fail to Execute Because They're Too Internally Focused," *Harvard Business Review*, November 13, 2017, https://hbr.org/2017/11/executives-fail-to-execute-strategy-because-theyre-too-internally-focused.
2. Paula Bernier, "Reports: Customer Satisfaction on the Decline," *Contact Center Solutions*, October 27, 2017, https://callcenterinfo.tmcnet.com/Analysis/articles/435223-reports-customer-satisfaction-on-decline.htm.
3. Jeff Boss, "Employee Turnover Is the Highest It's Been in 10 Years. Here's What to Do About It," *Forbes*, February 26, 2018, https://www.forbes.com/sites/jeffboss/2018/02/26/employee-turnover-is-the-highest-its-been-in-10-years-heres-what-to-do-about-it/#e5dc1a8478cc.
4. Wolf Richter, "A Great Debt Unwind Has Begun," *Business Insider*, June 6, 2017, https://www.businessinsider.com/commercial-business-bankruptcies-2017-6.
5. "Service Economy: Definition and Characteristics," *Study.com*, August 4, 2018, https://study.com/academy/lesson/service-economy-definition-characteristics.html.
6. "Service Economy," *Wikipedia*, May 25, 2018, https://en.wikipedia.org/wiki/Service_economy.
7. Christopher P. Skroupa, "How Intangible Assets Are Affecting Company Value in the Stock Market," *Forbes*, November 1, 2017, https://www.forbes.com/sites/christopherskroupa/2017/11/01/how-intangible-assets-are-affecting-company-value-in-the-stock-market/#67a020e42b8e.
8. Sijwang, "Disney's MyMagic+: Transforming the Theme Park Experience," *Harvard Business School*, April 5, 2017, https://digit.hbs.org/submission/disneys-mymagic-transforming-the-theme-park-experience.

9. B. Joseph Pine II and James H. Gilmore, "Welcome to the Experience Economy," *Harvard Business Review*, July–August 1998, https://hbr.org/1998/07/welcome-to-the-experience-economy.

10. Chris Mills, "Apple Breaks Stock Market Record by Closing with Market Cap Over $1 Trillion," *BGR*, August 2, 2018, https://bgr.com/2018/08/02/apple-1-trillion-valuation-share-price-at-close.

11. Anthony Mirhaydari, "The Fiscal Times," June 8, 2017, https://www.thefiscaltimes.com/Columns/2017/06/08/Even-Wall-Street-Warns-Market-Weird.

CHAPTER 1

1. Susan Fowler, "Reflecting on One Very, Very Strange Year at Uber," February 19, 2017, https://www.susanjfowler.com/blog/2017/2/19/reflecting-on-one-very-strange-year-at-uber.

2. Fowler, "Reflecting on One Very, Very Strange Year."

3. Mike Isaac, "Inside Uber's Aggressive, Unrestrained Workplace Culture," *The New York Times*, February 22, 2017, https://www.nytimes.com/2017/02/22/technology/uber-workplace-culture.html.

4. Isaac, "Inside Uber's Aggressive, Unrestrained Workplace Culture."

5. Jodi Kantor and David Streitfeld, "Inside Amazon: Wrestling Big Ideas in a Bruising Workplace," *The New York Times*, August 15, 2015, https://www.nytimes.com/2015/08/16/technology/inside-amazon-wrestling-big-ideas-in-a-bruising-workplace.html.

6. Michael B. Sauter, "The Worst Companies to Work For," *24/7 Wall St.*, June 5, 2017, https://247wallst.com/special-report/2017/06/05/the-worst-companies-to-work-for-3/5/.

7. Evan Comen, Samuel Stebbins, and Thomas C. Frohlich, "10 Worst Companies to Work For," *Huffington Post*, June 10, 2016.

8. Comen, Stebbins, and Frohlich, "10 Worst Companies."

9. Louis V. Gerstner, *Who Says Elephants Can't Dance?* (New York: HarperCollins, 2003).

10. Tali Sharot, "The Optimism Bias," *ScienceDirect*, December 2011, https://www.sciencedirect.com/science/article/pii/S0960982211011912.

11. Sharot, "The Optimism Bias."

12. Sharot, "The Optimism Bias."

13. Uri Berliner, "Wells Fargo Admits to Nearly Twice as Many Possible Fake Accounts—3.5 Million," *NPR*, August 31, 2017, https://www.npr.org

/sections/thetwo-way/2017/08/31/547550804/wells-fargo-admits-to-nearly-twice-as-many-possible-fake-accounts-3-5-million.

14. "The Wells Fargo Account Scandal: A Timeline," *Forbes*.

15. Anthony Bolante, "How Wells Fargo Encouraged Employees to Commit Fraud," *The Conversation*, October 6, 2016, http://theconversation.com/how-wells-fargo-encouraged-employees-to-commit-fraud-66615.

16. Chris Arnold, "Former Wells Fargo Employees Describe Toxic Sales Culture, Even at HQ," *NPR*, October 4, 2016, https://www.npr.org/2016/10/04/496508361/former-wells-fargo-employees-describe-toxic-sales-culture-even-at-hq.

17. Ali Montag, "Billionaire Ray Dalio: Bridgewater's Radically Transparent Culture Evolved from Painful Mistakes," *CNBC*, September 13, 2017, https://www.cnbc.com/2017/09/12/bridgewaters-ray-dalio-the-leadership-strategy-behind-my-success.html.

18. Montag, "Billionaire Ray Dalio: Bridgewater's Radically Transparent Culture Evolved from Painful Mistakes."

19. Omar Akhtar, "The Hatred and Bitterness Between Two of the World's Most Popular Brands," *Fortune*, March 22, 2013, fortune.com/2013/03/22/the-hatred-and-bitterness-behind-two-of-the-worlds-most-popular-brands.

20. "Strategy Quotes," *BrainyQuote*, April 16, 2018, https://www.brainyquote.com/topics/strategy.

21. Greg McKeown, *Essentialism: The Disciplined Pursuit of Less* (New York: Crown Publishing Group, 2014).

22. McKeown, *Essentialism*.

23. Dallin H. Oaks, "Good, Better, Best," *The Church of Jesus Christ of Latter-Day Saints*, October 2007, https://www.lds.org/general-conference/2007/10/good-better-best?lang=eng.

CHAPTER 2

1. Jill Grozalsky, "Customer Journey Mapping: Navigating a Course to Better Customer Relations," *CMSWire*, June 4, 2018, https://www.cmswire.com/customer-experience/customer-journey-mapping-navigating-a-course-to-better-customer-relations.

2. Todd Henderson, "The Real Reason United Won't Be Fined for Dragging David Dao Off That Plane," *Fortune*, September 13, 2017, http://fortune.com/2017/09/13/united-airlines-david-dao-department-of-transportation/.

3. Cadie Thompson, "United Was Plagued with a Huge Issue Even Before Dragging a Customer Off a Plane," *Business Insider*, April 25, 2017, http://www.businessinsider.com/united-rated-worst-full-service-us-airline-2017-4.

4. Leanna Garfield, "The United Airlines Boycott is Not Backing Down—Here's How It Could Affect Sales," *Business Insider*, April 18, 2017, http://www.businessinsider.com/united-airlines-scandal-boycott-sales-2017-4.

5. Elizabeth Wellington, "8 Cringeworthy Customer Service Stories," *Help Scout*, August 22, 2017, https://www.helpscout.net/blog/bad-customer-service-stories.

6. Kelvin Claveria, "Why Most Companies Are Not Customer-Centric Yet," *VisionCritical*, July 13, 2014, https://www.visioncritical.com/brian-solis-qa/.

7. "Greater Boston," *Wikipedia*, March 8, 2018, https://en.wikipedia.org/wiki/Greater_Boston.

8. Adam Millsap, "Not Everyone Likes City Living and Cheaper Housing Won't Change That," *Forbes*, April 11, 2017, https://www.forbes.com/sites/adammillsap/2017/04/11/not-everyone-likes-city-living-and-cheaper-housing-wont-change-that/#7fe9af691b4b.

9. Jon Gorey, "City vs. Suburbs: A New Study Breaks Down Exactly How Much More it Costs for Families to Live an Urban Life," *Apartment Therapy*, March 16, 2017, https://www.apartmenttherapy.com/city-vs-suburbs-a-new-study-breaks-down-exactly-how-much-more-it-costs-for-families-to-live-an-urban-life-243163.

10. Beau Dure, "Millennials Continue Urbanization of America, Leaving Small Towns," *NPR*, October 21, 2014, https://www.npr.org/2014/10/21/357723069/millennials-continue-urbanization-of-america-leaving-small-towns.

11. "Millennials Prefer Cities to Suburbs, Subways to Driveways," *Neilson*, March 4, 2014, http://www.nielsen.com/us/en/insights/news/2014/millennials-prefer-cities-to-suburbs-subways-to-driveways.html.

12. Ilana E. Strauss, "The Original Sharing Economy," *The Atlantic*, January 3, 2017, https://www.theatlantic.com/business/archive/2017/01/original-sharing-economy/511955/.

13. Blake Morgan, "NOwnership, No Problem: Why Millennials Value Experiences Over Owning Things," *Forbes*, Jun 1, 2015, https://www.forbes.com/sites/blakemorgan/2015/06/01/nownershipnoproblem-nowners-millennials-value-experiences-over-ownership/#1f6260b15406.

14. Shep Hyken, "Personalized Customer Experience Increases Revenue and Loyalty," *Forbes*, October 29, 2017, https://www.forbes.com/sites

/shephyken/2017/10/29/personalized-customer-experience-increases -revenue-and-loyalty/#2c3f3b7a4bd6.

15. Elizabeth Spaulding and Christopher Perry, "Making it Personal: Rules for Success in Product Customization," *Bain & Company*, September 16, 2013, http://www.bain.com/publications/articles/making-it-personal-rules-for -success-in-product-customization.aspx.
16. Spalding and Perry, "Making it Personal."
17. T.T. Bock and T. Linner, "Mass Customization in a Knowledge-Based Construction Industry for Sustainable High-performance Building Production," Technishce Universitat Munchen, http://www.irbnet.de /daten/iconda/CIB18865.pdf.
18. Nick Johnson, "How Your Customers' Expectations Have Changed in the Age of the Customer," July 7, 2017, https://www.salesforce.com /blog/2017/07/customers-expectations-in-age-of-the-customer.html.
19. Marc Saltzman, "Online Grocery Delivery: How Amazon Prime Compares to the Competition," *USA Today*, February 21, 2018, https://www.usatoday .com/story/tech/columnist/saltzman/2018/02/21/online-grocery-delivery -how-amazon-prime-now-compares-competition/344531002/.
20. Christopher Muther, "Instant Gratification Is Making Us Perpetually Impatient," *Boston Globe*, February 2, 2013, https://www.bostonglobe .com/lifestyle/style/2013/02/01/the-growing-culture-impatience -where-instant-gratification-makes-crave-more-instant-gratification /q8tWDNGeJB2mm45fQxtTQP/story.html.
21. Muther, "Instant Gratification."
22. Hayley Peterson, "These are the Major Differences Between People Who Shop at Whole Foods and Aldi," *Business Insider*, May 31, 2015, http://www .businessinsider.com/whole-foods-customers-vs-aldi-2015-5.
23. Peterson, "These are the Major Differences."
24. Peterson, "These are the Major Differences."
25. Clayton M. Christensen, Taddy Hall, Karen Dillon, and David S. Duncan, "Know Your Customers' 'Jobs to be Done.'" *Harvard Business Review*, September 2016, https://hbr.org/2016/09/know-your-customers-jobs-to -be-done.
26. "Uber: Finding the Way, Creating Possibilities for Riders, Drivers, and Cities," *Uber*, March 1, 2018, https://www.uber.com/our-story/.
27. Alyson Shontell and Anna Mazarkis, "Dropbox Founder Reveals How He Built a $10B Company in His 20's – Even Though Steve Jobs Told Him

Apple Would Destroy It," *Business Insider*, June 12, 2017, http://www.businessinsider.com/dropbox-founder-and-ceo-drew-houston-interview-2017-6.

28. Michael Skok, "4 Steps to Building a Compelling Value Proposition," *Entrepreneur*, June 14, 2013, https://www.forbes.com/sites/michaelskok/2013/06/14/4-steps-to-building-a-compelling-value-proposition/#a1304b146958.

29. "Theodore Levitt," *Wikiquote*, 2016, https://en.wikiquote.org/wiki/Theodore_Levitt.

30. Ben Gilbert, "25 of the Biggest Failed Products from the World's Biggest Companies," *Business Insider*, December 29, 2016, http://www.businessinsider.com/biggest-product-flops-in-history-2016-12.

31. "How Do I Return or Exchange My Book?" *Audible*, April 22, 2018, http://audible.custhelp.com/app/answers/detail/a_id/4592/~/how-do-i-return-or-exchange-my-book%3F.

32. Brad Tuttle, "Here's a Good Indication of How Much People Hate Car Dealerships," *Time*, April 17, 2015, http://time.com/money/3826562/buying-cars-online-hate-car-dealerships/.

33. Paula Skier, "4 Reasons People Hate Buying a Car, and What Auto Companies Can Do About It," *VisionCritical*, January 18, 2017, https://www.visioncritical.com/why-people-hate-buying-cars/.

34. Tuttle, "Here's a Good Indication of How Much People Hate Car Dealerships."

35. Gail McGovern and YoungMe Moon, "Companies and the Customers Who Hate Them," *Harvard Business Review*, June 2007, https://hbr.org/2007/06/companies-and-the-customers-who-hate-them.

36. McGovern and Moon, "Companies and the Customers Who Hate Them."

37. "Virgin Mobile Cell Phone Plans—Prepaid/Monthly/Pay as You Go Plans," *BuzzMobile.US*, April 22, 2018, http://buzzmobile.us/virgin-mobile-cell-phone-plans/.

38. Keith H. Hammonds, "Michael Porter's Big Ideas," *Fast Company*, February 28, 2001, https://www.fastcompany.com/42485/michael-porters-big-ideas.

39. Brandon Gaille, "22 Notable McDonalds [sic] Customer Demographics," April 19, 2015, https://brandongaille.com/22-notable-mcdonalds-customer-demographics/.

40. Ben Gilbert, "25 of the Biggest Failed Products."

41. Kate Taylor, "McDonald's is Bringing Back One of Its Most Expensive Failures—With One Major Difference," *Business Insider*, January 3, 2018, http://www.businessinsider.com/mcdonalds-tests-archburger-after-90s-flop-2018-1.

42. "History," *Minute Clinic*, March 6, 2018, https://www.cvs.com/minuteclinic/visit/about-us/history.

43. Kendra Cherry, "Motivation: Psychological Factors That Guide Behavior," *Verywell Mind*, November 7, 2017, https://www.verywellmind.com/what-is-motivation-2795378.

44. Peter Noel Murray, PhD, "How Emotions Influence What We Buy," *Psychology Today*, February 26, 2013, https://www.psychologytoday.com/us/blog/inside-the-consumer-mind/201302/how-emotions-influence-what-we-buy.

45. "Consumer Behavior," *Wikipedia*, February 26, 2018, https://en.wikipedia.org/wiki/Consumer_behaviour.

46. Carmen Nobel, "What Neuroscience Tells Us About Consumer Desire," *Harvard Business School Working Knowledge*, March 26, 2012, https://hbswk.hbs.edu/item/what-neuroscience-tells-us-about-consumer-desire.

47. Nobel, "What Neuroscience Tells Us About Consumer Desire."

48. Melissa Dahl, "Yes Shopping Can Be Addictive," *Elle Magazine*, January 6, 2017

49. Nobel, "What Neuroscience Tells Us About Consumer Desire."

50. Rikke Dam and Teo Siang, "5 Stages in the Design Thinking Process," *Interaction Design Foundation*, March 29, 2018, https://www.interaction-design.org/literature/article/5-stages-in-the-de-process.

51. Dam and Siang, "5 Stages in the Design Thinking Process."

52. Dam and Siang, "5 Stages in the Design Thinking Process."

53. Bryce DelGrande, "Which Big Companies Use Design Thinking?" *Quora*, March 6, 2016, https://www.quora.com/Which-big-companies-use-Design-Thinking.

54. Wendy L. Billings, "Effect of Store Atmosphere on Shopping Behavior," *Illinois Wesleyan University*, 1990.

55. Michael Bond, "The Hidden Ways that Architecture Affects How You Feel," *BBC*, June 6, 2017, http://www.bbc.com/future/story/20170605-the-psychology-behind-your-citys-design.

56. Cassandra Girard, "Meet the Scent Marketing Firm Winning the Battle for Your Nose," *NBC News*, July 24, 2017, https://www.nbcnews.com/business/your-business/meet-scent-marketing-firm-winning-battle-your-nose-n783761.

57. "Ecommerce Market Research – The Future?" *Smith Hanley & Associates*, May 8, 2017, http://www.smithhanley.com/2017/05/08/ecommerce-market-research-future/.

58. Chris Isidore, "Retail's Toughest Year: A Record For Store Closings," *CNN Money*, December 27, 2017, http://money.cnn.com/2017/12/26/news/companies/retail-toughest-year-store-closings/index.html.

59. Chris Campbell, "Online Reviews Are the New Social Proof," *Entrepreneur*, September 27, 2016, https://www.entrepreneur.com/article/281600.

60. Indrajit Sinha, "Cost Transparency: The Net's Real Threat to Prices and Brands," *Harvard Business Review*, March–April 2000, https://hbr.org/2000/03/cost-transparency-the-nets-real-threat-to-prices-and-brands.

61. Daniel Keyes, "Amazon Captured 4% of US Retail Sales in 2017," *Business Insider*, January 9, 2018, https://www.businessinsider.com/amazon-captured-4-of-us-retail-sales-in-2017-2018-1.

62. Wayne Duggan, "Amazon is on the Path to $1 Trillion Valuation," *U.S. News*, November 14, 2017, https://money.usnews.com/investing/stock-market-news/articles/2017-11-14/amazon-com-inc-amzn-valuation-stock.

63. Sonia Thompson, "What is the Secret to Amazon's Huge Success? Jeff Bezos Credits Commitment to These 3 Principles," *Entrepreneur*, November 6, 2017, https://www.entrepreneur.com/article/302253.

64. Thompson, "What is the Secret?"

65. "Happy Holidays from Our Associates," *Amazon*, March 7, 2018, https://www.amazon.com/p/feature/cdkk293z8nzm7q8.

66. "Amazon Knows Who You Are," *Wired*, March 27, 2005, https://www.wired.com/2005/03/amazon-knows-who-you-are/.

67. Kit Heaton, "How One Second Could Cost Amazon $1.6 Billion in Sales," *Fast Company*, March 15, 2012, https://www.fastcompany.com/1825005/how-one-second-could-cost-amazon-16-billion-sales.

68. "Jeff Bezos Quotes," *Brainy Quote*, March 8, 2018, https://www.brainyquote.com/authors/jeff_bezos.

CHAPTER 3

1. "The Waterside Inn," *Wikipedia*, April 2, 2018, https://en.wikipedia.org/wiki/The_Waterside_Inn.

2. "A Leading Light in the World of Gastronomy," April 30, 2018, https://www.waterside-inn.co.uk/.

3. Eugene Kim, "Pinterest, Last Valued at $11 Billion is Expected To Do About $169 Million in Sales This Year," *Business Insider*, October 17, 2015, www.businessinsider.com/pinterest-financials-are-leaked-2015-10.

4. "Enduring Ideas: The SCP Framework," *McKinsey Quarterly*, July 2008.

5. "Economic Trends in Tobacco," *Centers for Disease Control and Prevention*, November 16, 2017, https://www.cdc.gov/tobacco/data_statistics/fact_sheets/economics/econ_facts/index.htm.

6. Shobhit Seth, "Safest Industries to Invest In," *Investopedia*, May 1, 2018, https://www.investopedia.com/articles/investing/052815/safest-industries-invest.asp.

7. "1970 Full List," *Fortune 500*, May 14, 2018, http://archive.fortune.com/magazines/fortune/fortune500_archive/full/1970/1.html.

8. "Fulfillment by Amazon,"*AmazonServices*, May 1, 2018, https://services.amazon.com/fulfillment-by-amazon/benefits.html.

9. Leena Rao, "This Lesser-Known Amazon Business is Growing Fast," *Fortune*, January 5, 2016, http://fortune.com/2016/01/05/amazon-sellers-holidays/.

10. "Supplier List," *Apple*, February 2018, https://images.apple.com/supplier-responsibility/pdf/Apple-Supplier-List.pdf.

11. Reinhardt Krause, "Lumentum Has Apple iPhone 3D Sensor Design Win in the Bag: Analyst," *Investor's Business Daily*, May 4, 2017, https://www.investors.com/news/technology/lumentum-holdings-earnings/.

12. Vince Dixon, "What do Starbucks Locations Really Say About Income and Diversity in America?" *Eater*, November 20, 2015, https://www.eater.com/a/starbucks-income-map.

13. Devra Gertenstein, "The Average Profits for a Small Café," *Chron*, March 20, 2018, http://smallbusiness.chron.com/average-profits-small-cafe-30768.html.

14. Kyle Emory, "Walmart's Rural Dominance: A Brick & Mortar Advantage in an eCommerce Battle," *Harvard Business School*, November 15, 2017, https://rctom.hbs.org/submission/walmarts-rural-dominance-a-brick-mortar-advantage-in-an-ecommerce-battle/.

15. Tiffany Hsu, "Wal-Mart's Fresh Produce Promise: Fewer Middlemen, Faster Groceries," *Los Angeles Times*, June 3, 2013, http://articles.latimes.com/2013/jun/03/business/la-fi-mo-walmart-fresh-produce-grocery-20130603.

16. Rama, "Technology is Transforming Agriculture. Here's How," *3Dponics*, October 11, 2017, https://www.3dponics.com/blog/technology-is-transforming-agriculture-heres-how/.

17. Mansoor Iqbal, "Higher R&D Spending Doesn't Mean Greater Innovation," *The New Economy*, June 6, 2017, https://www.theneweconomy.com/strategy/money-cant-buy-innovation.

18. Jeff, "How Much Cash Do Apple and Google Have?" *STEM to Business*, May 2, 2017, http://www.stemtobusiness.com/how-much-cash-do-apple-and-google-have/.

19. Meghana Keshavan, "5 Reasons Why No One Has Built a Better EpiPen," *Stat*, September 9, 2016, https://www.statnews.com/2016/09/09/epipen-lack-of-innovation.

20. Chris Woodward and Mary Jo Layton, "Massive Price Increases on EpiPens Raise Alarm," *USA Today*, August 25, 2016, https://www.usatoday.com/story/money/business/2016/08/22/two-senators-urge-scrutiny-epipen-price-boost/89129620.

21. "Shipping and Delivery," *Zappos.com*, May 2, 2018, https://luxury.zappos.com/c/shipping-and-returns.

22. "What Zappos Can Teach Us About the Supply Chain," *OpenText*, February 15, 2011, https://blogs.opentext.com/what-zappos-com-can-teach-us-about-the-supply-chain.

23. Barry Glassman, "What Zappos Taught Us About Creating the Ultimate Client Experience," *Forbes*, May 13, 2013, https://www.forbes.com/sites/advisor/2013/05/13/what-zappos-taught-us-about-creating-the-ultimate-client-experience/#7418508b20fb.

24. Catherine Clifford, "What Richard Branson Learned When Coke Put Virgin Cola Out of Business," *CNBC*, February 7, 2017, https://www.cnbc.com/2017/02/07/what-richard-branson-learned-when-coke-put-virgin-cola-out-of-business.html.

25. Billund, "Lego's Turnaround: Picking Up the Pieces," *The Economist*, October 26, 2006, https://www.economist.com/node/8083013.

26. Billund, "Lego's Turnaround."

27. Roar Rude Trangbaek, "Successful Lego Strategy Delivers Continued Growth," *LEGO*, February 21, 2013, https://www.lego.com/en-gb/aboutus/news-room/2013/february/annual-result-2012.

28. Donald Sull, Rebecca Homkes, and Charles Sull, "Why Strategy Execution Unravels – and What to Do About It," *Harvard Business Review*, March 2015, https://hbr.org/2015/03/why-strategy-execution-unravelsand-what-to-do-about-it.

29. "Meet the Middle Performers – the Untapped Potential of Your Business," *Cornerstone*, March 8, 2011, https://www.cornerstoneondemand.com/2011-3-08+Meet+the+Middle+Performers+%E2%80%93+the+Untapped+Potential+of+Your+Business.

CHAPTER 4

1. Martin Hirt, "Is Your Strategy Good Enough to Move You Up on the Power Curve?" *McKinsey & Company*, January 30, 2018, https://www.mckinsey.com/business-functions/strategy-and-corporate-finance/our-insights/the-strategy-and-corporate-finance-blog/is-your-strategy-good-enough-to-move-you-up-on-the-power-curve.
2. Chris Bradley, Martin Hirt, and Sven Smit, "Strategy to Beat the Odds," *McKinsey Quarterly*, February 2018, https://www.mckinsey.com/business-functions/strategy-and-corporate-finance/our-insights/strategy-to-beat-the-odds.
3. Tom Jackson, "Adapt or Die: Future of Construction Will Require Contractors to Embrace Technology," *Equipment World*, February 10, 2017, https://www.equipmentworld.com/adapt-or-die-future-of-construction-will-require-contractors-to-embrace-technology/.
4. Richard Wray, "Boo.com Spent Fast and Died Young, but Its Legacy Shaped Internet Retailing," *The Guardian*, May 16, 2005, https://www.theguardian.com/technology/2005/may/16/media.business.
5. Wray, "Boo.com Spent Fast and Died Young."
6. Wray, "Boo.com Spent Fast and Died Young."
7. "History of Bitcoin," *Wikipedia*, June 25, 2018, https://en.wikipedia.org/wiki/History_of_bitcoin.
8. "Bitcoin's Price Swings Wildly, Touching Above $19,000," *Los Angeles Times*, December 7, 2017, http://www.latimes.com/business/la-fi-bitcoin-20171207-story.html.
9. Billy Bambrough, "The Bitcoin Price is Down 50% This Year Alone – Here's Why," *Forbes*, June 10, 2018, https://www.forbes.com/sites/billybambrough/2018/06/10/the-bitcoin-price-is-down-50-this-year-alone-heres-why/#70fc4d636801/.
10. Sean Burch, "Millennials Ride the Bitcoin Rollercoaster," *The Wrap*, February 15, 2018, https://www.thewrap.com/millennials-ride-the-bitcoin-rollercoaster/.
11. "Milton Friedman Quotes," *Goodreads*, June 25, 2018, https://www.goodreads.com/quotes/240845-there-is-one-and-only-one-social-responsibility-of-business-to.

12. "The Evolving Landscape for EPCs in US Renewables," *BloombergNEF*, October 14, 2014, https://about.bnef.com/blog/evolving-landscape-epcs-us-renewables/.

13. Damon Darlin, "Falling Costs of Big Screen TV's to Keep Falling," *New York Times*, August 20, 2005, https://www.nytimes.com/2005/08/20/technology/falling-costs-of-bigscreen-tvs-to-keep-falling.html.

14. Marco Bertini and Luc Wathieu, "How to Stop from Fixating on Price," *Harvard Business Review*, May 2010, https://hbr.org/2010/05/how-to-stop-customers-from-fixating-on-price.

15. Cameron Wolf, "Louis Vuitton Releases Its Most Expensive Leather Handbag," *Racked*, November 24, 2015, https://www.racked.com/2015/11/24/9793508/louis-vuitton-most-expensive-bag.

16. Matthew Plowright, "Louis Vuitton's Brand Fades in China," *Financial Times*, April 23, 2015, https://www.ft.com/content/17fb8d56-e99d-11e4-a687-00144feab7de.

17. Mariane Davids, "5 Shocking Statistics from Manufacturers Who Turned to Robotics," *Robotiq*, July 31, 2017, https://blog.robotiq.com/5-shocking-statistics-from-manufacturers-who-turned-to-robotics.

18. Mariane Davids, "5 Shocking Statistics."

19. "Global Online Project Management Software Market to Reach US $6.08 billion by 2025 – Transparency Market Research," *PR Newswire*, October 27, 2017, https://www.prnewswire.com/news-releases/global-online-project-management-software-market-to-reach-us608-bn-by-2025---transparency-market-research-653591643.html.

20. *Jetsmarter*, July 7, 2018, https://jetsmarter.com/.

21. "Kraft Heinz Revenue 2011–2018," *Macrotrends*, March 31, 2018, https://www.macrotrends.net/stocks/charts/KHC/kraft-heinz/revenue.

22. Sara Spary, "Heinz Ketchup Returns to 'It Has to be Heinz' in First Pan European TV Campaign for Seven Years," *Campaign*, September 29, 2014, https://www.campaignlive.co.uk/article/heinz-ketchup-returns-it-heinz-first-pan-european-tv-campaign-seven-years/1314571.

23. "Kraft Heinz Revenue 2011–2018."

24. Lauren Thomas, "Nike's China Sales Are Booming, as Demand Wanes in North America," *CNBC*, September 26, 2017, https://www.cnbc.com/2017/09/26/nike-q1-2018-earnings.html.

25. Erin Cullum, "Update! See Which Unexpected New Lay's Flavor Won the $1 Million Contest," October 11, 2017, https://www.popsugar.com/food/New-Lay-Flavor-Contest-Winners-2017-43731175.

26. "4 Brand Extensions and Why They are Successful," *Washington State University*, https://onlinemba.wsu.edu/resources/all/articles/4-brand-extensions-and-why-they-were-successful.

27. "Blue Ocean Strategic Moves," *Blueoceanstrategy.com*, July 11, 2018, https://www.blueoceanstrategy.com/about-the-authors/.

28. Dominic Barton and Mark Wiseman, "The Cost of Confusing Shareholder Value and Long-Term Profit," *Financial Times*, March 31, 2015, https://www.ft.com/content/bce20202-d703-11e4-97c3-00144feab7de.

29. "Warren Buffet: How He Does It," *Investopedia*, June 20, 2018, https://www.investopedia.com/articles/01/071801.asp.

30. Justin Fox, "At Amazon, It's All About Cash Flow," *Harvard Business Review*, October 20, 2014, https://hbr.org/2014/10/at-amazon-its-all-about-cash-flow.

31. Kimberly Chin, "Apple's 'Resilient and Recurring Cash Flow' Generation Means Investors Can Stop Worrying About the iPhone," *Business Insider*, March 9, 2018, https://markets.businessinsider.com/news/stocks/apple-stock-price-ongoing-cash-flow-generation-means-investors-can-stop-worrying-iphone-2018-3-1018560401.

32. Matt Hunter and Anita Balakrishnan, "Apple's Cash Pile Hits $285.1 Billion, a Record," *CNBC*, February 1, 2018, https://www.cnbc.com/2018/02/01/apple-earnings-q1-2018-how-much-money-does-apple-have.html.

33. Sarah Kessler, "The Optimist's Guide to the Robot Apocalypse," *Quartz*, March 9, 2017, https://qz.com/904285/the-optimists-guide-to-the-robot-apocalypse/.

34. Gene Zaino, "The Impact of Automation on the Independent Workforce," *Forbes*, May 2, 2017, https://www.forbes.com/sites/forbeshumanresourcescouncil/2017/05/02/the-impact-of-automation-on-the-independent-workforce/#48987e7e75c5.

35. "3 Ways Automation and AI Amplify the Role of Firstline Workers," *Forbes*, January 8, 2018, https://www.forbes.com/sites/insights-microsoft/2018/01/08/3-ways-automation-and-ai-amplify-the-role-of-firstline-workers/#b82799f3b5c2.

36. "Views. Visions. Insights. The Evolving Role of Today's CFO," *Ernst & Young*, 2011, https://www.ey.com/Publication/vwLUAssets/Americas_CFO_ViewsVisionInsights_062012/$FILE/Americas_CFO_ViewsVisionInsights_062012.pdf.

CHAPTER 5

1. "Employees Quotes," *BrainyQuote*, May 30, 2018, https://www.brainyquote.com/quotes/klaus_schwab_745787?src=t_employees.
2. George Klemp, "5 Ways to Win Today's War for Talent," *Fast Company*, September 19, 2014, https://www.fastcompany.com/3035836/5-ways-to-win-todays-war-for-talent.
3. Julia Carpenter, "The Rise of Diversity and Inclusion Jobs," *CNN Money*, August 21, 2018, https://money.cnn.com/2018/08/21/pf/diversity-inclusion-positions/index.html.
4. Jeanette Settembre, "Millennials Are Taking Over the Workforce," *New York Post*, April 17, 2018, https://nypost.com/2018/04/17/millennials-are-taking-over-the-workforce/.
5. Ken Makovsky, "Behind the Southwest Airlines Culture," *Forbes*, November 21, 2013, https://www.forbes.com/sites/kenmakovsky/2013/11/21/behind-the-southwest-airlines-culture/#64203a843798.Sujan
6. Sujan Patel, "10 Examples of Companies with Fantastic Cultures," Entrepreneur, August 6, 2015, https://www.entrepreneur.com/article/249174.
7. Chip and Dan Heath, *The Power of Moments* (New York: Simon & Schuster, 2017).
8. John E. Hunter and Ronda F. Hunter, "Validity and Utility of Alternative Predictors of Job Performance," *Michigan State University*, 1984, https://www.uam.es/personal_pdi/psicologia/pei/diferencias/Hunter1984JobPerformance.pdf.
9. Scott Keller and Matt Meaney, "Attracting and Retaining the Right Talent," *McKinsey & Company*, https://www.mckinsey.com/business-functions/organization/our-insights/attracting-and-retaining-the-right-talent.
10. Tomas Chamorro-Premuzic, Seymour Adler, and Robert B. Kaiser, "What Science Says About High-Potential Employees," *Harvard Business Review*, October 3, 2017, https://hbr.org/2017/10/what-science-says-about-identifying-high-potential-employees.
11. Sydney Finkelstein, *Superbosses: How Exceptional Leaders Master the Flow of Talent* (New York: Penguin Random House, 2016).
12. Sydney Finkelstein, "How to Hire Like a Superboss," *Harvard Business Review*, February 9, 2016, https://hbr.org/2016/02/how-to-hire-like-a-superboss.

13. David Wentworth, "Top Spending Trends for Training, 2016–2017," *Training*, November 30, 2016, https://trainingmag.com/top-spending-trends-training-2016-2017/.

14. "2017 Training Industry Report," *Training*, November–December 2017, https://pubs.royle.com/publication/?i=448382#{%22issue_id%22:448382,%22page%22:22}.

15. Zachary Crockett, "How a Janitor at Frito-Lay Invented Flamin' Hot Cheetos," *The Hustle*, November 29, 2017, https://thehustle.co/hot-cheetos-inventor/.

16. Crockett, "How a Janitor at Frito-Lay Invented Flamin' Hot Cheetos."

17. Crockett, "How a Janitor at Frito-Lay Invented Flamin' Hot Cheetos."

18. Travis Andrews, "The Flamin' Hot Cheetos Movie: How a Frito-Lay Janitor Created One of America's Most Popular Snacks," *The Washington Post*, February 23, 2018, https://www.washingtonpost.com/news/morning-mix/wp/2018/02/23/the-flamin-hot-cheetos-movie-how-a-frito-lay-janitor-created-one-of-americas-most-popular-snacks/?noredirect=on&utm_term=.5f86520fb3ff.

19. "Teacher Quotes," *BrainyQuote*, June 11, 2018.

20. David W. Ballard, "Managers Aren't Doing Enough to Train the Employees for the Future," *Harvard Business Review*, November 14, 2017, https://hbr.org/2017/11/managers-arent-doing-enough-to-train-employees-for-the-future.

21. "Companies Aren't Investing Enough in Training Younger Employees," *Panopto*, May 23, 2018, https://www.panopto.com/blog/does-your-organization-spend-enough-on-training-young-workers/.

22. Roberta Holland, "Companies Waste Billions of Dollars on Ineffective Corporate Training," *Harvard Business Review*, July 25, 2016, https://www.forbes.com/sites/hbsworkingknowledge/2016/07/25/companies-waste-billions-of-dollars-on-ineffective-corporate-training/#fd6cd9a4d222.

23. Mary Bart, "Reap the Benefits of Experiential Learning Without Leaving the Classroom," *Faculty Focus*, November 9, 2012, https://www.facultyfocus.com/articles/course-design-ideas/reap-the-benefits-of-experiential-learning-without-leaving-the-classroom/.

24. "Brooklyn Bridge," *History*, 2010, https://www.history.com/topics/brooklyn-bridge.

25. "The Inspirational Story of the Brooklyn Bridge," *Conscious Panda*, June 13, 2018, http://consciouspanda.com/the-inspirational-story-of-the-brooklyn-bridge/.

26. "Emily Warren Roebling," *Wikipedia*, June 7, 2018, https://en.wikipedia.org/wiki/Emily_Warren_Roebling.

27. Matt Valentine, "How 5 of the World's Most Successful People Handle Meetings,"*Goalcast*, July 23, 2018, https://www.goalcast.com/2018/07/23/how-successful-people-handle-meetings.

28. Behnam Tabrizi, "75% of Cross-Functional Teams Are Dysfunctional," *Harvard Business Review*, June 23, 2015, https://hbr.org/2015/06/75-of-cross-functional-teams-are-dysfunctional.

29. Jan Gleisner, "Non-verbal Communication Percentage," *Silent Communicator*, March 20, 2016, https://www.silentcommunication.org/single-post/2016/03/20/17-Non-verbal-communication-percentage.

30. Vivian Hunt, Dennis Layton, and Sara Prince, "Why Diversity Matters," *McKinsey & Company*, January 2015, https://www.mckinsey.com/business-functions/organization/our-insights/why-diversity-matters.

31. Tomas Chamorro-Premuzic, "Does Diversity Actually Increase Creativity?" *Harvard Business Review*, June 28, 2017, https://hbr.org/2017/06/does-diversity-actually-increase-creativity.

32. Alex "Sandy" Pentland, "The New Science of Building Great Teams," *Harvard Business Review*, April 2012, https://hbr.org/2012/04/the-new-science-of-building-great-teams.

33. "What is Deep-Level Diversity?" *IGI Global*, June 18, 2018, https://www.igi-global.com/dictionary/which-matters-more/53266.

34. Teresa Amabile and Steven J. Kramer, "The Power of Small Wins," *Harvard Business Review*, May 2011, https://hbr.org/2011/05/the-power-of-small-wins.

35. "Quotes on the Importance of Saying Thank You," *Ellevate*, June 20, 2018, https://www.ellevatenetwork.com/articles/8726-quotes-on-the-importance-of-saying-thank-you.

CHAPTER 6

1. "Distinctive Brain Patterns Help Habits Form," *Science Daily*, February 8, 2018, https://www.sciencedaily.com/releases/2018/02/180208120923.htm.

2. "Leonardo da Vinci Quotes," *Brainy Quote*, October 8, 2018, https://www.brainyquote.com/quotes/leonardo_da_vinci_107812.

3. Michael Goldstein, "Dislocation and Its Discontents: Ride-Sharing's Impact on the Taxi Industry," *Forbes*, June 8, 2018, https://www.forbes.com/sites/michaelgoldstein/2018/06/08/uber-lyft-taxi-drivers/#6dc8755c59f0.

4. Gregory Ferenstein, "This Is Exactly How Taxis Should Respond to Uber," January 14, 2015, *Venturebeat*, https://venturebeat.com/2015/01/14/this-is-exactly-how-taxis-should-respond-to-uber/.
5. David Z. Morris, "6th New York City Cab Driver Takes His Life in Crisis Blamed on Uber," *Fortune*, June 16, 2018, http://fortune.com/2018/06/16/new-york-cab-driver-suicide-uber.
6. Jeff Siegel, "Uber, Lyft Continue to Destroy the Taxi Industry," *Energy & Capital*, July 17, 2017, https://www.energyandcapital.com/articles/uber-lyft-continue-to-destroy-the-taxi-industry/5970.
7. Jason Snead, "If Taxis Want to Survive, They Should Learn from Uber," *The Heritage Foundation*, April 17, 2018, https://www.heritage.org/transportation/commentary/if-taxis-want-survive-they-should-learn-uber.
8. Doug Buchanan, "Chick-fil-A's Growth 'Almost Too Astounding to Believe,'" *Columbus Business First*, July 5, 2017, https://www.bizjournals.com/columbus/news/2017/07/05/chick-fil-as-growth-almost-too-astounding-to.html.
9. Rich Duprey, "Burger King's Big Bet on Fast Food May Go Bust," *The Motley Fool*, March 2, 2017, https://www.fool.com/investing/2017/03/02/burger-kings-big-bet-on-fast-food-may-go-bust.aspx.
10. Joan Magretta, "Jim Collins, Meet Michael Porter," *Harvard Business Review*, December 15, 2011, https://hbr.org/2011/12/jim-collins-meet-michael-porte.
11. "George S. Patton Quotes," *BrainyQuote*, October 16, 2018, https://www.brainyquote.com/quotes/george_s_patton_159766.
12. Hayley Peterson, "Why Chick-Fil-A's Restaurants Sell 3 Times as Much as KFC's," *Business Insider*, May 10, 2016, https://www.businessinsider.com/why-chick-fil-a-is-so-successful-2016-5.
13. Jeff Dahms, "4 Lessons in Employee Empowerment, Courtesy of Chick-fil-A," *CSP Happenings*, October 15, 2018, http://www.csp.com/chick-fil-a/#.W8TP7PZFxu1.
14. Michelle Darrisaw, "WATCH: Here's the Real Reason Why Chick-fil-A is Closed on Sundays" *Southern Living*, October 5, 2017, https://www.southernliving.com/news/real-reason-chick-fil-a-closes-on-sunday.
15. "Chick-fil-A Donations: Where Does the Foundation Donate Money?" *The Chicken Wire*, June 19, 2018, https://thechickenwire.chick-fil-a.com/Inside-Chick-fil-A/Chick-fil-A-Donations-Where-Does-the-Foundation-Donate-Money.

16. Hayley Peterson, "Why Chick-fil-A is Beating Every Other Fast-Food Chain in the US," *Business Insider*, October 4, 2016, https://www.businessinsider.com/why-chick-fil-a-is-so-successful-2016-10.

17. Emmie Martin, Tanza Loudenback, and Alexa Pipia, "The 25 Best Fast-Food Chains in America," *Business Insider*, May 9, 2016, https://www.businessinsider.com/the-best-fast-food-chains-in-america-2016-5.

18. Laura Diamond, "Chick-fil-A Opens Innovation Center in Tech Square," *Georgia Tech News Center*, January 25, 2018, https://www.news.gatech.edu/2018/01/24/chick-fil-opens-innovation-center-tech-square.

19. Sean Ward, "How Does Chick-fil-A's Drive-Thru Move So Fast?" *The Chicken Wire*, July 24, 2017, https://thechickenwire.chick-fil-a.com/Inside-Chick-fil-A/How-Does-Chick-fil-As-Drive-Thru-Move-So-Fast.

20. Cameron Sperance and Bisnow Boston, "Everybody Wants Chick-fil-A: Why the Chicken Chain is Dominating Fast Food," *Bisnow*, June 7, 2018, https://www.bisnow.com/national/news/retail/how-2020-will-be-the-year-of-the-chick-fil-a-89287.

21. Eric Ries, *The Lean Startup: How Today's Entrepreneurs Use Continuous Innovation to Create Radically Successful Businesses* (New York: Crown Business, 2011).

22. Gerstner, *Who Says Elephants Can't Dance?*

23. Donald Sull, Rebecca Homkes, and Charles Sull, "Why Strategy Execution Unravels—and What to Do About It," *Harvard Business Review*, March 2015, https://hbr.org/2015/03/why-strategy-execution-unravelsand-what-to-do-about-it.

24. "Habit Quotes," *Brainy Quote*, October 21, 2018, https://www.brainyquote.com/topics/habit.

CONCLUSION

1. Rickie Longfellow, "Back in Time: The Hastings Cutoff and Highway 80 Tragedy of the Donner Party," *Highway History*, June 27, 2017, https://www.fhwa.dot.gov/infrastructure/back0104.cfm.

2. "Donner Party," *Wikipedia*, October 17, 2018, https://en.wikipedia.org/wiki/Donner_Party.

3. Longfellow, "Back in Time: The Hastings Cutoff."

4. Anna Khomina, "Remember, Never Take No Cut-Offs, and Hurry Along as Fast as You Can," *U.S. History Scene*, October 22, 2018, http://ushistoryscene.com/article/donner-reed-party.

INDEX

A

D

E

F

G

H

I

M

N

O

P

Q

R

S

T

ABOUT THE AUTHOR

Author, CFO of an international billion-dollar company, and management consultant Steve Coughran has over two decades of experience driving business excellence. Known for his extensive research and writing on strategic growth and corporate financial management, Steve challenges conventional wisdom, earning the reputation of an "energetic trailblazer." He is an expert on strategy and an acclaimed keynote speaker with over twenty years of experience driving corporate excellence.

Steve has launched and managed three cross-industry companies, gaining a deep understanding of the competitive business environment. He is passionate about spreading his knowledge of strategy and finance with others, developing and leading programs such as the Strategic Financial Leadership Academy and Growth-Driven Leadership and teaching a Strategic Financial Leadership course at the University of Denver.

Steve is a CPA, earned his MBA from the Fuqua School of Business at Duke University, and studied international business across four continents. He advanced his specialization in strategy through study at the Executive Education Program at the Tuck School of Business at Dartmouth College. Steve lives with his wife Lalana and two children, Ava and Max, in Chattanooga, Tennessee. When he's not working, he enjoys running and has completed five marathons.